Mother at Seven

VERONIKA GASPARYAN

Mother at Seven

The Shocking True Story of an Armenian Girl's Stolen Childhood and Her Family's Unspeakable, Cruel Betrayal

by

Veronika Gasparyan

Visit our website at **www.StillwaterPress.com** for more information.

First Stillwater River Publications Edition

ISBN-10: 0-692-72141-X
ISBN-13: 978-0-692-72141-4
Library of Congress Control Number: 2016946289

1 2 3 4 5 6 7 8 9 10
Written by Veronika Gasparyan
Cover Design by Dawn M. Porter
Published by Stillwater River Publications, Glocester, RI, USA.

Publisher's Cataloging-In-Publication Data
(Prepared by The Donohue Group, Inc.)

Names: Gasparyan, Veronika.
Title: Mother at seven : the shocking true story of an Armenian girl's stolen childhood and her family's unspeakable, cruel betrayal / by Veronika Gasparyan.
Description: First Stillwater River Publications edition. | Glocester, RI, USA : Stillwater River Publications, [2016]
Identifiers: LCCN 2016946289 | ISBN 978-0-692-72141-4 | ISBN 0-692-72141-X
Subjects: LCSH: Gasparyan, Veronika--Family. | Abused children--Russia (Federation)--Sochi--Biography. | Abused children--Family relationships--Russia (Federation)--Sochi. | Families--Russia (Federation)--Sochi. | LCGFT: Autobiographies.
Classification: LCC DK510.75.G37 A3 2016 | DDC 947.086092--dc23

Dedication

To my grandfather, Sergey Movsesovitch Israelyan,
who dared me to survive
and is watching over me from heaven.

In my mind, learning to fly was a very logical alternative.
I honestly saw no other way to free myself from this torture
other than to fly just like the birds did;
the birds were completely free.

~ Veronika Gasparyan

Mother at Seven

CHAPTER 1

On The Edge of the Window

I stood at the edge of the window in my family's fifth floor apartment and wondered if I could fly. Just a few hours earlier, after enjoying yet another dream with my beloved and beautiful brown eagle, I made up my mind that today would be the day. Today I would finally be brave. Today I was going to fly away.

Most of the time, I considered Sundays to be my favorite day of the week. I would spend them alone watching over my baby brother which I felt was a wonderful way to spend a weekend. I always cherished Sundays the most because unlike the rest of the week, we were left alone and we were able to do the fun things that we weren't allowed to do on any other day.

Even though this was the fifteenth day in a row and I hadn't been allowed to go outside, I still felt strangely happy and joyful from the moment I woke up that morning. In fact, I somehow knew that this day was going to be different and unique even though I hadn't yet figured out what it was that made me feel that way. After all, I was only a little over eight years-old, and I did not understand everything in this world so easily. Despite my predicament, and despite the distractions of my one year-old baby brother who was needy and quite a handful, my mind was still so full of hope. I yearned for brighter days.

It was now 11 a.m. and my regular morning routine was finished. It usually took about three hours to complete my chores, but on Sundays they always took longer because I would pause to play with the baby and have fun. It felt better to be doing things around the house at my own speed without the pressure of adults watching over my shoulder. And now even my baby brother was happy, sporting a set of fresh, clean clothes and rounded belly full of food.

I looked down from the window and could see my friends and classmates playing outside as they usually did on the weekend. I, on the other hand, couldn't go outside. It wasn't just because my parents had forbidden it, but it was also because I didn't want to leave my brother alone. So all I could do was watch everyone from my balcony window and enjoy the bright summer sunbeams as they shone through the glass and warmed my face.

There are definitely advantages to living on the top floor of an apartment building — the strong heat from the sun and the breathtaking views are two of them. For some reason, looking out at our great view always made me feel calm and at peace with the world. The front yard of our building was big — at least five acres — and had all kinds of interesting things growing in it. There were many different varieties of fruit trees, colorful flowers, pretty bushes, and an endless carpet of thick green grass. There were also manmade features like playgrounds, swings, tables with chairs, and other interesting things for kids to play on. There was even a section set aside for personal gardens that our neighbors created for themselves.

These little gardens produced an amazing variety of fruit and greens that helped folks save money and avoid the high prices found at the stores and bazaars. Unfortunately for all of us kids, their gardens were fenced in, and we couldn't get any of the fruit or vegetables from them. (Except of course about once or twice each month when someone would forget to lock his gate!)

There were ninety apartments in the building that housed at least thirty kids of school age and their families. The building's big front yard was important for so many of us. On any given Sunday, especially in the morning, you would find at least fifteen children playing there at one time. It didn't matter how warm or how cold it was, or even what season it was, because all I knew was that I loved living here and I didn't want to be in any other country or city on Earth.

On this particular Sunday, since it was summer vacation, there were even more kids scattered around the yard than usual and they were doing all sorts of fun things. Just like most Sunday mornings, I was right there with my nose pressed against the window watching them play and have fun. Even though I couldn't physically be with them, no one could stop me from imagining that I was. After all, it seemed like that is exactly what children should be doing on a sunny Sunday during summer school vacation. Some of my friends were on the swings and each kid was trying to fly higher than all the other kids. Some were climbing the fruit trees, probably trying to get the bigger, juicier apples, pears, and plums that grew at the top. A few of the other friends were drawing hopscotch patterns on the driveways with colored chalk, while a couple of my closest friends were resting in the thick green grass with their hands spread apart wide, probably enjoying the warm and shining sun just like I was.

None of the kids called my name or asked me to come out because they already knew the answer they were going to get. Since the day my brother was born, I hadn't been out to play. Every time they came up to my door to ask me to come out and join them, I wouldn't be allowed. In fact, I would be punished if they shouted my name from the yard too many times, and then I wouldn't feel like going outside anyway. My friends got the point after they tried to get me out a few times, and now they just went about their business and acted like I didn't exist. What else could they do?

After a few minutes of watching my friends play, I thought again about the eagle in my dream and wondered why he had been acting so strange. I remembered feeling a smile cross my face the moment I woke up; the dream had been so vivid! Then suddenly, all the details of that dream poured back into my memory like a roaring ocean wave.

In my dream, a beautiful brown eagle with very large wings and a bright, white head would fly over our building and across the front yard every Sunday morning. He would always fly away before noontime, as if he had to fly off to some other child's dream or back to that wonderful, happy place he must have come from. Every time he visited, I would notice that our clock read 11 a.m. and it was always Sunday. I had never seen this beautiful eagle in real life, although I looked for him many times while watching other birds fly above our play yard.

This time, instead of just cruising past me through the air on his large, powerful wings like he usually did, he flew right up to my fifth floor balcony window and every time he made a circle in the air he would come a bit closer. Even though I was standing behind the glass window, I could still feel the gentle wind blow against my cheeks as he flew by. I know it made no sense that I could feel the breeze through glass, but in a child's dream, I suppose anything is possible.

I also could see his head in much more detail, and I was captivated by his eyes and the way he looked at me. His eyes were round and looked human, not what you'd find on any normal bird. He looked at me like he was a real person who was lost in deep and serious thought. I always wondered why I saw him only in my dreams

4

on Sunday mornings, but I knew that one day it would all make perfect sense — either in my dreams or in real life. After all, every story I had ever read or movie I had ever watched at that point in my life, always made perfect sense at the end.

The most significant thing I remembered from the dream was what the eagle said to me, in a human voice.

I know you've been thinking of flying away,
and I know that you've been in terrible pain.
It is now time for you to fly.
So please, come and fly away with me,
this morning — today!

With all the details of my dream now fully settled into my consciousness, I realized that I may have finally found the answer I had been looking for. Flying away was how I could end my pain and misery. I had thought about killing myself before, but I wasn't brave enough to come up with a way to do it, nor at just eight years old did I fully understand what dying really meant. Now, with a clear mind and encouraging words from my trustworthy eagle guide, there was no better time to try something so hopeful. It was a beautiful Sunday morning just like in my dreams, and it was 11 a.m., right when the eagle always would visit. It was time. It was meant to be.

All of my chores were done, no adults were around, and no one would be coming home for at least a few more hours. I looked around to see if my baby brother was still lying on my parents' bed where I left him. Sure enough, he was there and deeply asleep, covered up with his favorite thin blanket.

The enclosed balcony that I stood on was right next to my parent's bedroom and only a few feet away from where the baby was sleeping. When I looked at him, I suddenly felt the need to walk over and give him one last goodbye, so I gently placed a long kiss on his warm forehead and whispered softly into his ear, "I am ready my little baby. I am going to fly away now!"

I know I was only a little over eight years of age and my life should have been carefree and happy, but sadly, it was far from it. The only happiness I ever felt was when I practiced playing piano — my favorite musical instrument — or watched over my little brother. It was so hard to say goodbye.

Although both of these things were beautiful gifts to me, it was not enough to override the terrifying life I lived day after day. The constant suffering, neglect, sick games, and sadistic torture I was enduring had become unbearable. I just could not find the courage and strength in my tired, little body to continue to endure the animalistic abuse any longer.

Understand that my life had not always been so horrible; in fact it had been pretty great up until the day my baby brother was born. I tried to understand what I had done wrong to deserve such mistreatment and neglect. I thought I had obeyed everything I had been told to do, and did it in a timely manner, too. I never wanted anyone to be upset or disappointed with me.

But nothing was good enough now and I prayed that the torturous treatment wouldn't get worse. I needed to know when it would end and I worried that perhaps it never would. Now I was simply too tired and needed to go somewhere and get away from it all, somewhere where there was no pain, no suffering, and no one who could harm me physically or emotionally any longer.

Those thoughts and needs battled inside me because at the same time, I loved my baby brother deeply and was afraid to leave him there alone without me. He was the only reason I had not tried to do something to stop the abuse and why I had been putting up with the sadism and neglect for so long. He held the biggest place in my heart and to me it felt like he wasn't my brother at all, but more like a son. Since the day he came home from the hospital, I spent nearly every moment, day and night, caring for him just like a real mother would.

With all that conflict inside me, I knew that if I didn't fly away at that very moment, now that I felt ready, then I might never be able to; that I might never be free. I knew I could not continue living this way, and felt that I would not survive much longer if I didn't do something about it right there and then.

At least that was my belief at that moment. It would be some time before I would understand and discover how much inner strength and willpower I had in me — a power I would use to fight and survive the unimaginable, horrific treatment and sick games that would get much worse as I grew older.

Unfortunately for me, Russia had no child protective services department, no police who wanted to become involved in what some people would simply call "discipline," and no neighbors who would come and check on me. Even when I would scream, beg for my life, beg for forgiveness, and bang on the thin walls of our apartment pleading for someone to come to my rescue, no one in our building would even bother to ring our doorbell.

Many times I thought about just running away, but I always realized and understood that I couldn't do it. After all, where would I go? Even if I did leave the house, the only person I would consider running to was my favorite human being in the world — my guardian angel Grandpa. If I did run to him, my mother would simply go and get me, since he was her father, after all. I knew my punishment for running away would be much harsher and far more painful than usual. So what was the point in going through that? In my mind, learning to fly was a very logical alternative. I honestly saw no other way to free myself from this torture other than to fly just like the birds did; they were completely free.

Every time I saw them in the sky, freely flying through it, shooting up and down and riding the waves of air, I sensed they were so happy and cheerful. When not soaring, they would sit on the tree branches whenever they felt like it and sing their favorite melodies to whoever was listening. They would come down to the ground to drink from small, refreshing puddles, and fly back up under the control of nothing but their own free will. They would jump from branch to branch on the trees and check to see if the fruit was ripe and ready to be eaten for breakfast, lunch or dinner. And most importantly, they could fly away every fall to warmer, safer places of their own choosing, and not worry about anything. When thinking of escaping the hell I lived in, flying away just like they did seemed to be a perfect and peaceful way to escape.

On most Sundays, my parents wouldn't be home during the day. My father was an ER doctor who worked 24-hour shifts most of the time, with random days off. My mother was a piano teacher but was still on maternity leave, which in Russia at that time meant she received 36 months paid time off from work. Although she was not working at that time, she was rarely home on the weekends, especially during the day. She would spend this time with her friends doing manicures, pedicures, facials, hairstyles, and other things to make her look better. It seemed to me that ever since she had a second baby, she had become obsessed with her body and her image. It was something that I hadn't noticed in her before.

I knew that no one was coming home for at least a few more hours. My baby brother could not really talk yet, but I taught him some simple words that he used with me every day. He was not able to tattle on me or get me in trouble even if he wanted to. Everything seemed to be in place. I thought again about those caring and special words the eagle had told me in my dream the night before.

I stood on the balcony next to the window and looked through the glass to reassure myself that the decision I was about to make was the right one. This was it. To succeed, I knew I had to collect together all the courage I could muster and stay brave.

I hoped I would fly off to some secret place that only good and kind people know about, and where everyone is accepted. I wanted it to be a place where I would meet a new, good family and kind parents who would be there waiting for a good, brave little girl like me to join them. Maybe those parents also had an unfair, terrible and painful life, which made them fly away too, just like I was about to do. Maybe, just maybe, they had succeeded and were now just wishing for a little girl to love them so their family would be complete. If I succeeded, I would have a new, happy, and loving home with parents who would say that they love me and who would never even think of hurting me.

I was becoming anxious and a little nervous. I looked back to make sure my baby brother was still asleep because I didn't want him to see me fly — just in case I didn't succeed on my first try! Sure enough, he was still in the same spot where I left him, laying there on his belly with his cute little head turned towards me. He looked so calm and at peace, and had a smile on his face, with his chubby, rosy cheeks shining from the sunbeams that were covering him. He looked like he was having a happy dream and it made me feel warm within just to know that he was safe and pain-free.

I remembered whispering to him, "If you only knew what's going on around you, you would not be such a calm and happy baby. I did everything I could to shelter you from all the bad, negative, and painful things that this house has to offer." I thought it was sad that I had to endure all the pain and abuse just to be able to provide him with that peace.

And with that thought, I turned my head away from him and stood up onto a small chair which was next to the short dresser right below the window level. As I took my first step up, I felt strangely happy and accomplished within, but I had to stay focused to complete what I started. Otherwise, all the work I did to work up this courage would be for nothing.

I took another step up and onto the dresser which was firmly pressed against the wall right below the edge of the window. I stood straight up. The only thing separating my whole body from the sky outside was one thin layer of glass. A fear of heights took over and I started to shake a little, but I managed to stay focused and stayed absorbed in what I was doing. I now had to open the window, without making any noise, so as not to wake the baby.

The windows we had were very old-fashioned and were framed on the top below the ceiling, and on the bottom, to hold the glass in place. They were called sliding windows which meant they literally had no handles anywhere on them. The only way to open them was to slide them in opposite directions from the middle of the window to the sides by pressing your fingers and palms firmly against the glass. Let me just say that most of the children I knew would not be able to slide them open with such ease and would need the help of an adult. But since I was not physically weak at all, I could open and close those windows with just a little more than a usual use of strength. After all, I had good training doing all the daily household chores, carrying heavy grocery bags up to the fifth floor, and holding my chubby baby brother for a hundred different reasons throughout the day.

I pressed both my hands down on the glass at face level and slid the glass windows open, away from each other. As soon as there was a small opening just a few inches wide, a fresh and strong wave of warm wind rushed in. It came right at me and I tried to inhale it all. I instantly felt its freshness and warmth rush deep into my lungs and it felt wonderful; but at the same time, it made me feel a little nervous. The opening I made went all the way from the bottom of my feet to above my head near the ceiling, and it was at least three feet higher than I was. For some reason my shaking stopped, and I felt even more brave and ready. But I knew I had to slide the windows open even wider.

I was so eager. All I could think about was that I was just a few seconds away from freedom and a new, painless existence.

I pressed my palms harder against the glass to give my body more leverage so I could slide the windows wider. As I pushed the glass panes further apart, I realized that the opening was now big enough for my whole body to slip through. I don't know why I didn't stop at that moment since I had plenty of room, but I wanted to open the windows even more and I pushed the glass apart. Now the only things that held me from falling over the edge of that window and into the summer air were my two small hands that were firmly grasping the glass at the left and right sides of the opening.

With both sides of the window now open, I could see everything and everyone below much more clearly. It surprised me a bit that no one looked up and saw me standing there. Although I was still inside upon the dresser, it was at the same level as the edge. Still, it's funny no one noticed a fully dressed girl standing on the highest floor of the building, her skirt fluttering in the summer wind like an unfurled flag.

On the other hand, who would think of looking up towards my window and who would consider that a little girl would stand there in the first place? They seemed so busy playing and having fun with each other. Why would they notice or think of me at that moment, not that I really wanted them to anyway. The last thing I needed was for them to see my try to fly and to fail. How embarrassing! I was already a big failure, or at least that's what I was told daily at home. So with that on my mind, I put aside any ideas of screaming and shouting "hello" to any of them, and said to myself, "There is no way I will ever let anyone see me fail! They will not remember me as a failure!"

Now I only had one more important step to take, which was to move my feet off of the dresser and onto the window's edge. Even though it was literally only a couple of inches away, it was thin and sharp and didn't look very comfortable.

I took a deep breath and looked back at my little brother one more time. I just wanted to make sure he was still asleep. I then slowly stepped up onto the edge of the window with my right foot first and then with the left. My heart started to beat so hard and so fast that I felt light-headed. I quickly closed my eyes and tried to keep myself balanced. I wanted to open my eyes and to scream to the whole world, as loudly as possible. I wanted to tell everyone that I was a uniquely strong and very courageous girl. If I were really a failure, as my family thought I was, I wouldn't have been standing on that edge, high up, and unprotected.

I felt unstable and had no choice but to open my eyes, even if it was just a bit. I started to focus my mind and look for whatever was left of my strength to open them wide. I did and to my surprise, the scary feelings I had a moment earlier, all went away. My nervousness wasn't there either. To my disbelief, I actually found myself smiling into the summer air. Maybe it was because the sun was warm and felt soft on my face or maybe it was because I felt that I finally was doing something right, as well as important — something for my own good.

A warm feeling came over me inside and out and I became so happy within, that my body felt physically lighter than usual. It felt like I was in heaven, which I had pictured many times in my head. I knew from reading different stories that heaven was bright, warm, kind, loving, and accepting. I figured maybe that's the beautiful place where birds flew to every fall.

All of a sudden my face changed. I realized that if I did this, I would be leaving my baby behind, alone, with no one to care for him or to protect him from anything or anyone.

Being a mother at seven changed a lot of things in my life. Most of all it changed my feeling of responsibility not only for myself, but also for another human being. It really bothered me that he would not be able to protect himself against difficult or dangerous situations. A second later, I felt my heart fill with sadness and feelings of guilt. It was the kind that a real mother would feel if forced to leave her only child behind. I tried very hard not to think about it because I noticed that I was getting carried away with those thoughts. I was afraid that if I thought about it too much, I might change my mind. I stopped myself and took one last deep breath of fresh air. It was time to let my hands go so they could turn into the little wings I would need to fly out of that window.

As soon as I let go with one hand I became very unstable. Without second guessing myself, I looked up for strength and guidance. The endless sky was clear and blue, no matter which direction I looked. The only thing I saw other than blue sky were two small, almost see-through, white clouds. They were both shaped like puffy hearts which made me believe they were placed there as a sign that everything would be OK.

While my eyes focused on those hearts for a split second, I noticed something else in the air far away. Whatever it was, it was coming at me in a fast and steady manner. At first I thought it was someone's kite, but as the object got closer, I became confused and somewhat curious. I opened up my eyes as wide as I could just to make sure I was seeing it clearly.

It was the eagle! It was the beautiful brown eagle from my dreams! He looked exactly as I remembered, with large powerful wings and a big white head. And he was flying straight toward me!

A few seconds later he was not more than twenty feet away. I stood there in a numb state of mind without moving at all. It looked like he was going to fly right into me! Then right in front of my eyes, he made a wide, smooth turn. But he did come close enough to give me a moment to look right into his eyes. It was almost like he wanted me to. What I saw in them was the same deepness and seriousness that I would have seen in the eyes of someone who had lived a very tough life; like someone who had survived a war or had seen terrible things happen in front of him.

The eagle started to groove the air in steady circles right in front of my window. Every time he came closer, he would make a sharp turn to start a new circle. It almost felt like he was trying to tell me something: like not being scared, not doubting myself or like flying away with him was OK and safe.

All of a sudden, a terrifying thought raced through my mind, "If I don't hurry, he might fly away! Would he just fly away without taking me with him to that beautiful place that he and other birds must have come from?" Without a second thought, I shouted out to him just loudly enough for him to hear, "Eagle, please wait! I'm coming with you! Don't fly away without me! Take me to my new home!"

The eagle heard me and turned his head my way, just as he was flying away to start another circle. When I shouted, he almost came to a complete stop right in the air and turned his whole body to face me. Looking straight into my eyes, he started to move his powerful wings back and forth to be able to stay in one spot. That's when I realized it was time and he was waiting for me to jump. I was ready.

I slowly closed my eyes and took my last deep breath. I let one hand go and was just another second away from letting my little hands become a beautiful child's wings. I let go with my second hand and smiled.

"I am free now!"

CHAPTER 2
New Baby, New Life

I was born in the Soviet Union, presently Russia, in 1981 in a beautiful city called Sochi. Many people might be familiar with it because the 2014 Winter Olympic Games were held there a few years ago. The city was founded in 1838 and is located in a rare subtropical climate. The city skirts the coast of the Black Sea for over 90 miles, but only takes up about 1361 square miles altogether. Almost year round visitors can enjoy beautiful winter activities up on the snow-filled mountains. At the same time, down at sea level, the water is warm enough to swim in for more than half of the year.

It is not uncommon to see a gorgeous and colorful Macaw parrot sitting on a palm or a banana tree; yet, in the winter months, the temperature could drop to as low as 30 degrees and snow could arrive unexpectedly. Then the next thing you know, those same palm trees could be covered in a blanket of white snow. It is a rare, beautiful and unique scene that not many people will get to see in their lifetimes. I will remember those images forever.

The population of Sochi is only about 380,000 people; yet they have over 10,000 policemen who work there. That's a remarkable statistic: one out of every thirty-eight people. I always thought this to be an interesting fact because although there were plenty of "protectors" around, people of any age could still get away with very cruel and terrible behavior not only towards animals or people their own age, but also towards weaker groups. These groups included the elderly, sick, handicapped, and even children — their own or someone else's. It was also not uncommon to see kids after dark, torturing different animals in the corners of the dark alleys or in the park, or for parents to be disciplining their children right out in the street in front of everyone. Some would discipline them in their apartments with open windows. As a result, other people could hear this and know that the child was being punished for bad behavior.

Unlike other countries, to live in an apartment building in Sochi carried more prestige and was more expensive than having a house on the outskirts of the city. Most of these residential houses in Sochi were five stories high and were very long with six entrances at the same distance from each other. Each entrance had access to fifteen apartments with three on each floor. Some of the buildings were built one across from the other, with two or three in a row while others were built right next to each another, maybe about fifty feet apart. If you were to look at them from an airplane, they would look like boxes of matches, lined up and ready or like a row of soldiers preparing to attack a city or a castle.

Although I was born and raised in Sochi, Russia, I am full-blooded Armenian and my parents' Armenian roots go back many generations. The Armenian people have different national origins from Russians, but both nationalities are very friendly toward each other. I was brought up in very traditional, old-fashioned and strict ways, where being a girl was the last thing you wanted to be. Boys were loved and cherished much more because they were to continue the last name of the family; while girls were usually treated as maids, helpers, and future housewives in training. You would think that because I was not born and raised in Armenia itself that our family would adopt more of the Russian traditions which are very similar to America's, with more freedom and equality shared between the sexes. What was even stranger was that from my first day of kindergarten, I was not allowed to have any Russian friends. There were many Russian kids that I played with outside, or knew from the school, but none of them could come to our apartment or spend any time with me alone. I think it's because my family didn't want me to adapt or learn things that would go against their old-fashioned and peculiar beliefs. God forbid I would learn how to speak my mind! I could understand their point at times, because every time I was with Russian friends, I found myself acting differently at home. I would be happier, louder, more outspoken, more verbal and much more confident. And that is NOT how a good Armenian girl is supposed to be. An Armenian girl is supposed to be: quiet; forgiving; patient; selfless; predictable and obedient to adults and males of any age.

In my case, having to act one way at home and to act totally different outside, was not an easy task to accomplish. I could not be myself everywhere I went. If someone were to ask me about my personality and which nationality I was more similar to, I could only describe myself one way: I have both Armenian and Russian traits and behaviors in me.

But none of this had anything to do with my life until I turned seven years old. Before that I had been a very happy little girl. I loved to read children's books, play with my friends, spend time with my relatives, and practice playing the piano, at which I always exceeded my age level. I always wanted to be the best at everything, so to perform better than kids my age was very important to me. Many days I practiced for countless hours and did so every chance I got. I felt that my parents loved me and that all of my relatives thought the world of me.

There was nothing negative or sad around me at all and I assumed that my life would always be bright and happy. Unfortunately, that would not be the case, and it all dramatically changed after one day that I mistakenly thought was going to make my life so much better.

That day was in early April 1988 when my beautiful baby brother entered this world. I remember that day like it was yesterday. I was all dressed up waiting for my dad to pick me up so we could go to the hospital and meet the new addition to our happy family. I had a big smile on my face the whole ride there. I remember asking my dad all kinds of questions about the baby, and I recall him being so happy about having a son. Now he knew that his last name would live on for at least another generation. I asked him what his name would be, and he answered proudly.

"I have decided to call him Tigran, after the Armenian king of the 1st Century BC, Tigran the Great!"

"Wow, dad that is so amazing! Now you will have two very serious names in the family! My name is Veronika, which means she who brings victory, and the baby's name is Tigran whom you named after the great king!" I said with great pride echoing in my voice.

When we arrived at the hospital, I jumped out of the car before my dad had even fully stopped it. I charged up half a dozen stairs and flew through the main entrance and into the lobby. My dad was not even inside the building yet, and I was already at the information desk trying to get high enough on my tippy-toes to talk to the receptionist.

"I'm here to pick up my baby!" I screamed with excitement to the person that I could not even see.

A heavy set lady in her late 50's, wearing big round reading glasses, got off the chair and looked at me over the edge of the counter. She was wearing bright red lipstick and was fixing up her big old-fashioned hair-do which she must have sprayed three bottles of hairspray on just to get it to stay in place.

"Where are your parents, noisy little girl"? She asked with a very serious and annoyed expression.

"My dad is coming in any minute! But I can't wait for him and I want to see my baby right away!" I demanded.

"This is a hospital, not a playground, so wait for your father right here and do NOT make any noise!" she replied sternly.

With a sad face, I turned around and slowly walked back towards the entrance, dragging my feet. My dad was already coming up the stairs and my smile came right back.

"Daddy, hurry up. Baby is waiting for us to go get him"! I screamed out loud.

The receptionist got up and told my dad that I needed to be quiet or she would ask me to wait outside. When I heard that, I calmed right down and tried to contain my excitement as much as possible. My dad signed some paperwork and nervously stood next to me while the receptionist went through the door behind her. A few minutes later, one of the doors on our left opened and a nurse wheeled my mother out.

My new little brother looked so cute in my mother's arms. She held him close and stared at him with a smile. She didn't even move her eyes off of him to look up at us. I had never seen her in such a mesmerized state and filled with that much happiness. I ran up to her and started to make happy noises, careful to not be too loud. I was trying not to wake or scare the baby, although he seemed not to mind the sounds and activity around him at all. He looked very confused but I heard that newborns don't see clearly for the first few weeks. I thought he actually looked quite funny. I took another step forward and came up very close to the baby's face.

"Hello my little baby! I have waited for you for sooooo long! Now you are going to play with me, and eat with me, and sleep with me, and watch TV with me, and…" I said at a very fast pace until I was interrupted.

As I spoke, my mother became unusually angry and her face changed from happy to annoyed. She looked right at me and with a raised voice said, "You are standing WAY too close to him. You are WAY too loud for him. You are being quite annoying and obnoxious, so just move away so the baby and I can breathe!"

My face froze and I slowly took a step back in total shock. My eyes opened wide and I started to move quietly backwards. My dad was too busy staring at his newborn to realize how mean my mother had just been. As I was slowly moving back, my mother kept her eyes set right on me. Her actions reminded me of a lioness who was trying to protect her cub. When I was far enough away, she moved her eyes off of me and looked back at the baby. Her face changed again, and now her eyes were loving and bright.

After few minutes, my dad went to sign more papers and told the receptionist that he was going to get the car. My dad left the lobby while my mother was still staring at the baby and touching his hair. She did not even look at me.

When my dad came back, he grabbed the baby and helped my mother out of the wheelchair and down the stairs. For a moment, I thought they had forgotten about me because they did not even call me to go with them. I ran out after them and climbed into the front seat of the car. My mother gave me another stern and unhappy look, and I figured she was probably still mad at me for being too loud. It felt very awkward, as if she didn't want me there at all, and I stayed quiet for the entire ride home.

That day was nothing like I had imagined and dreamed it would be. When my mother screamed at me in the hospital, it was the first time she had ever raised her voice at me or displayed any type of anger toward me. I stared out of the car window and I tried to figure out what went wrong. I couldn't figure out why she reacted the way she did. I wish I knew how dramatically my life was about to change. I wish I would have at least somehow prepared myself for it. My brother's birth was the start of my nightmares and the constant fights for survival that I would face for many years to come.

From that day forward, everything my mother did around the house was now passed on to me. She told me that in addition to keeping the house clean, I had to step up and care of my newborn brother, too. I was definitely confused because although my mother was on maternity leave, she did minimal work throughout the day for the house, baby, or me. When I was home, all she would do was watch TV in her bed, do her nails, try on different make up, experiment with fancy hairdos, and read magazines about the body and skin. All of this made me wonder if that was what she did when I was a newborn, because when I was only a few months old, my parents put me in daycare where I stayed until the first grade. I thought it was odd because there should be no need for daycare if a mother is home on maternity leave for the first three years of the baby's life. She must have had her reasons for doing it.

All I knew is that I now had to keep the house spotless, keep some food in the fridge, the laundry done without a washer or drier, dishes washed, and whatever else she would tell me to do. And while I did all this, I was to take care of the new baby, take care of myself, do my school work and practice the piano. I literally took on the full role of a new mother.

The baby I thought was my brother was now my full-time son. I had to feed him, clean him, rock him to sleep, wash him and do everything that babies require when they are that little. Diapers and other supplies were scarce back in 1988 Russia, and that made it even harder. I had to wash him in the sink every time he would go to the bathroom, and then wash his dirty underwear and pants from the "poo-poo" he would do. Not a fun thing at all.

All the new motherly responsibilities were passed on to me right before I was about to finish first grade in both my regular school and music school. I was very smart, a straight "A" student, energetic, and had an unlimited drive with everything I did. Now, with just a couple of weeks before the school year ended, I was up all night with a newborn and then completely tired throughout the whole next day. I started to miss school as well as piano lessons regularly. If I didn't already have straight "A's", I would have had problems with my teachers in both schools, but thankfully, somehow, I still ended the year with high honors.

The political and economic issues in the country around this time affected our daily life in dramatic ways. The Soviet Union was dissolving. The price of food was going up fast while the supply of food was declining. My father was not making much money because in Russia, doctors and teachers had some of the lowest paying salaries. It was getting hard to survive and basic things like milk, eggs, bread, meat, and even baby formula were hard to come by. My mother's breast feeding was not enough for the baby and we had to add baby formula to his diet. There was a city-wide system in place for being able to buy those products and everyone had to follow it.

I am still not sure how, being a seven year-old girl that this all became my responsibility, but it all became part of my daily duties. If I wanted to eat, then I had to go out there and fight to get the food myself.

My daily schedule was quite astonishing. I had to get up between 4:30 a.m. and 5:00 a.m. and take care of the baby's needs. Then I would get dressed and run out of the house to the first factory that was opening around 7:00 a.m. where I could turn in glass bottles for money. The line was always long, but I had to stay in it to return the bottles to get cash. I would redeem anything I could find, including what we had used the previous day, as well as whatever I could find on the streets and in the garbage areas around our building.

After visiting the first factory, I had to go to four others and stand in long lines to get supplies like bread, milk, eggs, meat, and baby formula. I noticed right away that in every line, I was the only young child, and definitely the only girl. That made it hard because adults and older boys would try to cut in the line in front of me. On many occasions I was physically pushed out of the line and had to fight my way back in.

I did see some mothers with their own little babies in line, but only about one out of every 10-15 people. The majority of people in line were men of all different ages from high school to their late sixties. Most of the factories were about six miles away from the house and far apart from one another. The whole morning routine would usually take me six to eight hours to complete. City buses were off limits for me because they cost too much money and were completely full most of the time. On the few occasions when I tried to get on them, adults would push me out, so I chose to run instead. By the time I did get home, my mother would be annoyed and pissed-off that it took me so long.

After a few weeks of standing in those lines, I started to think to myself why I, a seven year-old girl, would have to be the one doing this almost every day. This responsibility was transforming me into a person I did not want to be. I was becoming a fighter who had to make sure that every single battle was won. The prize was food which I thought I should be provided by my parents. After all, isn't that why all those adults were standing in lines? Wasn't it to bring home food for their kids? Although my dad worked long hours in ER, why was I the one who was not home with the baby or at school where I should be? My mother should have been the one from our family to stand in line, with the baby or without him. If I were doing what my mother should be doing, then I was not a big sister, I was a mother, a mother at seven.

From the end of April, throughout the whole summer and all the way to the first day of school, I dealt with it and kept the aggravation to myself. I assumed that it would all change when I started second grade in September.

When there were only a few days left of that summer, I asked my mother to get me a couple of new things that I thought I deserved and had earned. "Mother, can you get me a new dress and a pair of shoes, please? My shoes are very small and look kind of old and worn out. They are actually starting to hurt my big toes and the back of my feet."

"We have no money to spend on the extra things like that right now," she answered me with a quick and irritated tone.

"But mother, I have blisters and walk barefoot most of the time!" I said back to her with tearful disappointment.

"Just put some butter or a cream on them and cover them with a bandage," she answered, "plus, you won't need anything new, because you won't be going to school on the first day. Your dad was supposed to be off but now he has to work, and I am not standing in line with your brother and running around the city with him between the factories!" she said to me with a raised voice and an angry look on her face.

What she said shocked me and I didn't know how to respond. I was very upset and it bothered me greatly that I was going to miss the first day of second grade.

The first day of school was not the only one I missed. In September alone, I missed over ten school days, which meant I was attending classes only two to three days per week at best. My friends and classmates started to notice that I was often absent from school. They also noticed that I had stopped going outside to play in the evening and on the weekends. I was already an infrequent visitor to the front play yard during that summer, but now I wasn't going out at all.

After a few weeks I noticed that my friendships with classmates and friends from the building had started to fade away. The only days I was able to attend school was when my father was off work and was able to do my routine for me.

It was not long before my "A" student status, of which I was so proud, was gone. In fact, after just a couple of months into the academic year, the only class I had an "A" in was music, and that was only because I had a natural gift in that subject and could pick up new material in mere minutes. With slowly dropping grades and disappearing friendships, I was becoming increasingly depressed.

As soon as I would come in the door from anywhere, my mother would just hand the baby right over to me. It did not matter to her that I just walked in and had not yet taken off my shoes or even gone to the bathroom. It did not matter that I had not yet eaten anything or had homework to do. She would just tell me when the baby ate last, was changed last, and took a nap last. From that moment on, I was to take care of him, without a break, until around 5:00 a.m. the next morning at which point I would have to get ready for my routine all over again or go to school.

Since I was with the baby every possible moment, I was the one who taught him many new things. I showed him how to drink from a sippy cup, hold a spoon, sit up, crawl, say letters and words, and even walk. It felt wonderfully rewarding and gave me a feeling of accomplishment and satisfaction in what was otherwise a depressing existence.

From the beginning of that school year, I was very obedient and did what I was told without questioning either of my parents. But as the end of the first quarter approached and my grades were still going down, I started to realize that I was heading in the wrong direction. It was getting very difficult for me to keep up with the homework, classwork and now even my piano lessons.

I started to complain to my mother about not being able to go to school, read, play piano, and do my homework. I didn't really talk to my dad about it because I did not see him much and it seemed like my mother was the one making all the decisions in our family. I was quite hopeful that my mother would help me and make some household changes to get me back on track. After all, that's what I thought mothers were supposed to do.

With winter slowly approaching and the weather changing to constant rains and lower temperatures, the morning routines were becoming harder and harder to complete. There were longer lines, shorter tempers, daily fights and constant arguments over spots in line and fewer hours the factories were open. There were times when adults grabbed the bags of food right out of my hands, right after I bought them. It was aggravating and started getting me angry about the whole situation that I was in.

With a full daily schedule and no time for anything else, my life became dark and miserable. In just a few months, I went from being a social and lovable girl to having almost no friends and no time to enjoy anything other than time with the baby. Even my teachers started to notice that something was very wrong in both my attendance and in the way I was dressed. I was constantly hungry and I would eat the other students' leftover food in the school cafeteria. I would leave class a few minutes earlier than everyone else so no one would see me grab whatever was left from the kids who had the lunch before us.

The teachers never gave me a hard time about anything, but the kids were a different story. When I would show up at the school, they would make fun of me saying that I hate the school and would rather sit home with a baby all day. They typically targeted me in the cafeteria or right after school, before I left for home. Since many kids in school were from my building and knew why I was always home, they probably were the ones who initially created the common insults about me. But even the kids that I had never seen before would point their fingers at me and taunt me as I walked by:

"Look who decided to show up! Mother at seven! Where is your baby? Go home and take care of your newborn! Mooooooother at seven! Moooooother at seven!"

I was already sad and depressed about my life in general, but now I was developing a serious complex because I was being bullied. Lately, because of all of this, I didn't mind missing school when I had to. I also started to lose weight, and even when I had an appetite, I was rarely able to eat much. At point the best meals I had were the leftovers I could get my hands on in the school cafeteria. When I wasn't in school, I was usually very hungry. There was just never enough to eat at home, and the baby and my mother always came first.

At the end of November, I decided to tell my mother that no matter who depended on me or for what, I could not miss so many days of school anymore. Being a teacher, she should have known that education should be a number one priority for any child, especially someone my age. I felt a bit of hesitation talking to her about it since we didn't have the same relationship we had before the new baby arrived. She was like my best friend right up until then. She used to brush my hair and then put it into a thick, long braid or two. She read books and sang to me, and baked my favorite cakes. But that was all in the past. None of those things had happened for a while now, so to me it felt like I was going to talk to a total stranger.

She was sitting in the kitchen, which had become her favorite place to be, sipping coffee and looking through some fancy magazine. I approached her very quietly.

"Mother, I have to talk to you about something very important."

"Go ahead" she answered me, without looking up.

"I am not doing that well in school anymore and I have to catch up on a couple of months' worth of homework. Also, most of my "A's" have now became "B's" and "C's" and I might be failing a couple of my classes," I explained to her in a calm but worried manner. To my surprise, she did not seem too concerned with anything I said. Instead, she acted very annoyed with my explanation.

"You should work harder to bring your grades back up to 'A's'," she answered.

"I'm trying to do it Mother, but to bring my grades up, I have to be in school every day," I said with the bravest voice that I could muster.

"You are obviously not trying hard enough and that's why you are standing here annoying me," she added with sarcasm.

"I don't have time and that is the problem. I cannot continue to be the one to get the food for the house most mornings."

As soon I said that, she looked up from her magazine and stared right at me. "You will continue doing what you are doing and if you give me any trouble, I will have to deal with you in another way," she said with an angrier voice than before.

I did not know what to say since it was the first time I had stood up for myself and been shot down. I was lost on what my next step should be and was definitely unprepared, so I left the kitchen and went back into the living room. After few minutes of thinking about our conversation, I decided not to go out to the factories the next morning, but to go to school instead. I decided to disobey my mother and to stand up for myself and do the right thing for me. I didn't take her warnings about disobeying her too seriously.

As usual, I woke up around 4:30 a.m. The baby slept in his crib next to the couch in the living room. The living room was where I lived most of the time and the couch was my bed. Having the crib next to me was working out quite well, because it made it easier for me to wake up in the middle of the night if the baby cried and needed to be fed and changed.

I cleaned and fed my baby brother, brought him quietly to my mother's bedroom, and placed him on my dad's side of the bed since he wasn't yet back from his 24-hour shift. I then grabbed all my books and ran out of the house. I never had a backpack, so I had to carry the books in my arms pretty much all day. The school was about five miles away, but I never minded walking the distance. It was much better than the dozens of miles I had to walk and run between home and those factories.

I was very excited as I made my way to school. It felt good inside to finally stand up for myself and to do what I believed in. Even though I ran most of the way, I was still very late to my first class and I didn't arrive until it was almost over. As usual, it was OK with my teacher, and I just tried to enjoy every minute of my classes and lunch as much as I could.

When I got home, I immediately sensed something wasn't right. The front door was unlocked, like I was expected to come home at that exact time and it was quiet. There were no usual sounds, like from the baby, the TV, or music from the radio. I slowly opened the door and took a few steps inside.

"Mom?" "Dad?" There was no answer.

I walked into the kitchen and saw my parents sitting at the table across from each other. There was another man, with his back towards me as well, sitting between them. He turned around and I quickly recognized him from when he came to our house for a party a few months back. He was in his early 40's, a little over six feet tall, skinny, with thick brown hair, and strange, triangle-shaped eyebrows. In the past, I was told he was a distant uncle, and also happened to be my dad's best friend from many years in medical school.

After a few seconds, my dad broke the silence. "Do you remember Uncle Armen"? he asked.

"Yes" I answered as I nodded my head.

"Your mother called him here because last night she realized that you are entering the age when you are going to start to disobey her and me. With my busy work schedule and not being home and available that much, she needs help from someone else to discipline you, just in case," he said.

"What is discipline?" I asked.

"It's when you don't listen to your mother or me. That is when Uncle Armen will make sure that you do and you have to obey her, me, and him now," my dad replied back. "Understand"?

"OK." Still confused, I just looked at him and then I ran into the living room. My baby brother was sleeping in his crib, so I took out my books and started on my homework. I could smell the baby's dirty undies and felt bad because I knew that he had probably not been changed in at least a few hours. I didn't want to wake him so I planned to change him as soon as he woke on his own.

About twenty minutes later, he woke up and started to cry. Before I could pick him up, my mother walked into the living room. Without saying a word to me or even looking at me, she grabbed the baby from the crib and left the room in a rush. It surprised me, because when I was home, I was the one who was supposed to be caring for him. A few minutes later, while I was reading one of my homework assignments aloud, Uncle Armen walked into the room. I could see he was very angry as he had a tense look on his face. I was confused, since it was only the second or third time I had ever seen him and I didn't know why he had such a strange facial expression. As he started to slowly move toward me, he unclasped his black leather belt and took it off. It was like a slow motion movie and I was not sure what exactly he was doing. I actually thought it was kind of funny.

As he came closer, he folded his belt in half and grabbed the buckle side of it with his right hand. I was not moving because I honestly had no idea what he was about to do or why. Without taking his eyes off of me, he raised his hand and hit me across my wrists with his leather belt. I paused for a second, in complete shock; then suddenly a sharp pain raced through my whole body. I let out a piercing scream and my eyes filled with tears from the pain. My wrists turned bright red, with the perfect imprint of his belt lines across them. I immediately moved my hands off of the books and under the table. Without waiting more than a few seconds, he raised his hand again, and this time since my hands were under the table, the belt slashed across my upper arms. I screamed even louder.

"Your father is in the shower and you mother doesn't want to hear it, so do not scream. Screaming is useless at this moment," he said to me as I shot off my chair and ran into the corner.

He took a few big steps toward me and raised his hand again. Thinking that he was aiming for my hands, I quickly put them behind me; but that didn't stop him and within a few more seconds the belt landed right across my face. I screamed again and grabbed my right cheek, now burning from the pain. I crawled from one side of the room to the other, trying to get under the piano. As I was struggling to crawl away as fast as I could, I felt a very hard hit on my back from the belt. The strength of it made me fall from my knees and onto my stomach. As I tried to cover the spot that just got hit, I felt another hit. and that one hurt even worse since it landed on the exact same place.

I screamed as loudly as I could: "Maaaa!" "Mommy!" "Mommmmmyyy!" " Daddddyyy!"

I tried to grab the loose end of the belt to stop him from using it on me while at the same time I was begging him to stop. For some reason this made him angrier and he hit me again. This time the belt landed on the other side of my face, and now my whole face and body were enveloped in a terrible, burning pain. After a couple more hits, I managed to escape from that corner and I ran out of the living room. Seeing that my dad was in the shower, I ran into the kitchen. I figured there must be a reason why my mother hadn't come to my rescue or heard me calling her name so many times. I had to find her.

As I made my way to the kitchen, I froze in place. My mother was sitting only a few feet away reading a women's fashion magazine while my brother sat on her right leg. She had a cup of hot, freshly-brewed coffee in front of her along with assorted chocolate candy. I hadn't even seen candy in months. She did not even look up at me or move even though I was standing next to the table. My whole face was covered in tears and my breathing was heavy. I couldn't understand why she wasn't paying any attention to me.

Armen walked into the kitchen and I immediately crawled under the kitchen table, pleading for my mother to stop him. She did not say a word. A few seconds later, my brother started to cry, probably from hearing me cry. Armen moved close to the table but the baby became cried even louder. Now my mother was getting annoyed with both of us crying and was making some aggravated sounds of her own.

I couldn't comprehend why she still hadn't stopped Armen because it should be clearly every mother's responsibility to protect her children. After all, that's the trust that bonds a mother and her child together forever.

A minute later, Armen was actually the one who ended it.

"I think she got enough punishment this first time."

"Are you sure she has learned her lesson?" my mother asked him back.

"Yes, I think so. She got about a dozen hits all over."

"OK, fine. If you say she is all set, then she is."

When I heard my mother say those things, my heart almost broke. I felt such a deep emotional pain from hearing her say those words that I stopped wiping my tears and froze right there on the floor under that table. I felt betrayed. All the good things she had ever done for me disappeared from my memory in an instant.

I stayed under the table for at least two hours until after Armen left. My father finished his shower and both of my parents went to their bedroom with my brother. During those two hours, no one even checked on me. No one asked if I was OK or if I was even alive. The whole time I was under that table, I felt completely deceived by both of my parents; by my mother for asking Armen to beat me up, so harshly and painfully and by my father who let it happen and didn't say anything to Armen or my mother. It was mind-boggling to know that I would experience such betrayal at such a young age while others live their whole lives without knowing what betrayal is.

I was getting very thirsty and my wounds were burning and becoming more swollen. I desperately needed some cold water to cool them off, so I came out from under the table and ran into the bathroom. My whole body was in excruciating pain and my wounds were very tender. An uncontrollable amount of tears started to flow from my eyes again as I put cold water on most of the spots where he hit me. At that moment I was in both physical agony and indescribable emotional pain.

My stomach was making a growling sound, so I went to the kitchen to look for something to eat. I saw one leftover boiled egg on a plate and grabbed it. I swallowed it almost whole as I ran back into the living room. I slammed the door behind me and put up two chairs against it so no one could get in. I tried to lie down on the sofa but the whole back of my body was in pain from the beating. The only painless position I could find was to sit on the edge of the couch so the backs of my legs weren't touching it and my back didn't touch it either. With my hands down by my sides and my back now bent forward, I sat there in a state of complete shock trying to understand what had just happened to me and what I was supposed to do now.

This was the first time that I had ever felt such a terribly unbearable pain on both my body and in my heart. I promised myself that I would never disobey anyone in my life again, but I did not keep that promise. That beating was just the beginning of the tortures I would experience in this new hell.

After that first beating, Uncle Armen became an almost-daily visitor to our house. No matter what I did, right or wrong, if my mother was not satisfied with it, she would threaten me with more discipline from him. Many times she would call him right in front of me and an hour or two later, he would just show up at our house to do what he did the best; beat me as badly as he wanted to until he got tired, or until my baby brother would somehow crawl toward us. I grew to believe that he deeply enjoyed watching me suffer and writhe in pain.

Now, after almost a year of trying to survive these beatings and doing whatever I could to make them stop, here I was on a beautiful Sunday morning standing on the edge of my balcony window, ready to end my misery and pain by flying away with my dream eagle.

This moment was supposed to be my wildest dream to ever come true, but it didn't play out as I wished it would have. Just as I was about to jump, I felt something small, soft and warm grasp my right ankle. I opened my eyes and looked down to see what it was, then quickly grabbed the glass to keep my balance. As I turned my head and looked down, I saw my baby brother holding my ankle with his pudgy little hand. One of his legs was already on top of the dresser.

I was so confused that I couldn't say a word, yet it seemed to me that the baby was aware of what was happening.

"Veya? You go? Food! Veya, story! Veya, play! Veyaaa!"

I stood there on the edge completely frozen and looked at him not knowing what to do. I even looked over at the bed to see if he was really holding onto me or if I was lost in some strange kind of dream. The bed was empty and his blanket was hanging half way to the floor. It really was he, and not only was he holding one ankle, but he was trying to grab my other ankle with his other hand, too.

I felt his other little hand grab me, and he was holding me firmly by both of my feet. He looked at me with a wide, fearless smile across his face even though he was very close to the edge. If he would haves moved just a little further forward, he would have fallen out of the fifth floor window. I was in too much shock to think about that. Everything was happening too fast.

With the last bit of strength I had left, I said, "Tiko, please go away! I can't stay here and I can't take you with me! If I don't succeed in flying on this first try, then I will stay here with you; but for now please go to the living room and play! I will try to come back for you. Please just let go of my feet!"

My eyes started to well up with tears as I pleaded with him to let go, but the little guy just wouldn't give up. I was getting scared, anxious, and confused. I didn't want to push him away because if I did, he would fall off of the dresser and get hurt. It was also getting harder for me to hold onto the glass as my fingers were getting numb.

My mind had been clear but now so many things were starting to fill it, that I started to lose my balance. I moved my right foot off of the window's edge and back onto the top of dresser. I then blocked the gap in the window with my other foot so the baby wouldn't fall out of the window by mistake. He looked very uncomfortable, and I realized that it must have been hard for him to hold on to me for that long. I moved my second foot off of the window and back onto the top of the dresser. As I did that, all kinds of pain and negativity filled my body and mind and I was right back where I started. It was the same feeling of dread that I had lived with for so many months now, leading up to this morning.

"If I could just push him away or down to the chair or the floor," I thought to myself; but he was still looking right at me with his big brown eyes and his beautiful, innocent smile. I had to do something while my brave self was still here at the edge of this window. I was getting mad as I realized that my dream was disappearing with every passing second and I was doing nothing about it.

Hoping I could get him to understand this time, I addressed him again. "Baby, I cannot stay. Don't you understand that? I just cannot do it! I cannot handle the torture, neglect and abuse. You have to take care of yourself now or find someone else who can. Now please, if you love me, let me go! Let me go for all the good that I have done for you"!

"Veya. I poo-poo. Hungry, play, story." was all I heard back.

Just minutes ago, I was about to be freed from it all, and would never have to deal with the emotional or physical pain ever again. Now my dream was disappearing because of that child and the realization of that started to fill my mind. I knew that if I stayed, I may never again find the courage to be this brave and to end the misery and hell I was in.

"Oh! My God! Where is the eagle?" I screamed out loud.

I spun my head back around as fast as I could. I had become so wrapped up with what was happening that I forgot that the eagle was waiting for me. As I looked up to the spot where I saw him last, I realized he was not there any longer. He was leaving! The only thing I could still see was his barely-visible outline disappearing far away into the summer sky. He had become tired of waiting and left me behind.

I shouted to him "Please wait" but he did not even turn his head or move off his course. His body was becoming smaller and smaller by the second until I could no longer see him along the horizon.

I stood and stared out for several seconds with an empty heart and eyes full of tears. Then I turned back around toward my baby brother and saw him in the same spot. He was still holding on to me with both of his little arms without realizing what he had just done. My tears flowed from my eyes and rolled down my face, over the dresser and onto the baby's arms.

"Do you have any idea what you just did? I might never get a chance or find enough courage to fly away and to free myself ever again!" I screamed at him.

He showed no reaction and I decided to take control of my anger and calm myself down. As I became more aware of what I was doing and the danger the baby was in standing up so high, my reality started to settle back in and with that my motherly instinct, which I had developed so well, took over both my mind and my body. To keep the baby safe, I decided to quickly close the windows back together and get him down. My fingers and palms were in pain and so were the bottoms of my feet which now felt heavy and numb. The fresh air was coming in less and less, as the glass came together and closed. I realized that my dream was now gone and that I was not going anywhere. I now needed to get down as fast as possible, clean the windows and pick up the small mess we had made.

Although I still had a few hours before either of my parents came home, my feeling of worry was growing with every passing moment. I got down off of the dresser, grabbed the baby, and left the balcony, picking his blanket up off of the floor on the way.

We went into the kitchen where I sat him in his high chair in order to feed him a freshly-cut banana. He was getting excited and was clapping his cute little hands together as I prepared his food.

It was at that moment I realized that I just did something only a real mother would do for her baby. I had made a pure and unconditional sacrifice to give up on my dreams of inner and outer peace and a chance to be in heaven even though my beautiful brown eagle had come to help me and to take me with him. A feeling that I did not know little girls were capable of having, over powered me. It was a pure and selfless motherly instinct that most mothers possess from the moment they start to carry their babies in their bellies or from the minute they see their babies for the first time.

I knew that I was voluntarily staying in this abusive, neglectful, slavery-like hell. Even if I were to survive until I was old enough to run away, knows if I would ever be brave enough to try to do it.

Still lost in my thoughts, I put the bib on him and started to feed him the banana. He was looking right at me and smiling as he chewed his food using only the few front teeth he had. I felt his hand on my other hand and I looked down. I saw him firmly holding my fingers, as if he was afraid for me to leave.

After he was finished eating, I washed the spoon and his small dish; then I brought him to the bathroom to wash up. That whole time he was still smiling, but I surely wasn't. Then I brought him into the living room and set him on the couch.

"Sit here while I go clean the fingerprints off of the balcony window, and don't move!" I said to him in a strict manner.

All of a sudden I heard a loud knock on the front door. I got nervous because neither of my parents ever came home that early on a Sunday, and Uncle Armen never visited on Sunday either.

I told the baby to be quiet and went to the door to check and see who it was. I stood up on a small chair so I was able to see through the peep hole. As soon as I saw who it was, my knees and body started to shake.

My heart beat very fast and I felt lightheaded. I asked myself, "How can this be and why now, on Sunday, when we are alone? Please, no," I whispered to myself.

I got down from the chair and slowly slid my body down against the door until it hit the floor. All of a sudden, my back felt the very hard knocking through the door, and this time it was not coming from a hand, but a foot: a big, strong, angry foot. I knew I only had a few more seconds to open the door before he was going to get very mad.

The image of my beautiful eagle came back into my mind for a split second and then instantly disappeared as I moved to open the chain on the door. My left hand slowly grabbed the only lock we had and I turned it open. The moment the door was unlocked, he swung it open with a very powerful force, knocking the chair and me back to the floor.

"This is it," I said to myself. "This is it."

CHAPTER 3
Little Feet in the River

U ncle Armen was one of those people who could get upset at every little thing no matter how good a mood he was in. He reminded me of the stepmother from the fairy tale "Cinderella." No matter what I would do, even if it was exactly what he asked me to do, he would still pick on me and find something negative or wrong with it.

As he opened the barely-unlocked door with the force of his shoulder, I was thrown to the floor a few feet away. He walked right in and saw that he had knocked me down and that I was frightened and shaking from head to toe. I became even more scared when he looked at me and said:

"Give me just ONE reason why it took you so long to unlock the door, just ONE!"

"Aaaaah… I… I… don't know why. I… I… I… was with the baby in the living room and then I… I… I… heard the knocking and came to the door right away," I answered with a very quiet and shaky voice.

"I knocked for at least two minutes, so don't lie to me! Don't ever lie to me!" he shouted as he walked up and put his shoe right on my stomach.

"I swear I was with the baby in the living room when I heard the knocks," I answered back to him while starting to cough from the pressure of his foot pushing harder and harder into my stomach.

"That's it" he said. "Now get up and go into the corner and stand on your knees for the next three hours!"

"I can't get up. Please move your foot!" I begged as I tried to wiggle away.

"Get up now or I will smash your face," he warned with a very angry stare.

"I can't move, uncle! Please move your foot off of my stomach and I will get right up and go to the corner," I mumbled, while coughing and trying to catch my breath.

He bent down and smacked me across my face. Then, as hard as he could, he pushed his booted foot into my stomach. The pain was beyond any belt or spanking I had ever received before. It was a terrible feeling and wasn't something I could even describe. I let out a squawking sound but he warned me that if the baby heard me, he would make my next disciplinary session last much longer. I covered my mouth with my hands and he moved his foot off of my stomach. I instinctively crawled into a ball to try to recover from the strange yet awful pain. And as I did that, he kicked my thigh and told me to get off of the floor and go into the corner immediately. I slowly got up and crawled to the spot; it was a spot with which I had become very familiar.

The corner was by the front door in the foyer, and as I got on my knees to start my punishment, Armen went to the kitchen to get a plastic bag and some dry beans to fill it. Forcing me to kneel on the beans was just one of the sick methods of discipline he had been us-ing on me for the past few months. Though it may not sound too bad, the pain was unimaginable.

It was actually not too bad for the first few minutes, but soon after my knees would become hard, sore, and numb. I am not sure where he got those large beans or where he learned such a terrible method of torture, but that punishment surely served its purpose very well.

When he came back with the bag, it looked much larger than usual, but I didn't question him. He laid it down in front of me and told me to put my knees on it. I knew I only had about ten minutes before the pain would become so intense that I would have to go into a special routine to overcome it.

I had actually developed a few techniques to numb the pain he inflicted on me. First, I would take very deep breaths, as many as I needed, and all in a row, until I would start to feel light-headed. Then I would repeat that every time the light-headed feelings started to go away. This made me feel like I was half asleep and half awake. It was almost like living in a dream.

As time went on, that method didn't have as strong a numbing effect on me as I wished it did, but still, it did work a little and was better than doing nothing at all about the pain. From the first time Armen hit me with the belt up until now, almost a year later, he had modified his abusive techniques to inflict as much pain and suffering as he could.

A couple of months after using only the leather part of the belt on me, he started to use the side with the metal buckle. The pain from that was absolutely unbearable and excruciating. It did not matter what part of my body the buckle hit; all the areas were bad. Every hit would leave an exact imprint of the actual buckle embedded on my skin, and if any of his lashes hit my face, I would have to stay home until the marks were gone. Apparently, my parents cared after all.

They didn't want someone to see the bruises and question why I had them.

I could never understand why they worried about that, because even when I had a few visible marks on my face or neck, teachers never asked where I got them or even who did it to me. All I knew at that point was that I must have deserved the abuse, and whatever Armen was doing was simply trying to make me a better girl. It made sense to me that only bad kids would get in trouble and earn the right to be disciplined.

After a while, even the belt with its leather and buckle wasn't good enough for Uncle Armen. He started to use other odd and sadistic torture methods.

He would pick a night, usually when my dad was on his 24-hour shift at the ER, and would stay at our house until the next morning. After my mother would take my brother into her bedroom and go to sleep, he would purposely keep me from falling asleep. He would turn on all the lights in the living room and force me to sit upright on a chair. If I ever closed my eyes, even for a split second, he would hit me with the metal buckle as hard as he could, either on my legs or on my arms. If I screamed, I would be so brutally beaten the next day that I wouldn't be able to sit down for at least two to three days. I always feared he would add another layer of punishment and keep me away from any food or water which I found harder to deal with than the pain. I stayed as quiet as I could and rarely made a sound and on those occasions when I did close my eyes, he would hit me with the belt to wake me up. I realized later that he must have had to really prepare for our "disciplinary" sessions, because I saw him drink a lot more tea during those evenings then he usually would. The tea helped him stay up late and gave him more energy.

Although I knew of many bad girls in our neighborhood, none of them were ever abused or tortured. I guessed they must have not been as bad as I was, or that they just didn't have an uncle like mine.

I even knew about kids who hit their own parents, stole money from them for extra snacks, slept at their friend's house against the parent's wishes and even missed school day after day. I didn't understand how I was fitting into this "bad girl" category, but I guessed that my parents and Uncle Armen knew better than I did; they were the adults, after all.

* * *

It was now around the middle of August. I had done everything I could to be a good girl for three straight days and hadn't done anything to get Uncle Armen or my parents angry. This was the longest I had gone without punishment since he had first started the beatings.

Because of that, as well as because I had completed all my daily chores, my mother allowed me to go and play outside, but just for couple of hours. It was a Saturday morning and she had her friend over to our apartment. They were coloring each other's hair. Armen and my dad weren't home so as soon as my mother said I could go out, I took a quick drink of water from the kitchen faucet and rushed toward the front door. I was so happy to finally be able to go and play outside that even the worn-out flip-flops that I kept gluing back together were not going to stop me from going.

"Where are you going alone?" My mother screamed out.

"What do you mean alone? I thought you said I could go outside and play?" I answered.

"Yes, you can go outside, but obviously not alone! Take your brother with you. He needs fresh air and I am too busy to watch him at this moment," she responded.

I paused for a second, and in a disappointed voice, told my brother to go get his shoes and a hat. It was cute how eagerly he crawled to get his things. He was very happy to go outside, especially with me, but I surely was not happy about it. I just wanted to play with my friends for a change, and be free for couple of hours, without having to be responsible for my baby brother.

My mother didn't even see us leave as she was too busy gossiping with her friend. The baby wasn't yet walking around with ease and most of the time crawled from room to room, so I just carried him on my back so he wouldn't slow me down. As soon as I closed the door, he held tightly to my neck as I made my way down the stairs.

When we arrived outside, I immediately found all my friends playing one of my favorite games — it was called "family" — a game I hadn't played in a year. As soon as they saw me they called me over because I was very good at that game and most of the time played the role of the father and the husband.

"Finally" said one of my friends who shared my first name. "No one ever wants to play the role of a father except you and we haven't been able to play the "family" game to the fullest since you last came outside!"

"I know. I'm sorry. I have been very busy, but I am here now!" I answered with a smile.

"OK, put the baby down and get ready to climb the plum tree with your 'daughters,' to get us something for 'dinner,'" she said happily. After all, in this game, she was the mother in our family and I was the father: our usual set up. It is quite ironic that I always played the father's role, considering how many other kids could have played it. Fathers are supposed to be the protectors and the money makers; and they are supposed to be strong both mentally and physically, or so I believed. I put my baby brother down in the grass just a few feet away from the tree.

"OK, children, let's do this. Let's get some fruit for mom," I said loudly, taking control.

I was the best tree climber in the neighborhood and always got the best and the biggest fruit from every tree. I climbed all kinds of trees — apple, pear, plum, and even cherry -- and I always climbed as high as possible. Sometimes I climbed so high I could see into the 3rd floor windows. After everyone ate the fruit I was able to pick, one of my friends announced an idea.

"Why don't all of us head to the river, just to see how high the water has gotten."

"That's a great idea! Let's go check it out," said my other friend while getting up off the ground and putting her new pink flip-flops back on.

I threw my two cents in. "Do we have to go over there because I don't think I'm allowed. I kind of have to be here right in the front, in case my mother calls me to go home." I added with a bit of disappointment, sadness and fear in my voice.

"Oh stop it Vera, come with us! We're only going to check the water level and be back here in the yard within a few minutes! No one will even know you left!" one of my friends answered, using my nickname.

I looked at my brother who was happy no matter what he did, as long as he did it with me. Then I looked up to the 5th floor kitchen window to make sure my mother and her friend weren't looking outside and I picked the baby up off of the ground. I was easy to convince when it came to doing or trying out fun stuff for a quick minute or two.

"OK, I will go, but only for a few minutes," I announced to everyone, still a little nervous but excited.

The river was about 100 feet away from our building, which only took five minutes of walking. The river was named after our city — Sochi — and connected the Caucasus Mountains to the Black Sea. The river was about twenty-eight miles long, but the part of the river near us was at its end. The sea was only about a mile away from that point.

Most of the year the river was shallow and most people could walk across it by getting only their legs wet, at the most to their knees. Sometimes there were weeks when the heavy rains or the snow melting from the mountains would increase the water level to as high as three or four feet. At least once each year the river would rise over ten feet and overflow, come out of its banks, and flood the nearby streets with a few feet of water.

As we were making our way to it, one of my friends started to talk about crossing the river over to the other side. After all it wasn't that deep. As soon as we arrived at the river, we looked over the cement railing and saw that water was at its low point, barely a couple of feet deep. Even though they promised that we were going to just look at the water level and go back, my friends then insisted on going down to the shoreline to touch the water and check the temperature.

There was an opening in the railing about 250 feet from where we were standing. It looked like the start of a small path that led from the river walk and right into the river. I had once watched a few older gentlemen sit there and try to catch fish. At the water level, the opening was about twenty feet wide and could fit ten people if they were sitting next to each other.

Without waiting, all my friends started to run toward it. I ran too, along with my brother, who was happily riding on my back, just like a cowboy on a wild horse.

After we all arrived and dipped our hands in the water, one of my more adventurous friends said that we should now all wade across it. Everyone agreed in an instant, but I hesitated.

"I can't walk over to the other side! My skirt will get wet and the baby might fall off of my back," I told them with great disappointment.

"Well, you can't stay here alone! It's boring!" one of them said trying to convince me. "Plus, you NEVER go outside, and who knows when you'll be able to come out again! Just leave the baby right here and he can watch us from the shore."

"I guess if I leave him to sit here, he won't fall off my back and he will be safely watching me," I said aloud with growing excitement. "But we have to be very fast or I might get into trouble."

A moment later, all of my friends started to walk one after the other into the water. When they were all a couple of feet from shore, they turned and waved me to follow them. I took the baby off of my back and set him down a few feet away from the edge. I didn't even realize that the time my mother had given me to play outside had expired.

"Just sit right there and do not move. I will be right back! Just sit and watch me cross over the river," I told the baby.

He smiled back at me and drooled on his little white bib which was already covered in food stains. I rolled up my skirt as high as I could, and stepped into the cold, yet refreshing water. It felt good on the bottom of my feet, since they had become dry and warm walking around without my flip flops for a couple of hours. I had left them behind at the tree because they were so worn out and about to break. I carefully took step after step, making sure I was not stepping on anything sharp or slippery. As I was making my way across, I was carried away by the excitement of what I was doing. After few minutes, I was already standing in the deepest part of the river, right in the middle. My friends were most of the way to the other side but that was OK; I wasn't in any rush, because this challenge was super fun and very exciting.

A moment later, my eyes opened as wide as they could and I realized that I had not even once turned my head to check on the baby. I moved my whole body back, with a super-fast speed. For the rest of my life, I will never forget what I saw.

My brother was sitting on the edge with his legs almost fully emerged in the water. He was wobbling and moving back and forth, while trying to touch the current with his little hands. I don't know how he made his way from where I left him all the way to the river's edge, but it didn't matter. I was petrified!

"Do NOT move! Do NOT rock! Stay still! I am coming to get you right now", I screamed out loud, while trying my best to stay calm.

The baby heard me, looked up, stopped moving for a split second and then continued rocking again. Realizing that at any moment he could fall right into the water, I started to head towards the shore as fast as I could. The water was making it impossible to run and my progress was slow and frustrating. My eyes were dead set on the baby and I was not even looking where I was stepping as I had done when I walked into the river. I felt sharp things on the bottom of the river cut my feet. The pain shot through my whole body but that was not what I was thinking about.

The thought of how I was a terrible sister to leave a little baby alone on the edge of the river was filling up my head. How selfish it was of me I thought, to want to have fun with my friends while I was supposed to watch him and stay with him every single moment.

The baby was rocking harder and harder. His legs were almost fully in the water, and the edge he was sitting on was becoming more submerged. It seemed like the river had become higher than when I first got in. The water was known to rise unexpectedly and rapidly; it's just that was the worst time for that to be happening.

When I was almost ten steps away from him, I heard very loud screams coming from somewhere higher up and far away. I didn't pay attention to them because I needed to keep my eyes on the baby. There was a good chance he was going to jump or fall into the river at any given moment, and I would have to be ready in case I had to dive in after him. Seconds later, the screaming became louder, and I recognized the voice at the same time that I saw my mother running toward the river entrance where the baby was sitting. It was one of the most terrifying moments of my life not only because at any second the baby could fall into the water and possibly drown, but also because my mother was completely freaking out and screaming at the top of her lungs.

Everything was happening so fast and when I was only a couple of steps away from the baby, my mother was already running down the river walk toward us. As I looked up at her, she reached out to grab him, but a second before she did, the baby jumped right into the river.

My mother let out the loudest scream that I have ever heard, dropped to her knees, and submerged both of her arms fully into the water after him. As she did that, I dove into the river to try to grab him somehow. He was already submerged, but by some miracle, I was able to grab him by his leg. I pushed him up out of the water and my mother pulled him out by his arms. He looked scared and was spitting water out of his mouth. She slapped him on his back as fast as possible, trying to make it easier for him to cough up all the water.

Meanwhile, I was still in the water, breathing heavily and totally afraid to come out. My mother pushed the baby into her chest and started to go up the path and onto the main river walk. When I could not see her anymore, I got out of the river and stood on the cement shore. I was completely exhausted and scared about what had just happened. I looked up to the other side of the river and saw all of my friends standing on the other side staring back at me in complete shock.

All of a sudden, I felt sharp pains coming from the bottom of my feet and my ankles. I looked down and realized they were all cut and bloody in at least a dozen places. The bottom of the river had a lot of sharp objects like broken glass, bottles, metal and other types of debris. I remembered that many kids from our neighborhood threw all kinds of bottles and junk in there for fun, sometimes just to see who could throw it the farthest. I guess they didn't need the money because they could have returned those bottles and could have gotten cash like I did. Whether it was from the broken glass or other things, there was no doubt my feet were cut quite badly. It looked like I had a bright red pair of ankle socks on.

I got up and made my way up to the main river walk. I looked down to wave to my friends who were still watching the whole thing from the other side. As I started to walk toward our building, I realized that I was not going to see them for a very long time, not after what I just did and I would be right.

As I made my way up the stairs to the 5th floor, all I could think about was what I was going to say to my mother. Other than apologizing, what else could I possibly do for her not to hate me or punish me too severely? It was bad enough that she didn't love me at all. Now, I guessed she would definitely hate me. I had almost killed her only son.

When I made it to our door I dropped to the floor right in front of it. I was so tired, so hungry, so thirsty, and I had to go to the bathroom really badly. Not to mention, my feet were killing me.

I knocked on the door a few times, but heard nothing back. I rang the doorbell a few times and still didn't hear anything in return. I didn't know what else to do, other than try and knock on the door much harder. Still there were no signs that anyone would open the door for me.

I wished someone else from the other two apartments on our floor were home so I could at least go to the bathroom and wash my bloody feet but it seemed like the whole 5th floor was silent. The apartment across from us had an older couple living there who were always very nice. The older lady would often ask my mother for sugar, salt, and other stuff whenever she ran out. My mother would gladly give it to her. At first, I thought it was because my mother was trying to be nice, but then I found out that she was only being generous because most of the time the lady returned twice the amount she borrowed. I tried knocking on her door, but she was also not home.

After sitting there for at least ten minutes, I decided to apologize to my mother right through the door. A few minutes later, and after I shouted "sorry" through the door at least a dozen times, she came up to the door and said, "I am not going to ever forgive you for what you did, so sit there and think deeply on what you have done."

"Mother, I know what I did was very terrible, but I will never do that again. I am very sorry," I answered her back through my tears. After hearing no response for at least another five minutes, I decided to tell her that both of my feet were cut.

"Mom, please let me in! I have to go to the bathroom badly! My belly hurts and my feet got all cut up and are bleeding from running in the water," I begged.

"Yeah, sure I will be right there. Hold on a minute," she answered, but her voice sounded like it was farther away.

A few more minutes passed and the door remained locked. I thought about going to the bathroom outside, but couldn't even move because of the belly ache. When I couldn't hold it in anymore, ashamed, and like an animal, I peed on myself right there while sitting on that floor. And then, without realizing it, I fell asleep.

I woke up a little later when my dad came home and wanted to know why I was lying there in such a terrible condition. I was a little confused at first, but then realized that I was still outside of the apartment. Without saying anything more, he grabbed me, knocked on the door and then pushed it open. To my surprise it was unlocked. My mother must have opened it after I fell asleep.

"I don't want to see that pig, so keep her out of my sight!" shouted my mother, as soon as she heard us come in.

"What is going on over here and why is she outside on the floor with bloody feet and completely wet clothes?" he asked her in an angry manner while looking me over. "She smells like pee," he added even louder.

"If I tell you what she did, you will kill her with your own two hands," my mother screamed back.

"It doesn't matter at this moment, because both of her legs are covered in blood and she is not in good condition."

"Trust me! You shouldn't care about her bleeding or even breathing! She almost killed my child! Is that something that I should be OK with?" she screamed back at him with more anger than before.

"I don't know who was trying to kill whom, but you and the baby look OK to me while Vera's clothes are completely wet. She smells like urine and both of her feet are covered in blood," my dad answered in an even angrier tone.

Before I was able to tell him that I peed myself only because my mother wouldn't open the door, he told me to go to the bathroom and clean up. He followed me there and took out a bottle of medicinal alcohol to clean up my wounds. The alcohol burned so badly that I screamed, but my dad didn't say anything. He knew that screaming helped me somewhat cope with the pain.

"I don't have time to listen to what happened, but we will talk about this tomorrow. I am on my break and have to go back to work," he said to me in an unhappy manner.

"Dad, please don't leave. Take me to work with you. I don't want to stay here today! I will sleep in the ambulance or in the waiting room until you finish," I begged.

"You can't come with me because I am working in the busiest department of the ER today and I have very difficult cases to deal with, non-stop," he answered. "Take a shower, eat, and put bandages on all of your cuts. We will talk tomorrow."

He then looked at his silver-toned Citizens wristwatch and left the bathroom. "I have to go now," he said to my mother as he walked out the door. "We will talk about everything tomorrow."

I quickly locked myself in the bathroom and lay down on the tile floor. I used to do that after I was beaten because the cold tiles felt better on my fresh, burning hot wounds. Now I was just too tired to even shower, eat, or change, so I just lay down and closed my eyes.

Although my dad didn't protect me from Uncle Armen's discipline, I still liked it when he was home because Armen would only use his belt on me and nothing else. He only used all the other types of punishments when my father had long shifts at work. Today was one of those days, and with what I did, I could only imagine how Armen was going to punish me for it.

I don't know how long I was out, but a very loud knock on the bathroom door woke me up. As I expected, it was Uncle Armen.

"Open the door right now before I break it down!" he screamed into the small area between the door and the wall.

"OK, OK, I'm getting up," I said very quietly, yet loud enough for him to hear me. I unlocked the door and before it was even fully open, Armen thrust his big hand out and grabbed me by my long, thick hair. All I thought to myself was, *here we go, time to start taking those deep breaths and holding the air in longer to feel less pain.*

"I know EVERYTHING," he screamed at me, while pulling me out of the bathroom, through the hallway, and into the living room. "I know what you did and how you planned that out," he added as he dragged me behind him. I didn't say a word and just continued deep breathing.

"What kind of eight year old plans such a terrible crime, so carefully and so calculated? What girl would attempt to kill her own brother in such a terrible way as by drowning him?!" he screamed right into my face. "You wanted him to be drowned in the water? That's great, because now you will not see water at all until you will be almost near death! I will make sure you are near death before you can have one drop of it."

"Kill who? Kill my baby? I would never do such a thing! It was a totally unplanned accident! A mistake of mine and I would..."

A huge hit from his wrist landed right on my face before I could even finish my explanation. He then threw me down on the floor and started to kick me with his brown leather loafers on my upper legs and lower belly. I curled into a ball and didn't make a sound. Deep breathing wasn't helping this time.

"Those small cuts on your feet will be the least of your concerns, low-life animal," he said to me as he took a few steps to grab something from behind the TV. I didn't even try to see what he went to get because I really couldn't move. All I wanted to do was starve myself of more oxygen so I could numb the pain I was in.

A few second later I heard a strange whistling sound, and then I felt something very sharp and cutting hit me on my upper leg. For a second I was confused about the type of a pain it was, because I hadn't felt anything like this in the past and didn't recognize it. A second later I uttered the strangest and loudest cry I had ever made. The pain went from sharp, to burning, to excruciating. Whatever that was, it could not be from this planet and was not meant to be used on any kind of living creature. My body straightened within a second and I looked down to see the spot which just got hit. All I saw was a thin red line of blood that ran the entire width of the front of my upper leg. Before I could figure out what I just saw, I heard another whistling sound, and now, knowing what kind of pain was coming, I covered my legs with my arms. My defense just made it worse and the second hit landed across my upper arm where the skin was even more sensitive. The same red line immediately appeared on my skin with the blood showing right through it, without coming out of it.

I could not comprehend what he was whipping me with or if the red lines were in fact my blood or something else. I turned my head toward him to try and see what was in his hand. I saw a tree branch! It was a perfectly cut, long, thin, polished tree branch. He must have brought it with him because we never had anything like that in the house. As I paused in complete shock, he told me that I needed to cooperate and let him do his job.

"Just so you know, this type of tool has been used on very bad people for centuries. It cuts your skin and could leave a permanent scar if I hit you too hard with it," he said calmly and very close to my face. "You do NOT want this to land on your face or neck Trust me! Plus, you should be thankful that I took my time to prepare this new, beautiful whip just for you! I promise it is going to make you a better person," he added.

I couldn't stop crying and coughing at the same time, which was making Armen angrier. "Every time you scream I will add one more slash," he said.

"Hhhhow mmmany do I have to get ttttoday,Uncle"? I asked him through hiccups and tears that had taken over my body.

"I told your mother that you needed ten, but she insisted on fifteen. I can do twelve if you stay quiet and not make any sounds at all," he answered in a convincing tone. I agreed to twelve knowing that the first two were already done.

The next ten whips landed all over my body: on my hands, legs, butt, and arms. At that point I could not even think straight and it felt like the pain completely controlled me. Every single inch of my body burned. I lay on the hardwood floor like a lifeless doll and just stared into space. I felt like I was physically there but my soul was off somewhere else.

"OK, you are done for today," he said with a hint of sarcasm as he threw the whip down right next to me. "Oh yeah, and that was just the physical part of your punishment. You also cannot have any food or water for the next 24 hours."

After he left the living room, I lay on the floor for at least another fifteen minutes, half on my belly and half on my side. My head was turned to the left in an uncomfortable position. I whispered to myself, "This isn't a living room any longer. It's a dead room now." If someone saw me at that moment, he would think I was a corpse like the ones I would see in the horror movies which my mother loved to watch on TV.

A few minutes later, when my breathing stabilized and the full effect of whipping started to overtake my body, agonizing pain filled every single cut. My bloody feet were nothing compared to the agony I was feeling from these fresh wounds.

When I was able to slowly move, I got up on all fours and crawled to the full-size mirror we had in the corner. I gradually rose to my feet and stood right in front of it. I looked into it to see what damage my body had endured this time. I turned to the side, then looked at my back and then at my arms and legs.

My feet were still covered in dried blood, but my collection of wounds had gotten bigger with new red lines that were now all over my fully exhausted body. As I stood there, continuing looking at myself in the mirror, I said to myself, "This man took his time, created the whip, made sure that he whipped me carefully and perfectly, and even spaced the bloody red lines at the same length from one another. He is actually a great artist, to paint my body in such a strange, yet perfect way."

I then came very close to the mirror, touched it with my forehead and whispered to my own reflection. "You are not a girl! You are a painting: a beautiful, one of a kind painting! Just like all the rare paintings, you will survive! You will be priceless and you will live forever!"

CHAPTER 4

A Two Year-Old Soldier Goes to War

When I started my second year of school, things didn't get any better for me. Nothing I did was good enough and nothing I said was taken seriously. No one in the house cared how I felt or cared about the way my life was turning out. The one good thing that happened by the time September rolled around was that the food supply in the city was becoming more stable and accessible. The factories started to stay open much longer and I was able to get to them at any time during the day I wanted.

Without having to miss as many days of school, I was hoping that my grades would start to go back up. Unfortunately for me, the academic damage was already done and I was behind my peers on the material by over half a year.

It was not easy. There were many new students that seemed to stay to themselves and were not friendly toward me at all. I think much of that had to do with my appearance, but there was not much

I could do about that. The shoes I was wearing were secondhand — acquired from one of our relatives — and my backpack was still nothing but a plastic grocery bag. On most days I didn't have clean clothes on and smelled like sweat from wearing the same thing, especially since the weather was still hot. I don't know if the other kids could smell the odor coming from me, but I never judged them or got upset at them. I just figured they would change their minds as soon as they got to know me better. Then they would see that I am not the same on the inside as I am on the outside.

It's kind of funny, because one of my favorite quotes of all time was: "Don't judge a book by its cover," which I preached to all my friends. It used to get me mad when they would treat other kids badly or neglect them if they were different. Poor or rich, unattractive or beautiful, heavy or skinny, very smart or not smart at all, we were still all children, and most of our lives were out of our own control.

I tried my best while I was in school, but I started to realize it really didn't matter because between not being able to do my homework on a daily basis and already being so much behind, it was almost impossible to catch up. I was still blaming myself for that, because I thought I should have known better. I was very well aware that if I continued to get bad grades, I would face the possibility that I would have to stay back a year. Not having good grades was also what got me in the most trouble.

At home I got blamed for doing badly in school; while at school, teachers just seemed to be disappointed and sad about my work. They knew of my abilities, and how good a student I had been, but now they were just watching me slip down lower and lower. When I did get a good grade, the teachers would write it in with a smile and even add a plus sign next to it. However, every time I got a grade lower than a "B", they would shake their heads and take a deep breath before writing it into my agenda. They looked frustrated that I was failing day after day. Sadly, they never questioned me on any of that or even showed any curiosity as to why my homework was not done most of the time I came to school.

I never received any praise when I brought "A's" or "B's" home. I was told that it was expected and I should have nothing but all "A's" anyway. I couldn't understand that, but didn't really want to question anyone at the house that much. Last year, when I did question my situation, it was the first time I felt the terrible pain from the leather belt.

It seemed like my life was stuck in some kind of vicious circle. I would get bad grades in school, come home to do the daily chores, and then submit to my assigned punishment that varied, depending on how bad the grades were or in what subject they were in. After that, it would be time for my "motherly" duties with my baby brother and the next thing I knew, it was late at night and I was too exhausted to do any of my homework anyway. The results of all this were obvious the next day in school because I would be clueless in most of my subjects and totally lost on what to do with the homework.

Things weren't looking too good for me. I started to feel down, picked myself apart, and stopped doing even small things for myself that I would usually do quite often: things like brushing my hair, taking a shower when allowed, or even brushing my teeth. The only thing that was getting better was the way I played piano. I felt that music was the only thing that was there for me, no matter what happened that day or the next. It was something that carried me away from reality and to beautiful places which I imagined when I performed. It was actually very interesting, because only a few months into that school year, I was performing at two levels, or I should say, two grades above all of my classmates. When I was only eight and half years old, I was already playing quite difficult pieces for my age and they included works by composers such as Bach, Mozart, and Beethoven.

My piano teacher was one of the best teachers in the city, and I think the most emotional one as well. She was very skinny, in her mid-forties and dressed very conservatively, almost like she was still living in the 1950's or 60's. Despite still being young, she had gray hair, but it was nicely made up into a bob-style haircut. She was so into the music that she used to actually demonstrate it to me with body language and by making sounds I thought were funny. Depending on what piece of music I was working on, she would do a specific dance or a move, to make me see it, live it and feel it. She just wanted me to play it to perfection.

There was one time, when I was working on playing the famous music piece by Nikolai Rimski-Korsakov, called "Flight of the Bumblebee". She stood on her chair, jumped off of it and tried to flap her hands in the air as she landed on the floor. She was acting like a bee that was trying to fly. That was her way of explaining to me how I should feel when I touched the piano keys. I remember thinking to myself, "Good thing she doesn't have to demonstrate the "Dance of Swords, by Aram Khachaturian"! The last thing I wanted her to do was to pull out the swords and start showing me on how to use them!

Even though she had her own unusual approach to teaching, I still appreciated and respected the passion she had for it. We had an almost silent understanding. We both believed in one another. I truly felt that she played a major role in the love I developed for the piano as well as the high level of performance I demonstrated year after year. Being great at playing piano gave me great opportunities to participate in concerts and perform at competitions.

I was very fortunate, because other than being an amazing teacher, she was also one of very few who would praise me and compliment me every chance she had. She didn't even have to do it because most of those competitions were required for each student to graduate and move up. But she always did. She would even do things for me and they weren't even her responsibilities. She would share her dinner with me before the lesson started and she would surprise me with a present on my birthday. She would even get me a little something for the holidays. She did all that even though she was essentially quite poor and it made me love her much more than any another teacher.

Other than from her, I only received presents from my closest relatives and usually only from my father's side. Most of them would visit us during the winter holidays and would only stay at our apartment for a few days.

My favorite visitor was my grandmother on my dad's side. She had an old-fashioned Armenian name, Geganush, which means beautiful and sweet. Both of those things were true. When I used to look through old pictures of her and my grandfather, who died a couple years before I was born, they looked like such a beautiful couple.

She was the only grandmother I ever knew, because my mother's mom, who I was named after, had passed away before I came into this world. I thought I was very lucky to still have one grandma, especially because of the way she acted around me. I knew she loved me very much and I was by far her favorite. I don't know why she loved me more than the other grandkids, but my dad being her only son must have had something to do with it; also it could be because I looked just like him!

Unfortunately, most of the time, my grandma didn't stay at our house for more than a few days. She and my mother didn't get along well. I never heard my grandma say anything bad about my mom but I did hear my mother talk about her to my dad. I guess she made it clear that my grandma was someone she couldn't stand. I wish I knew why, but no one ever answered that question when I would ask.

Her longest stays were usually when she visited us for the holidays at the end of December. She stayed in the living room with me and we slept together on the sofa that opened up into a small bed. Those were the best days and nights I had.

She would even help me to take care of my baby brother so I could catch up on my schoolwork and practice piano. She would sit and listen to me play. After we put the baby to sleep, we would stay up late and talk about all kinds of things and many different people. I loved listening to the many old stories she used to tell.

She told me about how in the early 1900's, her family escaped from the Armenian Genocide and was able to flee before the Turks killed them all. She said there were more than 1.5 million Armenians who weren't able to escape and were killed in cold blood in all kinds of sadistic ways. She used to get really upset and cry when she talked about what the Armenian Genocide had done to many of our generations and how unfair it was that Turkey wouldn't recognize it due to some political issues. She would tell me how many innocent families she knew who were executed just for the territory and land they lived on. Then she would smile and say, "Oh, Vera, Vera! After the genocide nightmare ended, I met your grandfather. Gaspar was so handsome and kind and was a very brave, highly-ranked soldier. He helped me and my family move farther away from the Turks into a village deep in Armenia, and then we got married! He was so talented and played many musical instruments. He could fix anything and could even build a whole house!"

I used to love hearing about it because I never met him, and really wished I had. After all, my last name had his first name in it. She gave me a book, called *Armenian Genocide*, which I read in a couple of weeks. I never forgot any of the nightmares that I read in it. After learning about all the different ways Turks tortured Armenian women, kids and families, I started to realize that some of the things in the book were very similar to the techniques that Armen was using on me. It was almost like he had read that book to look for some sick ideas.

I remember asking my grandma, "Gram, it seems like our nationality has been mistreated a lot. Maybe my life is bad because I am an Armenian or do you think that I'm possibly cursed?"

To that she would just smile and say, "Everything will be all right! Believe me! EVERYTHING will be all right."

She only knew about a very small amount of brutality Armen was putting me through and probably nothing more than him using the belt on me. She really hated him and the way he treated me but she couldn't do much about it. Even if she would tell my father to have it stopped he wouldn't do much about it, because in our house, my mother was the boss.

At least when Gram was there, she would not allow the abuse to go on. She had no issues standing up to Armen even though she was only about five feet tall and weighed not more than one hundred and twenty pounds. The last time she visited us about a month earlier, she walked in just as Armen was in the middle of disciplining me with his belt. I still remember it now because it became a surprisingly funny memory.

When she got home and heard me crying and begging for him to stop, she ran right into the living room and saw me on the floor. I was under the piano and Armen was standing over me beating me with his belt. In less than a second, she was right next to him screaming in Armenian and grabbing the belt out of his hand. After she got the belt away from him, she continued swearing and calling him names and she started to hit him with the belt, without even looking at where it was landing.

"You are a son-of-a-bitch devil and a monster! Stay away from my granddaughter, you sick, ugly pig! I will show you how to behave," she shouted, mixing several Armenian and Russian words together.

"What are you doing you crazy old woman! Stop immediately! You are hurting me!" Armen screamed while trying to cover himself.

It was such an amusing scene that the tears stopped streaming down my face and were replaced by a wide and happy smile. A few moments later, he ran out of the living room almost knocking my mother off her feet as she was coming into the living room to see what was going on. I guess she suddenly became worried when she heard Armen scream.

Even after he ran out of the living room, my grandma was still very angry at both him and my parents. She helped me get up, fixed my hair and wiped my tears. She then looked at me and her face changed from angry to calm, yet, it was still sad.

"I am only staying for three days this time," she said, "but when you turn seventeen, you can come and live with me. You remember that!"

"I know Gram, but how can I leave the baby here alone? I have to stay until he is old enough to come with me," I replied.

"We will figure it out! There is always a way out," she said.

I put my head on her lap and she played with my hair while I dreamed out loud. She would ask me what I wished for in the upcoming year. Those moments were the only times that I felt like an actual child, not a mother to one.

The wishes she talked about were a tradition which my family would follow every year on New Year's Eve. A few minutes before December 31st ended, the Russian president would address all the citizens of our country on national TV. Each of us would have a pen and a small piece of paper. While we listened to his speech, we would all think of what we wished for in the New Year and would write it down on our paper. The President would talk about the country and the year it had, as well as what had been accomplished. He would talk about the plans he had for all of us in the coming year. At the end of his address, he would wish all the people of Russia a Happy New Year and then at exactly midnight, the huge chimes on the Kremlin's tower clock in Moscow's Red Square would ring exactly twelve times. My dad would then open up a bottle of champagne and pour it into everyone's glass. After his toast, we would burn that little piece of paper with the candles that were placed on the dinner table.

I can remember what I wished for every single year since I was five years-old. I would always use every area of my small paper to write down as many wishes as possible, and they were all different from one another. The best part of writing so many wishes was that at least one of them would always come true. When I was five, I wished for a new outfit and I got a brand new dress for my birthday. When I was six, one of my wishes was to have a new baby in our family. And sure enough, I welcomed my baby brother into my life. When I was seven, one of my wishes was that at least one day each week Armen wouldn't touch me. That wish also came true because he rarely visited on Sundays, and even on those rare occasions that he did, he almost never disciplined me.

Now as we sat at the table and it was almost midnight, I finished writing my wishes faster than ever before. I actually remember that year's wish list word for word.

> *"I wish to die as soon as possible, but painlessly"*
> *"I wish for someone to kill me, for whatever reason"*
> *"I wish to find the strength to kill myself without pain"*
> *"I wish to get hit by a big car or a huge bus and die"*
> *"I wish to fall asleep and only wake up if I'm in heaven"*

When the clock on our TV turned to midnight, I folded the paper a few times so no one could see what I wrote, lit it on the candle in front of me and put it on a small plate so it would burn all the way down. There was no second-guessing about what I wanted or wished for in my life at that moment and I believed that if only one of those wishes came true, I would be a very lucky little girl.

One evening a couple of months later I was on my way home from music school. It was already dark outside and I was very tired. I had to switch two buses to get to the bus stop closest to my building. I was not being careful or attentive to my surroundings. After I got off the bus, I decided to quickly cross the main six lane road to get to the side path that led toward home. I went toward the front of the bus and decided to cross the street in front of it. The road was huge with two-way traffic. As I stepped from in front of my bus, out of nowhere another huge tall bus flew right at me at a very high speed. Before I was able to jump out of its way, it hit me hard on the left side of my body.

I don't know how far I flew, but it felt like it was at least fifty feet. I landed on my back and onto the right side of my body, with the top of my head hitting hard against the curb. The next thing I remember, a bunch of people were hovering over me and someone screamed to call the ambulance. Some guy bent over close to my face and told me not to move. A few people started to point fingers to different parts of my body saying that I broke my legs, my ankle, my right arm, my back, and who knows what else. At one point I was not even sure if I was dead or alive, because the way everybody hovered over me, I could no longer see the street lights or the sky.

The last thing I remembered was trying to cross the street in front of my bus, then another big bus… and that's it, nothing after that. I didn't feel any pain anywhere in my body, so I was not even sure what all that chaos was about. Then I heard some guy telling everyone that he had just called the ambulance from the payphone.

I didn't expect any help to arrive for some time, so I just closed my eyes and blocked everyone out. A sudden thought ran through my mind as I realized that the sudden appearance of the big bus was not a coincidence. I had, literally, asked for it. It was one of my New Year's Eve wishes that I wrote on the list and burned with the candle.

A few seconds later I heard the loud siren of an ambulance getting closer and closer. When it stopped I saw lots of bright lights between the heads of all the people that were hovering over me. The next thing I knew, I could see someone pushing people apart to get to me. As I opened my eyes wider, I realized my dad was standing there in his white doctor's coat with a very scared look in his eyes.

"Daddy! What you doing here?" I screamed out in excitement as I tried to sit up just a bit.

"Do NOT move!" my dad screamed back. "I need to check you first to see how many bones are broken."

"Broken?" I asked. "I don't think I broke anything. I don't have pain anywhere."

"That's impossible. You must have broken something; it's just that your body is in shock and you don't feel it right now," he answered while checking my feet and lower legs an inch at a time. "I... I... I... don't think you broke any bones! Can you move your legs and arms?"

"Yes, Dad, I can, very easily! Watch, I said while trying to get up, "but I think I scratched my arm."

As I got up and stood on both feet, all the people that were around us moved back like they were afraid of me. My dad and the male nurse that was with him grabbed the stretcher and slowly helped me on to it, and then they put me in the ambulance and we drove away. I surely was happy that every ambulance had a doctor onboard to take care of patients.

"Dad, can you please tell the driver to turn the sirens on just for few seconds? Pleeeease! I just want to feel important!" I asked him while I tried to make a cute and convincing face.

He told the driver to turn all the sirens on for one round, whatever that meant, and then he turned back to me.

"You don't realize how lucky you are and how perfectly your body landed after the hit. There isn't one broken bone in your whole body from what I can see," he said as he started to clean up the large scratch on the side of my right arm. "You could have easily died or busted your head open!" he added.

"Well, I guess I didn't, so maybe this isn't the time for any of my wishes to come true," I answered him with unexpected sarcasm. Then I turned my head to the left and away from him.

"What is that supposed to mean?" he asked somewhat confused.

"Nothing, Dad; it meant nothing" I answered with disappointment.

As I lay there all I could think about was how clueless my dad was about everything that was going on in my life each day. I mean, I surely knew that he had a very busy schedule and worked almost every day, but why wouldn't he make sure that I was OK? He still had not talked to me about the river incident when my brother almost drowned, even though quite some time had passed.

After checking over my entire body, my dad told his driver that I didn't need the hospital and that it was OK for him to just bring me home. He turned the ambulance around and started toward the apartment. When we arrived, my dad carried me all the way to the fifth floor. Uncle Armen was there and he and my mother were having tea in the kitchen. My mom was surprised that my dad had come by and had me with him, because he rarely did that when on one of his 24-hour shifts. My dad told her what happened and that by total chance it was his ambulance that was dispatched to the scene. Before going back to work, he told everyone that I needed to lie down for the rest of the night. He said he would check on me when he came back in the morning and if I was OK, then I would be allowed to go to school.

My mother didn't look too happy and just nodded her head, showing her agreement. He walked me into the living room and told me to lie down on the sofa.

"Only get up if you need to go to the bathroom," he said.

"Give her something to eat," he shouted to my mother on his way out of the house. "Oh, and keep the baby in the kitchen so she can sleep."

As soon as he shut the door behind him, I closed my eyes to take a nap. I was exhausted.

A second later I heard my mother's voice. "Vera, come get Tigran, he needs to go to sleep, and he missed his nap."

I got off of the couch and slowly walked to the kitchen dragging my feet behind me.

"Let's go baby, time for bed," I said to him in a soft and very tired voice. He got off of the chair and ran up to me.

"Shut the door behind you! We are watching a movie," my mother screamed at us as we made our way out of the kitchen.

I closed the door behind me and told the baby to lie down next to me so we could go to sleep together. He wasn't sleepy yet, but he still listened to me. He asked me to tell him one of his favorite stories: *The Three Little Pigs*. By now he knew every word of it, but he still wanted me to tell it in my own way and with my own sound effects. I couldn't say no to him but I felt absolutely no energy. Thankfully he fell asleep before I was finished and I was able to close my eyes again.

Hunger was taking over but I didn't want to get up until my mother went to bed and Uncle Armen left. He was usually gone before midnight. I heard that he lived far away from us and took a bus most days, since his car was always in the repair shop. I think he lived with his mother in some apartment, maybe forty-five minutes away, but I wasn't sure. I actually didn't know that much about him, other than he was somehow my uncle and I had to listen to him. I heard he was married once before but never had any children. Either way, he obviously didn't enjoy the company of whomever he lived with because he was at our apartment almost every day. Some days he would come early in the morning and would not leave until late at night. I guess this night was one of those nights.

It was almost midnight when he finally left and it was another half hour after that before my mother went into her bedroom. I waited fifteen more minutes and very quietly opened the living room door. Our hardwood floors were so sensitive that I had to be super careful and only take one step at a time. It wasn't the first time that I had to get out of the living room quietly in the middle of the night. By now I already knew which pieces of hardwood I could or could not step on. It was almost like a game of hopscotch, just without the numbers.

I slowly and carefully made my way through the hallway and into the kitchen. It still smelled like food in there, probably from the dinner they had earlier, but there weren't any leftovers. I just grabbed a stick of butter from the freezer and slowly went back toward the living room so I could eat something and then get a few hours of sleep.

In the morning, my dad checked me again and told me I seamed OK and to just watch how I felt throughout the day. During my classes I didn't feel too well, and unfortunately, I had two very important tests one after another. Both of the tests were in my two hardest subjects: Russian Literature and Math. I loved them both but struggled in them dramatically.

I ended up getting "C's" on both of them and my teachers wrote the grades in my agenda by the end of that same day. After school and on my way home, I was becoming nervous. My "C's" always got me in trouble.

When I arrived at our building and stood at our entrance, I didn't see my dad's car parked anywhere on the street. He probably had lots of errands to run or went food shopping. As soon as I got on the first set of stairs, I smelled Armen's strong cologne. I became very scared and knew that I was in trouble. I hoped that maybe he had been here earlier and just left, but I would be wrong.

When I got up to the fifth floor, I saw our door unlocked and open a little bit. The opened door meant I was expected home at around that time. I pushed it open and quietly ran from the hallway and into the living room which was on the left side, ten feet away from the front door. Our kitchen was on the right side and almost right after the main doorway, so no matter what, you would see the kitchen on the right as soon as you walked in. As I ran through the apartment, out of the corner of my eye, I noticed something unusual.

My mother and Armen were sitting at their regular spots at the table, but my baby brother was doing some kind of exercise. I wasn't exactly sure what it was, but for a split second it looked like he was doing squats or something similar to that. My brother was not even a full two years of age, so I wondered why he would be doing that kind of exercise at all. It seemed very strange to me. I wasn't worried about Uncle Armen abusing the baby because my mother would never let anything like that happen to my brother. She loved him too much — simply said. I must have seen her kiss and hug him at least a dozen times each and every day, not to mention that she told him that she loved him every chance she had.

With my concerns set aside, I took out my books and started on my homework. All of a sudden I heard a loud scream and then a cry from my baby brother. I became very worried because he rarely cried, and even when he did, it took a lot for him to start. I figured he probably fell down or something happened like that, but I kept my ears open in case it continued. After he cried for about another minute or so, I started to hear my mother screaming. Her reaction completely confused me and I got up to go to the door so I could hear them better. I couldn't make out exactly what she was mad about, so I decided to pretend that I needed to go to the bathroom. I opened the door and walked out of the living room, through the hallway and into the bathroom, which was on the right side before the kitchen. I was going to run by as if I wasn't even paying attention to what was going on in that kitchen. If asked why I was being nosey, I planned to say that I just had to pee. I was also very hungry, since the last time I had eaten was around noon-time in the school cafeteria. I thought that if my mother saw me again, she might invite me to eat something.

As I passed through the hallway my baby brother saw me and cried out, "Veyaaaa! Veyaaaa!" He sounded like he was in pain and I got so sick to my stomach that I couldn't just continue going about my business. I stopped right before the bathroom door and I looked at my baby brother and then up to Armen and my mother with confusion. What I saw was beyond disturbing and scary. Armen was holding my baby brother by his left ear and pulling him up. The baby was crying and trying to turn his head toward me to beg for help. I looked at my mother and saw her sitting at the table with the cup of coffee in her hands, but keeping her worried eyes fixed on the baby. Then she told Armen to let my brother go, but it was too late. At the exact same time that she said that, the bottom of the baby's ear ripped separating from his head, and bright red blood streaked down the baby's body.

As soon as I saw the blood, I snapped out of my dazed state of mind. The baby was making an agonizing high-pitched scream and it was a sound that I will never forget. I ran right to him and grabbed his hand. I was angry and livid and I looked right at Armen, then at my mother and then rushed the baby into the bathroom. He was crying and gasping for air. I could only imagine how much pain he was in.

My mother rushed in right behind us and tried to help me clean him up, but the blood was getting onto everything. I pushed the baby in front of me, blocking her from trying to touch him. She realized what I was doing and stormed angrily out of the bathroom..

The next thing I heard, over the baby's ear-piercing cry, was my mother screaming at the top of her lungs at Uncle Armen.

"ALL I TOLD YOU TO DO WAS TO MAKE THE BABY MANLIER AND STRONGER, NOT TO HURT HIM LIKE THIS!"

I didn't really have time to pay attention to them, so I tuned them out. The baby was hurt and needed my full attention. Having plenty of experience taking care of my own wounds, I knew exactly what I had to do. I grabbed the peroxide, lots of cotton balls, and moved the baby's head over the bathtub. I didn't want to pour the peroxide right into his open flesh because that would have burned and hurt him badly. I poured it instead onto the cotton balls and started to press it gently against his wound.

The baby screamed and cried so loud that I started to freak out. The blood was all over the white bathtub, his neck, and his shoulders. I could hear my mother still screaming at Armen somewhere on the other side of the house.

I was gently pressing the cotton against the baby's ear right at the spot where it detached from his upper neck. He was doing OK, but I was keeping his mind busy by talking to him and making him feel better.

"Look at you my little soldier! You are so brave! I saw you doing the squats like a really strong muscleman! You are such a good little boy! Vera loves you!"

"I am a good boy. I didn't do any bad things!" the baby mumbled back at me, struggling to talk through his hiccups.

I felt terrible for him. Tears started to roll uncontrollably down my own face.

"I am so sorry, baby. I was in the living room and didn't know what they were doing to you. You are such a nice boy and you did so well! You can be a marine after this, or join the Navy! Maybe you can even be a special forces agent — like KGB!" I added.

He just looked at me, his face soaked from his tears. Meanwhile, I realized that the white cotton had turned bright red and the blood had started to run down my wrist. I switched it with a new piece of cotton and I told the baby to hold it in place so I could get bigger bandages from the first aid box. I grabbed everything I needed and taped it all over his head and even around his neck to hold the bandage in place.

My mother was still arguing with Armen and ordering him never to touch her baby again. For a second there, I wished that she was arguing with him about me. She was acting like an angry lioness that was fighting off a pack of hyenas that were trying to attack her cub. It had become very obvious that she only felt that way about one of her children, not both. I wish I knew what I had ever done wrong and why I meant nothing to her. I wish I knew whatever it was that made her feel like I was not worth fighting for. I hoped that maybe one day I would understand, but maybe it was just wishful thinking.

CHAPTER 5
Wait and Hope

As my ninth birthday approached, my emotions were somewhere between confused and disappointed. I was sure that my mother hated every inch of me. I was also sure that there were only a handful of people who actually cared about me in any genuine way. For the rest, I didn't feel that I was worth much.

On an almost daily basis, I felt like a soldier in the army. I had to follow a rigid schedule and couldn't escape from it no matter what happened. I was less and less excited about things that had been important to me in the past, and even my favorite day of the year — my birthday — felt like it was not worth celebrating.

Seeing my friends enjoy things day after day, while my days were mostly dark and painful, made me feel discouraged and useless. I knew that I had many important roles which I had to play: a mother; a maid; a teacher; a student and even a punching bag. Even with all these responsibilities and roles, I felt totally unwanted and unneeded, almost like an abandoned piece of furniture.

I never stopped looking for answers as to why my journey was so harsh and painful, but I couldn't really find anything helpful. It seemed like I had to look for and use the life experiences of adults and grown-ups, not children, to find similarities and answers. My life was not like that of any other child and that is why I decided to find what I was looking for in more serious books written for older readers. All I wanted to know is what my exact purpose in life is, or was to be. That was all.

It felt like the answer was somewhere near me, yet I just could not find it. Maybe the need of finding it and the will to look for it drove me to read book after book and story after story. These were books that kids my age wouldn't even think of reading; books that would make normal children scared and give them nightmares, but not me. I was too hungry to get to the bottom of things. Since every character in any story I ever read had some kind of a role to play, meant that I must have one as well.

My grandfather on my mother's side had a huge library at his house that he amassed throughout his lifetime. There were hundreds of books on many different topics as well as from many different decades. Most of them were not children's books, with the closest to my age being a series of books by Alexandre Dumas. That was actually the author that I started with when I was still in first grade. Some of my favorites were *D'Artagnan and The Three Musketeers, The Count of Monte Cristo, The Black Tulip* and all the books from the Vicomte De Bragelonne series. These were just a few that I read before moving on to some more serious topics like the history of different kings and queens, both World War I and World War II, and other mesmerizing stories and true events.

The hardest books for me to read were about the Armenian and Jewish genocides of the 20th Century. Just the gruesome descriptions and the things human beings were capable of doing and surviving through, made me feel like my life was not as bad as I thought.

Most nights, when I was done with my chores and the baby was fast asleep, I would read for hours until I fell asleep with a book on my chest. I must have read tens of thousands of pages between the ages of seven and ten.

My grandpa used to tell me to be careful reading too much because the material in those books was way above my age group. Then he would also smile at me and tell me that I was very unique and extraordinary, and hadn't done many of the things that matched my age group anyway. He told me that he was just being protective but knew very well that I would understand most of the material I was reading. He was always so nice and kind to me and was very generous with compliments.

My "Deda," which is a Russian way of saying grandpa, was someone who I wished every person could have in his or her own life. He was someone who loved me unconditionally and made sure that I knew it. He used to say that to me every chance he had and it was something that I had never heard my mother or father say. He was also very kind and loving, and I never left his house without a kiss and a hug or without a stomach full of food.

He was in his sixties and his own mother was in her eighties. And it was only the two of them who lived together, since his wife, my grandmother, had died a couple of years before I was born. He told me many stories about their life together and how much he loved her. He always spoke so highly of her and I saw the love still shining in his eyes every time he said her name. He used to tell me that she was a very powerful and strong willed woman, and that I reminded him of her. I already knew a few things about them from many of my relatives and from the older neighbors who lived in our building. They told me that my grandparents were a power couple and well-known throughout the city and the region.

He became an important director of import and export at the Sochi seaport after he came back from World War II, and she was a director of a few large food store chains that could be found throughout the region. I knew they were well-known for sure, because every time he and I were going somewhere together, we would have to stop every twenty to thirty feet so he could talk to yet another person he knew well. Sometimes it would take us half an hour to walk a five- minute distance, although I never minded that because he would always talk about interesting stuff with people. I would just hold his hand and listen for as long as it took him to finish his conversations.

When it came to my grandmother Veronika, whom I was named after, I always wished I could have met her because I wanted to see first-hand what she was really like and if everything that people said about her was true. After all, how can one person be so missed and so loved?

My grandpa told me that the famous saying about no one being irreplaceable was not true and that she was proof of that. He told me that she worked long hours and was very involved in every project she ran, as well as in the peoples' lives who worked for her. He also told me that she died from some kind of heart condition after she suffered a heart attack and ended up in the hospital. I guess she was there for a long while and apparently did not get the care she needed to prolong her life and bring her to full recovery.

I asked him how she got along with my mother, since I was trying to compare my relationship to hers. He told me that they were like best friends, and since their birthdays were coincidentally on the same day, April 14th, they always celebrated it together. He also said that she died a couple of weeks after her 53rd birthday and that she took her last breath while my mother was holding her hand. That made me sad, but I didn't really feel that bad for my mom. It was just sad to think of a twenty three year old woman having her mother die in her arms.

My grandpa went to visit my grandmother at the cemetery every single Sunday no matter how hot or cold it was outside. When I was seven and eight years old, he took me only a few times each year because I was always stuck watching the baby. With my brother growing, and my dad now having most Sundays off, I was finally able to start going to the cemetery with him much more often. From the time I was almost nine and for the next few years, grandpa took me with him almost every single Sunday.

The spot where grandma was buried looked like something from a movie where the rich family had a big plot reserved for all their family members. My grandpa bought three spots next to each other, two for him and my grandma, and one for his mother. The headstones for his and grandma's spots were hand-carved, one-piece marble stones with their pictures carved right into the front. Everything around it was made from that same kind of marble, including the grave stones, the grave covers and even the flower vases on each side of the graves. There were even some three-foot tall columns made of that same marble. The whole area was surrounded by a very thick tungsten rope, all connected to those same columns. There was also a marble table and two benches so that people who came to visit could sit down and talk to those who had passed away. My grandpa definitely put lots of thought and effort into making these graves beautiful. It showed the love he always had for her.

When my grandma died, my grandpa wrote two quotes, one for her and one for him, which he had engraved on both gravestones. My grandma's stone read,

"There are so many things of yours you left for us. There are so much of ours you took with you, when left"

On his stone he engraved,

"Please trust me. I am far from being scared of death. There's nothing scarier than life, which destiny prepared"

It was the first week of April, and I asked my mother if she could go with me and my grandpa to the cemetery. I wanted her to see how nice he and I took care of it and how we kept the marble shiny and clean. She refused.

Unfortunately, when my grandma died, the whole family separated and stopped talking to each other. The house that they all lived in was sold and divided into three different condos.

My mother had a stepbrother, Andrey, who was very little when my grandma remarried. His dad died when Andrey was very small and my grandfather cared for him and raised him like he was his own son. My mother and Andrey didn't get along well, from what I heard, and after my grandma died, their connection went from minimal to zero. When I asked my mother about why she wasn't talking to her dad or her step-brother, she would just say that I was too little to understand. The only thing she would tell me was that she wanted her father to help her with everything instead of creating a new life for himself, so soon after her mother was gone. She also told me that she didn't think it was appropriate for him to have a girlfriend, although his wife had been dead for over ten years now.

I didn't see anything wrong with any of the things she was talking about, especially since when my grandma died, grandpa was in his early 50's. I didn't think his wife would want him to be alone for the rest of his life like my mother apparently wanted him to be. He was also very handsome, kind, loving, fun, healthy, smart, and just an amazing human being. But it was no surprise that yet again, she and I didn't see things the same way. I was just glad that she let me go with him every time he came to pick me up and that we were able to celebrate all of my birthdays together.

Both my birthday and my grandfather's birthday fell on May 2nd. Well, technically I was physically born on April 30th, but my mom changed it to May 2nd. She told me that she wanted my birthday to be the same as her father's since I was his only granddaughter and he requested that from her. I was super lucky that she did that because I loved having our birthdays together on the same day and celebrating them together, too.

* * *

A week after my ninth birthday, all of my final grades were in. I wasn't sure what my 3rd grade report card was going to look like, but I knew that it wasn't going to be pretty. On the last official school day of the year, my parents were called to the school by the secretary to attend a meeting with the principal. I had to wait after the last class for them to come and I knew quite well that they would not be hearing anything good in that meeting. What I didn't know at that moment is the bad things they were about to hear were actually quite horrible.

"I am very sorry, but unfortunately, we are not able to move your daughter to the 4th grade. Her grades in the main subjects were well below the minimum and she was absent for five times more school days than are allowable by the rules," said the principal to my parents. She had a deep, disappointed tone in her voice.

I thought I was going to melt right into my chair when I heard those words. I really wish I could have, because I also knew that Uncle Armen would have a field day with me over this news. It was just another excuse to abuse and torture me.

"Are there any other options for her that you can suggest, so she doesn't stay back?" my dad asked grasping at some sort of hope. My mother's face just turned from white to red.

"The only thing I can think of is for you to move her to another school, since a different school can't use outside grades to determine her grade level. That is the one good thing about that rule, so you should consider that." As she answered my dad, she looked at me sadly, almost as if she felt badly that any of those rules existed at all.

"The only other school we can put her in because of the location of our apartment is School Number 8. It's much harder and it's much farther from our house," my dad said back to her, hoping that something else could be done about it.

"I understand that, but rules are rules, and we can't break them for one specific child, although we all love her here. The only thing I can tell you is that if she has passing grades for the first two quarters at her new school, she can come back here and continue in the third quarter to finish 4th grade," she added.

"OK, well thank you for everything. We will go now since we definitely need to discuss this as a family," my dad said as he grabbed some paperwork and the report card off of her desk.

The moment he said that, I knew that I was in big trouble and that my summer would be the worst one yet. My parents stood up and headed to the door. I followed them slowly. Right before we left the principal's office, I turned around to wave to her. When I did, I noticed she was almost crying and had her right hand covering her mouth. I knew why she was upset. After all, she knew me for several years now and heard many things about me from my teachers. She definitely was aware that I was once a straight "A" student and I had slowly slipped down to achieving no "A's" at all, while failing three classes. She also saw the way I came to school, how often I didn't, and how dirty and hungry I was while I was there. She even walked into the cafeteria a few times while I was eating leftovers. On a few occasions, I was brought to her office by my teachers because my bruises were visible and I refused to tell them where I got them. I never told the principal the truth either because there was really no point in it. The first few times I mentioned it to them when it first started, they didn't do anything about it, so why bother. I just told them that I wasn't a good girl and it wasn't anyone else's fault but mine.

Either way, in a short few years, she witnessed a smart and intelligent girl go from being a great student to becoming one of the worst ones there. I didn't say anything to her when I walked away. There really wasn't much to say. I just smiled back, waved goodbye, and rushed after my parents.

I could tell that my dad was mad, although he wasn't saying anything to me or showing it with any gestures. My mother, on the other hand, was livid and wasn't afraid to show it. As soon as we left the school and started to walk home, she started to yell and call me all kinds of names.

"I cannot believe how retarded you are! You a pure pig and not a child! You couldn't even get passing grades, UGLY BITCH! I can't believe you just shamed me this way and made me sit there in front of the principal like I was some sort of stupid kid," she shouted back at me while I walked a few steps behind. "Wait until we get home and you will see who will be a troubled kid!" she added.

I didn't say anything back and just continued walking behind them, listening to the sound of my new flip-flops that I had just gotten for my birthday, slap the sidewalk. We were walking along the river and coming closer and closer to our building. I was so scared of the whole situation with the principal that I didn't even think to ask my parents who it was who was taking care of my brother.

When we came up the stairs they walked in first and left the door wide open for me. This was not a good sign. I was trying to sniff the air to see if Uncle Armen's cologne was present. I could not sense any. That was surely a relief, but it could also mean that he had been at our house all morning and the scent had faded.

I knew I was definitely in big trouble because my mother had never threatened me openly like that in the past. I slowly walked in, shaking with fear. At this point with Armen there or not, I still expected to receive a beating from my dad. As I opened the front door all the way, my feelings of terror were replaced with a completely shocking and amazing surprise. Apparently, my childish prayers, which I didn't believe in, were somehow answered on the way home, and all I was able to say and mumble under my breath was, "Thank you God." Standing in front of me was my grandma, holding my baby brother in her arms.

My mother was very angry at my grandma for some reason and shouted at her in a sarcastic tone, "Oh thank you for taking Tigran to the park -- just like I asked!" My dad didn't seem too angry anymore and grabbed my brother from her arms to cuddle and hug him.

"I am visiting for a couple of days, and just got to Sochi this morning" my grandma said to me with the smile.

I ran up to her and hugged her so tightly around her waist that she almost cried from my squeeze.

"Gram, you literally could NOT have picked a better time to visit!" I said with complete excitement as I loosened my grip.

I obviously knew that when she left, I would still be in huge trouble, but I was hoping that by then my parents would have calmed down a bit and wouldn't be too harsh on me. It also gave me time to behave well and do all the extra chores I could, to earn extra kindness from my mom, and therefore a lesser punishment.

Two days later, another blessing came into my life, or at least that is what I thought at the time. That night, right before my grandma was planning to leave, I overheard my parents talking in the kitchen about some kind of vacation that my mom wanted to take since the school year was now over. I didn't say anything to them or to my grandma, and just started to wish that they would go away as soon as possible.

It was now almost ten o'clock at night, and nothing was said to me or to grandma. I sat on the sofa and watched her pack the few bits of clothes she had with her. She was leaving the next morning around eleven. My baby brother was on the sofa as well, but already asleep from listening to us talk.

When she was finished packing, I moved the baby closer to the wall, opening the other side of the sofa for her so she could lie down. I would always sleep on the floor, next to the sofa, every time we had company. I didn't really like it, but unlike the times when Armen stayed over, it did it for my gram with pleasure. When Armen was sleeping on the sofa, I could never fall asleep or even close my eyes with any ease. I always thought that he might do something painful to me or hit me in the middle of the night. With gram, I slept like a baby even though our floors were hardwood and I was very uncomfortable.

Early the next morning, I felt someone's foot pushing into my upper leg. I opened up my eyes and saw my mother standing above me with her hand reaching out towards me holding a long "to-do" list. Then she woke my grandma and told her that they had decided to go away for two weeks and they would need her to stay to watch after us.

I was surprised that she didn't even kiss her son goodbye while he slept, but maybe she was just too happy to get away from all of us. I started to read my "to-do" list as soon as my mother left the living room. A minute later my dad poked his head into the room.

"Behave for grandma and listen to everything she says. We will be back before you know it," he said with excitement in his voice.

"Dad, can you leave us some money please?" I asked.

"We don't have much cash and have to take what we have with us, but the fridge is full and has enough food for the two weeks we will be gone. If you need more, ask grandpa to bring it to you," he responded.

"OK I guess. Have fun," I answered somewhat upset. "I hope Uncle Armen isn't coming here while you are away," I added, but my dad had already closed the living room door.

I turned to my grandma and said, "Gram how can they go on vacation, eat at fancy restaurants, visit beautiful landmarks, go to the beaches and take different mini-cruises, while supposedly they have no money? My mother has been saying that we cannot have a normal supply of food for the family and we can't afford to buy enough water." My grandma just shook her head and turned around to catch a little more sleep as it was still quite early.

"Don't you worry gram, I got it all covered! You don't have to do a thing. I will take care of everything for all three of us," I said to her hoping she was still listening.

A few minutes later I heard the front door open and then close. I figured they must have gone. I got up, picked my pillow and blanket off of the floor, folded the blanket and put them on the nearest chair. The baby and grandma were still sleeping, so I decided to go and start to make breakfast.

When I opened the fridge, I almost fell down. There was enough food for two, maybe three days tops. On the top shelf there was a gallon of milk, half of a dozen eggs, some leftovers from the previous night's dinner and a little low fat yogurt that no one could stomach. There was also a small container of sour cream, a little bit of cheese and some bologna on the top shelf. In the freezer, I saw one whole medium-size chicken and some frozen peas. I also spotted half a loaf of bread near the fridge and an almost empty bottle of Pepsi.

"I will have to make this work somehow," I whispered to myself. I took that same piece of paper with the chores and turned it over. It was time to draw up a daily schedule of our meals to make the food in the fridge last.

Food wasn't our only problem. We were also facing a water and electricity shortage which was present in our city and the region at this time. Because of the bad economy, the city had to ration its supplies very carefully. Knowing that most of the residents go away in June, they decided to use that month to cut down on how much water and electricity the city utilized. Starting at the end of May, they shut off the electricity every night from late evening into the early morning. The water supply was also monitored and heaped with even more restrictions, limiting peoples' access to only a couple of hours every two to three days. Even when it was on, the water pressure was so bad that people barely had enough time to fill up their jugs and buckets so they could have water to use later.

Those weeks my parents were away were very difficult. The only places that had more water than regular homes were hospitals and free-standing emergency rooms. My parents couldn't have picked a worse time to go on vacation. Just to go to the bathroom, we would have to fill the back of the toilet bowl at least half way, just enough for one flush. It was quite a mess.

With these restrictions in mind, I went to check on how much water was available for us to use since we had filled the container the day before. To my surprise, there wasn't much water left at all, probably because my mom used it to wash for her trip. I don't know why she couldn't do what I did and just jump into the sea for a quick swim; that was surely better than using up our drinking water. My dad was a bit more considerate and took showers at work in the emergency room's bathroom. That was smart and clever of him.

Overall, I was just surprised that they left us at such a difficult time. After all I was only nine, my baby brother was only two, and my grandma was in her late sixties. How could they go on vacation knowing we didn't have any food, money, electricity or the water we needed to simply survive? It just made no sense.

All I knew is that I had quite a few problems in front of me that needed to be resolved. Unfortunately, when I called my grandpa a few minutes later no one answered the phone. When I called my mother's second cousin, she told me that my grandpa took his mom and went to Georgia to visit his younger brother, so I couldn't count on him for any help. Asking other relatives for help was never an option because my mother told me many times that nothing should leave our walls and that no one should know anything about what's going on in our house. The last thing I wanted was to make my family look bad in the eyes of our relatives, so that option went out the door before I even thought of it.

I turned the piece of paper the long way and drew lines to make fourteen columns, one for each day, to cover the next two weeks. The most I could stretch the food we had without the baby and gram noticing anything wrong was five days and that was only if I wasn't going to eat any of it. Five days was not enough. I needed to cover fourteen days and I needed water for all of us to drink and to be able to wash the baby.

I had to come up with a plan on how to make enough money to provide food for the other week and two days and all fourteen days of it to feed myself. I took a fresh piece of paper and started to write down everything that came to my mind on how I could earn extra money. I wrote everything down in the order in which I felt the most comfortable doing them.

1. *Get the fruit off of the trees outside of the building and from my grandpa's garden to sell at the bazaar.*
2. *Hold a talent show or concert for the neighbors and collect some donations in the form of change or food.*
3. *Knock on neighbor's doors and see if they need me to do any chores like run out to get groceries, clean their house, and yard or take out their garbage.*
4. *Go to the church and sit next to the elderly people and beg for money. (emergency option only!)*

I heard my grandma call me, so I rushed back to the living room. "Can you clean up the baby while I will make the breakfast?" she asked in a kind voice.

"Yes Gram I will do that, but, I need to talk to you about the food and the water", I said with frustration. "We only have enough food for possibly five days. I have no idea why they left us in this predicament without money or supplies."

She looked at me with confusion and then started to search her pockets for something. I grabbed the baby off of the sofa and stood in front of her waiting to see what she was doing. I imagined she was hiding a thick stack of rubles (some wishful thinking!) but instead she pulled out a small handkerchief all tied up in a ball and she started to undo the knots. A minute later she opened it up and inside was one wrinkled ruble along with dozens of different coins that added up to almost four rubles more. She thrust her palm out to me and told me to take it.

"That's great grandma! This will buy us milk and a loaf of bread," I said knowing very well that it would not be nearly enough for that.

She smiled back at me and asked me what I needed help with. I told her that everything was going to be great, that I would be in charge of the fridge for the next two weeks and I would decide what to cook and what to feed everyone every day. She was OK with that and said that she would make sure that the baby was taken care of while I was busy. She sounded happy but also kind of sad. I wish I knew why, but I could only take a guess. I think that she had other plans for the next two weeks and now was stuck watching us, although if someone had asked me, it was more like I was watching them.

She must have read my mind because she looked right at me and said, "I am so glad to be here and spend time with you both."

"OK Gram!" I smiled. "I will clean the baby up and make some quick French toast from the bread and eggs. Then we can all go to the park and check out the cool trees! I will even show you the famous tree I was telling you about."

"Which tree is that? Is it the one you planted?" she asked.

"Oh. No! That one isn't famous! The one I want to show you is called The Friendship Tree. It was planted back in 1934 as a scientific experiment to create a new hybrid of citrus fruits. It was originally a lemon tree, but then other fruits were somehow added to it

88

like oranges, grapefruit and other kinds from the citrus family. There are 45 different types all together. Many famous people and presidents have come to see it. Scientists continue to inject it with new citrus types and the tree takes it in and adjusts to it. It's the only one of its kind in the world and you have to see it. The tree has lemons, clementines and oranges growing on it at the same time. There are 45 kinds and they are all different in taste.

"Wow, I can't believe such a thing exists! That's amazing! I definitely want to go see it today," she replied with excitement.

Sadly, that morning was the last time I would eat or drink water from my own home for the next two weeks. From that evening until my parents were back, I had to do every single thing I had written on that piece of paper. I wasn't proud of everything I had to do.

Picking the fruit was the easiest to do, because I gathered almost five pounds of plums and apples just from my grandpa's garden alone. I also collected cherries and pears from the trees in the front yard. Some of it I brought home for the baby and Gram, but most of it I sold at the bazaar because I needed to buy milk, a couple gallons of water, half a dozen eggs, and at least one loaf of bread.

The talent show that I organized also went very well and although I almost never came out to play with my friends anymore, they were excited to try something different and fun. I found ten girls from the building to help me and we performed different dances and sang songs by popular singers. We had to learn and practice literally a day before the show. We also came up with another idea that everyone enjoyed which was to recreate different scenes from the soap operas (the most popular being *Santa Barbara*) that our elderly neighbors watched on TV every day. I made tickets out of paper and used them to sell admittance to the "concert'. The tickets had a date, time, exact location, and a list of performers and what each of them was going to perform. As a price, I wrote:

"THE CONCERT IS FREE BUT ANY DONATION OR FOOD WOULD BE APPRECIATED AND CHERISHED"

The only problem was that I had to split the proceeds among eleven of us. But a little bit was better than nothing.

After the show was over, I spent a few days going around our building and others nearby to knock on doors in order to see if anyone had any work for me to do. I wasn't picky and was ready for anything. Maybe because I was eager, I got lucky and was booked-up for the first two days instantly. I was happy because being busy meant money.

I did all kinds of things for people. I cleaned their apartments, took out their garbage, ran out to the stores, walked their dogs, cleaned their cars and did yard work. I even cultivated the soil for those who had gardens out front. One of my favorite things to do was to paint the bottom of the damaged or fragile fruit trees with white paint so the tree bark could recover from the pests that attacked the trees while they were weak.

I wished people had paid me only with money, but with the bad economy, there were many who couldn't. Most of my customers were elderly and they lived alone with no one to help them. I didn't really want the money from them anyway because I felt badly taking their last few rubles, even if they had it. Ironically, they must have felt bad not paying me in the traditional way and did their best to make up for it. They gave me food, anything from apples, vegetables, honey, and walnuts, to a ready-to-eat hot meal and tasty homemade desserts. I brought it all to my brother and grandma.

The hardest thing that I did to feed my family was the last on my list. At the beginning of the second week as we were running short of our supply, the water didn't get turned on as usual and we had gone four days without a drop: the longest yet. The price per gallon of water had tripled overnight and whatever I earned wasn't even going to be close to enough. There wasn't enough time to work to earn what I needed because we needed the water now, and plus, who knew if I could get enough money anyway. Everyone was using what cash they did have to buy water for themselves. I had no choice but to do what I had to do.

I chose the furthest church from the center of the city but still within half an hour distance and headed there on the morning of the 8th day. After taking two buses, I arrived at around ten. When I walked up to the door, I saw quite a disturbing scene which I had only seen previously on TV.

There were ten old people, maybe in their late seventies or early eighties, who were sitting next to each other at both sides of the entrance. They all had their hands out waiting for someone to put money in their palms. The church was actually really busy with its doors wide open and quite a few people were coming in and going out. There were eight older ladies and two older men each sitting in rows across from each other.

I felt out of place and very ashamed to be asking for money right next to all of them. I really had no choice because I couldn't go home without having enough water for my family to drink and bathe the baby. So I came up to the end of the row and asked the older man if it was OK for me to sit next to him.

"Yes my child, sit here please. Do you want piece of bread? Are you hungry?" The man pulled an old, dry end piece of a roll from his pocket.

"Oh. No, No, No! I am not hungry at all, thank you very much. I am just trying to get a little money to buy some water and bread for my baby brother and my grandma," I answered while eye-balling the piece of bread he still held in his hand.

"OK. Then just sit here and put your hand up as high as you can because people don't like to bend over too low. Make sure that you don't look at them and keep your head down as much as possible," he added with a patient and thoughtful voice.

I did as he said and when I put my hand up, the older woman next to him turned her head to me. Without looking up she said, "If you sit here all day, at the end of it the church people will bring us bread and water. That's how we drink now, since the city has started to disconnect the water."

"I wish I could stay here all day and wait for the bread and water, but I can't because my family is waiting for me at home and they depend on me."

I copied her body language and did not pick up my head. A couple of minutes later, I felt something land in my palm, but I remembered not to look up even though I was curious to see how much it was. All of a sudden I felt another coin, then another and then something paper-like. I put my hand down, without moving my head and emptied the money into my other hand to count it. I had one paper ruble and over three rubles in coins, all within only fifteen minutes or so. I couldn't believe it.

I wasn't dressed any better than the older people and I was actually maybe dressed worse than they were. I wore a dirty white t-shirt and a thin light pink summer skirt that already had a few rips in it and spots on it. My flip flops weren't that old, but already there small holes worn under my heels because I wore the sandals everywhere, every day. My hair was its usual mess because I hadn't taken a shower in at least two weeks. I guess people must have assumed that I was homeless.

A couple of minutes later, more coins fell into my hand and it felt almost as if every person going in or out of the church was giving me something. I felt bad not even thanking people for the money and decided not to listen to the old man and to look up right after I got the next coin. I got another one within a minute and I looked right up the second I felt the metal hit my palm. To my surprise, the donor was a cute little girl not more than four or five years old, wearing a simple yet clean yellow dress. She had nicely combed hair with a thick braid that was long enough to rest on her chest. She was smiling at me, like we already knew each other.

"Why are you sitting here with all these old people?" she asked me. "Where is your mommy? I've never seen little girls here before, only you! You don't have parents? Do you have grandparents?"

"I do have parents but they are away right now and so is my grandpa. I have never done this before. I have to do it today, because I have to feed my little brother and my grandma," I answered her with a hint of shame and sadness in my voice.

"I also have a little brother, but I never do anything other than play with him. My mommy takes care of him, and me! I bet you can't wait for your parents to come back!"

Just then, her mother called her by first name, which was Katya, but she said Katusha, which was more of a loving, affectionate way of saying it. She waved goodbye to me and ran away. I checked the hands of others, and none of them had received any money yet. I didn't understand why, and my curiosity started to take over. The next time I felt a coin in my palm I looked straight up. This time I saw a middle-aged woman, dressed very conservatively, but with modern looking sunglasses and a scarf around her head.

"Thank you very much for the money. I need it to feed my little brother," I said.

"Why are you sitting here? Where are your parents? This is really ridiculous that you have to be here. I hope you know that." She was angry but had an understanding tone to her voice.

"My parents went away and didn't leave us much food so I am trying to make sure that my brother and grandma are fed," I replied back. "Can I please ask you just one question?"

"Yes, sure, go ahead", she answered, breaking a barely noticeable smile as she pulled down her sunglasses.

I paused for a moment. I was mesmerized by her long black eyelashes and unusually green eyes. "You are so pretty! But that isn't what I was going to say," I explained as her smile grew bigger. "I just wanted to ask you why you decided to give the money to me instead of to one of these elderly people."

"Well, to be honest with you, they are already very old, and probably have not much longer to live. You, on the other hand, are a little girl who obviously is either hungry or in great need of money for something very important with no place to get it," she answered me with patience. "I hope I will never see you here again," she added as she walked away.

After she left, I added up all the money I had received. I had over eight rubles, which was as much as I would have made working two or three days for different neighbors. I only needed five rubles to get a gallon of water and a loaf of bread. I really would have loved to have bought a piece of chocolate or a stick of gum with the extra money, or maybe a small roll just for myself, but I knew it wasn't the right thing to do.

I knew that these people had nothing in their hands and that no one wanted to give them any money. I took the other three rubles and divided it almost evenly into ten. Then I got up and gave each old person a share of it.

"I think if you look up and say 'thank you' to whoever is giving you the money, you will make them feel better, and it will show them that you appreciate whatever they were able to give you!" I said out loud with bit of sarcasm. "Someday when I have money, I will come back and bring you some of it. I promise," I said as I started to walk away.

When I turned around and looked one last time, I saw most of them had their heads up and not down like before. Who knows, maybe I taught them something useful. It's never too late to learn.

Many thoughts went through my mind as I walked to the bus stop. I wondered why they were all there in the first place. I felt badly for those people and the lives they were living. I thought that maybe they were bad parents but just treated their children poorly.

Maybe now that they are old, their children don't want to take care of them anymore. Maybe they just didn't have any children or other relatives to look after them, which is even worse. I knew one thing for sure. I could never let my parents or grandparents be in this situation, no matter how bad or mean they were to me, or how much pain they inflicted upon me. If I were a mean and heartless person then maybe I could do it, but that would make me just as bad as they were and I didn't want to be like that. For these old people, I felt nothing but sadness. I wished I could help them more right now or even stay there by the church and collect money for them, but I wasn't going to be able to do anything like that or even help them for at least a couple of years.

I got to the bus stop, bought the bread and a gallon of water at the kiosk, and made it home before it was two in the afternoon. Gram and the baby were happy to see me since I hadn't been home much over the past few days. I washed the baby using as little water as possible and then I went to see if the water system had been turned on while I was gone. I had placed buckets of all different sizes under each faucet and all the handles were turned to the open position in case the water came on unexpectedly. Unfortunately for us, the buckets were all still empty.

My grandma knew that I was out making money but she didn't know how hard it was. She also didn't know that I had been hungry for days now and was very thirsty, especially since it was getting hotter by the day.

Out of nowhere grandma looked at me and said, "Wait a minute! I haven't seen you eat anything at home for over a week now! You are eating and drinking, right?"

"Uh, yes... I am! Just not at home. I eat outside throughout the day. Do not worry about me. As long as you both are full, we are good," I answered trying to convince her with my smile.

I didn't lie to her. I did eat outside. I just didn't tell her what I ate or where I ate it. It wasn't as if she asked me for any details. The truth was that I really was starving day after day, and was eating things I couldn't tell her about.

I didn't use the food or water I earned or brought home for them because they weren't getting enough of it as it was. I felt a full responsibility for their well-being, and saw my role as being a mother to the baby and a daughter to my grandma. It was pretty much the role that my mother should have been playing, but when it came to satisfying my own hunger and thirst, I had to be much more creative.

From the day my parents left, I told grandma that I was sleeping in the living room on the sofa so she could sleep in my parents' bed with my baby brother. She saw nothing wrong with it, so it wasn't hard to talk her into that. What she didn't know was that I did that not only for her comfort, but also for another specific reason. I didn't want her to know that I left every night for an hour or so while they both slept.

For eight days I sneaked out of the apartment after midnight and went to the main garbage container area that served all four of our apartment buildings. There were six containers, one next to another and they were all very big. You could fit a dozen large garbage bags in each of them without a problem. These containers were always full and were emptied out by the city on Monday mornings.

I knew that it was the last thing I should have been doing, but other than eating the food which was meant to be for Gram and the baby, I saw no other way around it.

I would sit in the nearby bushes while wearing something dark, and would wait until most of the people had thrown their garbage out. It also really helped that there were no lights in the city at night and that no one ever saw me sitting in the bushes or going through the bags.

On rare occasions, lazy people would just leave their garbage bags next to the containers, but they were only doing me a favor. I could look through their trash in very efficient ways, however, most of the time I had to climb into each of those big metal containers to find something edible.

It was hard in the beginning, both mentally and physically. First of all, the whole climbing into the container thing was not as easy as I thought it would be. The garbage bags were mostly soft and I couldn't use them to push-off to climb back out. Second of all, since it was pitch black outside, every time I climbed into one of those containers I was taking a chance on falling and hurting myself. They were not always full, and sometimes I would fall almost to the bottom.

It was also very hard mentally. I had to overcome my pride and my self-worth to make myself eat other peoples' trash. I remember seeing homeless people looking through the garbage during the daylight and it always amazed me how they could do that right in front of other people. I had now developed some sort of respect for them and even looked up to them; they were better than I was. They didn't care what others thought of them or if anyone would make fun of them. God forbid that people would find out that I was hungry and in need; that was a weakness that I wasn't ready to show the world I had. After all, I was considered to be from such an "upscale" and educated family! My mother was a teacher and my dad was a doctor!

In the past, the only place I ever ate any leftovers was from the school cafeteria. And even that was something I disliked doing. I only did it when I was really hungry and when other kids couldn't see me.

Being surrounded by the trash bags filled with garbage was a whole lot different than in the cleaner school cafeteria. The smell that was coming out of these metal containers was just terrible and it was unbearable to be in there for more than a few minutes. It didn't help that there were a bunch of cats inside and outside of those containers, scratching the bags open and doing the same thing as I was, trying to find something to eat. It was difficult. Trying to figure out in the dark what I was touching inside a bag or even outside of it was terrifying. If it was too hard to guess, I had to try and smell it.

Some nights I got lucky and found chicken bones with some meat still on them or a leftover salad with half-eaten olives. Of course there were other times when I wasn't so lucky and had to really look hard through lots of trash for anything.

Sometimes when I thought it was food, it was really not. One time I came across a small plastic bag that was still warm. I thought it was soup and I got very excited, but after I made a small hole in it with my finger and drank some, I realized that it was someone's vomit. Another time I found a glass bowl filled with pasta and I assumed it had gotten thrown out by mistake, but when I opened it and ate some, I realized that one side of the bowl was broken and all the glass was now mixed in with the food. I only swallowed a little bit of it before I felt lots of sharp things in my mouth, but by then it had already scratched my gums, tongue and lips in few places.

I guess I wouldn't have had those issues if I looked through the trash during the daytime, but I wasn't that brave. What I didn't mind doing during the day was to climb the trees to pick the baby fruit that was still green. They were not yet ready to be eaten and I was told I could get very sick from eating it, but I didn't care.

When it came to the water I drank, it also didn't come from our rationed house supply. Since the river was mostly dried out, which usually it was in June, I drank the water from rain puddles. These puddles were on the street and around the buildings and I even drank the morning dew that collected in the flowers, grass, and leaves.

The most efficient and fastest way to get a drink was to drink the water directly from the puddles which I only did when no one could see me. I learned this had to be done very carefully, without disturbing the lower part of the puddle, where all the dirt, bugs and dead leaf bits were. For that I used a discarded straw that I found next to the milk shake and ice cream kiosk. It worked the best, especially for the deeper puddles. I still got some smaller pieces of dirt through the straw, but I could just spit that out.

Although the water from the ground tasted absolutely terrible, something was better than nothing. There was surely more than enough to satisfy my thirst.

When my parents came back from vacation in Bulgaria, they didn't even ask what we did or how we survived. My mother sent my dad out to buy some food and water the next morning, while checking to make sure that all the things she left for me on the "to do" list had been completed. My grandma was very mad at my mother and she packed up and left only a few hours after my parents came back, without talking to either of them. It was a good thing that gram didn't know what I had to do to provide her and my baby brother with food and water. If she found out, she would have made a huge deal about it and all our relatives would have found out. Now with gram gone, I knew that my "vacation" was over.

CHAPTER 6

Monday, Wednesday, Friday

While my parents were away on their two-week vacation, I lost quite a few pounds and started to feel sick. I was hoping my mother would notice that I was pale and tired, but as usual she wasn't around me for more than a few minutes, here and there.

Three days later, as soon as my dad went back to work, Uncle Armen came to visit. After my mother made something to eat, she called me and my brother to join them in the kitchen which didn't happen too often. It felt weird to be sitting there, all four of us, almost like a family but without my dad. I really disliked eating at the same table with Armen because it was never peaceful, but without a good meal in my stomach for over two weeks, I decided to suck it up and try to eat what I could.

I ate everything that was on my plate within a minute after I sat down. The atmosphere at the table was as tense as it had ever been whenever I was in Armen's presence. But as long as I was sitting there like a robot, I figured I would most likely be OK.

"Chew each piece of food exactly thirty-two times!" Armen demanded.

"I am trying but my teeth hurt and the food is already gone after I chewed it a few times," I answered. I felt weak, and spoke so low that it was hard even for me to hear it.

Changing the subject, Armen said, "So I was talking to your mother about the issues you had at school, and she said they threw you out for being stupid! Is that true?"

"They did let me go but I don't think it was because I was stupid. I think it was because I missed too many days of school. At least, that's what the principal said," I answered him quietly without looking up.

"No, no, no. It's because you are stupid and got bad grades, and now you have to do very good in this other school so that your old school can take you back like a little lost pet."

"I understand Uncle. I will do my best in the new school, although I heard it's much harder and the kids there are much smarter," I answered him quietly.

My mother and brother didn't say anything and just concentrated on their food. I don't think my mother really cared because she never interfered in anything Uncle Armen said or did to me. My baby brother was just as scared of him as I was, so he would never say much either.

"After talking to your mother about how we can prevent you from getting bad grades and doing badly in the new school in September, I came up with a great preventative schedule that she completely agreed with," Armen said to me after a long pause.

"You have a preventative schedule?" I asked confusedly.

"Yes that is correct," he replied.

"But how can we prevent something from happening?"

"Well, what we decided to do is schedule a half hour session three times per week — Monday, Wednesday, and Friday — from 4:00 to 4:30 in the afternoon right after you get back from school and right before you go to your music lesson. The sessions will consist of you lying face down on the sofa and me giving you between fifteen and thirty lashes on your back in those thirty minutes. Depending on how good you are and if you don't move, I might give you only fifteen. All this is just in CASE you get bad grades or don't behave," he explained with what sounded like genuine patience in his voice.

I was still very confused. I had never heard of disciplining a children before he or she got in trouble.

"Wait! Are you saying that if I get in trouble or have bad grades, there will be a separate discipline from the Monday, Wednesday, and Friday discipline?"

"That is correct. This is called prophylactic discipline, and it was used in the ancient world when slaves and animals were trained to not misbehave before something actually occurred," he clarified. "It really works. Trust me on that."

"But what if I wasn't going to misbehave? Then what would happen?" I asked trying to understand what he was trying to accomplish.

"Well, we can't hope that you will not because you have proven that you will do badly in school, even though what the elementary education teaches is very primitive and simplistic," he added while chewing on his food.

I was still completely confused by the whole idea because none of what he was saying made any kind of sense to me. I started to feel a little light-headed and sick to my stomach. I had felt sick for few days now, but hadn't really paid too much attention to the symptoms. A moment later, I got up from the table and ran into the bathroom, barely making it to the toilet bowl before throwing up everything I had just eaten. My brother ran after me, but I closed the bathroom door with my foot so he wouldn't see me in that condition. After I threw up, I felt even worse and had trouble getting up. I stayed on the bathroom floor until my mother came to check on me, about fifteen minutes later.

It turns out I was extremely ill and was rushed to the children's hospital with some sort of food poisoning, or at least that was the first diagnosis by the ambulance doctor. When I arrived I was quickly admitted and moved to the top floor for further testing. I don't remember what happened after that because they put me under a general anesthesia. I think they checked my intestines and my stomach with a camera, took a biopsy of my liver and conducted other serious tests. All I knew was that I had suddenly ended up in the ward of the hospital for dangerously sick kids. I knew I had to tell the doctors about what I had eaten over the past two weeks. They needed to know I had ingested dirty water, food from the garbage and un-ripe fruit from the trees. I had planned to tell my dad, but everything happened so fast that I never got the chance to do it.

I was scared and confused lying on the bed. I was surrounded by four walls of some thick, matte-finished clear plastic that was taped to the floor and attached to the ceiling. I felt like I was trapped inside a square plastic box. Although I was scared, I figured I was there only until they ran some tests because they didn't know what I had yet. It turned out that wasn't the case.

About an hour later, three people came up to the outside of the plastic wall and stood right where I could see them. They unzipped the plastic and walked in, quickly zipping the opening back up behind them. They were fully covered in what looked like some sort of space suit with strange face masks. Not one spot of their skin was exposed.

"Hello Veronika, you are probably confused about where you are, but do not worry, you are in good hands. This is the Sochi Children's Hospital and you are in the quarantined isolation zone because you have numerous infections and bacterial diseases in your body," said one of the doctors as he wrote some things down.

"Where is my dad? I want to talk to him please. I need to tell him something. Please call him now," I mumbled back, while starting to cry.

"I actually know your father quite well, and he is aware of your condition. We spoke to him over the phone about your tests and the test results. He is very concerned and worried that you may not recover well unless you fully cooperate with us and let us do what we need to do to help you. We are going to start by giving you different vaccinations and anti-virus medication as soon as possible," he explained.

"I don't know what you want from me! I just want to go home! Please let me call my dad or my grandpa! I have to go home! My baby brother will get scared! I never stay out all night, so I can't stay here! Pleeeeeease!" I begged the doctor.

I was simply freaking out because I had never really been in the hospital without a parent before, and getting all these tests done, the blood taking and all the medications and vaccinations I had to get were terrifying. The doctors didn't seem too confident that I was going to even make it.

"Under no circumstances can you leave this hospital, at least not until all of your test results show that you are no longer contagious. We know you are scared but you have to trust us," the doctor added.

"After we ask you a few questions, you will be able to talk to your father over the phone," said the female doctor.

"We need to know every place you have been in the past three weeks. We need to know every bit of food you remember eating, including meals and any raw things like meat, fish, fruit and vegetables. We need to know everything you had to drink and everyone you came into contact with and we need to know all that right now," said the first doctor.

"What do I have? Do I have a cold or food poisoning maybe or some kind of virus? I don't feel anything other than a body ache, a sore throat, and a little lightheadedness."

The female doctor answered in somewhat of a demanding but caring voice. "You have probably never heard of any of these things, but I will tell you what we have found. You have an intestinal worm, pinworms, mumps, a liver fluke, and Diphtheria, as well as food poisoning. We really need you to answer all our questions right now so that we can start to give you what your body needs immediately in order for you to get better. To be totally honest with you, we are completely shocked that you are not in a coma and that you are even still alive, so please try to cooperate with us the best you can."

I spent the next half hour telling them everything I had to eat and drink, as well as from where I got it. The only thing I changed from the real story was that I said that finding food in the dark in the garbage was a sick bet that I made with my friends. They didn't seem very convinced, and told me that it didn't make sense to them because I didn't come across as someone who would do things to deliberately harm myself. They also noted that I had lost over fifteen pounds in just two months. I guess the school nurse had recorded my weight the one time I went to see her about a stomach ache. It is definitely possible that even if they suspected that I wasn't being honest with them, they wouldn't make a huge deal out of it. My dad was a well-respected doctor in our city and was well-known through the region. If they did say something, it would almost certainly make my family look bad.

Right away that day, they started me on all kinds of painful shots and procedures every couple of hours. I also got to talk to my dad the next morning, but I was completely exhausted from staying awake all night in pain and discomfort. I don't even remember what we talked about other then he said that I was in good hands and that he knew I would get well soon.

For two weeks I had zero visitors other than the doctors and nurses whose faces I hadn't even seen. Anything that was done to me was done in that square plastic room. Different medical equipment, machines and other things came in and out of there all day. Most of the time I was giving blood, receiving blood, getting intravenous lines put in, vaccines, breathing vapors, drinking disgusting liquids and swallowing dozens of pills. I didn't eat much regular food and was fed through a vein in my arm. The only thing they gave me to drink was some chalky-looking liquid and a special creamy hot cereal that tasted terrible.

I was giving up by the hour, and the only time I got off the bed was when I really wanted to go to the bathroom; and even then I had to do that while a nurse was present. Then she took away whatever I did with her the minute I was done.

By the middle of the second week, I actually stopped talking to all the medical staff and just lay there like a lifeless body following their routine. I wasn't really sure what was happening to me or why I was behaving this way, but it felt like things were getting worse and that no one cared about me being alone and sick in the hospital.

One day, after my daily morning vaccination, I was supposed to go to sleep but didn't swallow the pills they gave me, spitting them out as soon as the nurse left. I waited for about half an hour, until I didn't hear any sounds or noises around me, and without getting off the bed, I grabbed one of the thin tubes that were all around me. Without any type of physical or mental preparation, I wrapped the tube around my neck and squeezed it as hard as I could. I don't know what came over me or why I did what I did, but I was trying very hard to keep myself from breathing. A few seconds later I let it go because I was too physically weak to continue. I breathed very heavy for a few minutes, gasping for air, but then grabbed the tube to try again. This time I would hold it closer to the middle so it would be easier to squeeze it hard.

Just as I was about to try it again, I heard some voices pass by in the hall outside my plastic room. Two men were talking to each other about something that they had just seen outside, and as they passed by my bed, one of them said, "Did you see that huge brown eagle flying over the front play yard? I have never seen anything like it. It's the largest bird that I've seen flying that low to the ground."

As soon as I heard that, my hands stopped squeezing and my whole body froze. "My eagle is here? Did he come back?" I whispered to myself as big tears flowed from my eyes. I didn't know why he came back, but I knew that he had to be here for a reason. Something made me stop for a moment -- a thought or a fear perhaps — I don't know for sure, but a few minutes later, while I was still frozen in place, the female doctor came in to check on me.

"WHAT DO YOU THINK YOU ARE DOING, YOU CRAZY CHILD?!" she screamed louder than my mother ever would. She ran up to my bed and started un-wrapping the cord from around my neck. "DOCTOR, DOCTOR, PLEASE COME HERE RIGHT AWAY! SHE IS TRYING TO KILL HERSELF," she screamed again and again.

The head doctor ran into the room with two nurses while the female doctor un-wrapped the cord and put a breathing mask on my face.

"YOU ARE ALMOST THERE! DO YOU UNDERSTAND THAT? You are ALMOST out of here! Fight a little longer! You know you can and I know you can! It's easy to give up, but your grandpa can't wait to see you. He calls every day to check on you!" the head doctor said with a voice that sounded like he was scared. I felt some sort of special connection develop right then and there between me and both of these doctors as they shouted. They were actually really worried and it didn't look like they saw me like one of their other patients. Their screaming and fear for my wellbeing showed me that they did care if I lived or died.

After all the craziness was over, they gave me an intravenous sleeping medication and I felt myself slowly fall asleep. The last thing

I remember thinking about was my friendly eagle that showed up at the hospital at the same moment as I was trying to end my life — again. If I had not heard those men talking about him in the hallway, I wouldn't have stopped and would have choked myself, this time successfully.

The following Monday, just a few days after my nervous breakdown, I received an unexpected surprise the moment I woke up. Both the head doctor and the female doctor were sitting in chairs right next to my bed. They didn't even disturb my sleep and waited for me to naturally open my eyes. I thought I was still in a dream, because they were dressed in their normal white doctors' coats without any masks. They were both smiling and the female doctor's eyes looked a little watery.

"Sweetie, you can now leave the quarantined floor and continue your treatments on the lower floor with the rest of the children," the female doctor said.

I stared at them for a minute before I smiled and put my arms up to them silently. They both came up to me at the same time and hugged me. I held them tightly, almost as if it would be the last time I would ever see my best friends again. I felt deep attachment to them at that moment, even more than I did a few days earlier when they had saved my life. The female doctor was crying as the head doctor walked around my bed to disconnect some wires. I think he just didn't want us to see he was getting emotional.

When he sat me into the wheelchair and opened up the plastic wall in front of me, I couldn't believe how big the hospital was. There were dozens of rooms and lots of big plants everywhere. We got into an elevator and went down a couple of floors. Before I even had a chance to realize that I had made it out alive, the elevator doors opened, and he wheeled me out to the second floor.

As we headed to the main play room, he said, "With your combination of conditions, you are by far the most challenging patient I have had to face in my whole career, but you did it. You are going to be healthy again!" he said in a proud yet caring voice.

When we arrived at the main area, I saw dozens of children from ages five to fifteen playing all kinds of games and laughing out loud. Many of them came to greet me and pointed to areas where they were playing so I could join them.

One little girl, who was not more than five or six years old wearing a pretty pink dress, hopped over to us singing something as she switched from one foot to another. Her long blond, braided hair looked very thick like it was taken off of a human-sized doll. I didn't believe it even looked like her real hair, but I didn't say anything out loud. When she came close, she asked my doctor if it would be OK if she kissed me on my cheek. He said yes, so she got on her tippy-toes and gave me a long, loud kiss. Then she moved one step away and put her little hand out to shake mine.

"My name is Maria and I've been here for six months now. I have a cancer in my head, but my mommy said there is a good chance I might be able to go home for the holidays," she said to me in an optimistically happy voice.

"Hi Maria, my name is Veronika and I have been upstairs in isolation for two weeks. I had many bad things inside me, but the doctor said I am OK now and I am allowed to play with others."

I stayed in that section of the hospital for a couple more weeks and I played with Maria all day long, almost every day. There were a few days, when I didn't see her, but other kids told me that she had some procedures done which made her too sick to play with others. I missed her a lot when I didn't see her, because despite her age she was very smart and knew a lot.

Maria and I could talk about everything and everyone. She was really an amazing and kind little girl and I felt that she was by far the best friend I had ever had. I told her that when I left the hospital, I would come back and visit with her the first chance I got; if not right away, definitely before she went home for the holidays.

On my last day there, when I only had a couple of hours left and was about to go home, Maria wouldn't leave my side, even to take her medication. She cried non-stop when she found out I was leaving, and so did I. When my father came to get me, I had almost no emotion or interest, other than asking him how my baby brother had been doing.

When we left the hospital, I looked right up to the second floor. Sure enough, Maria was staring at me through the window, still crying and waiving to me the whole time we were visible to each other.

I thought I would miss my home, my family and my friends, but the truth is I really didn't. The only one I really missed from my family was my baby brother who was beyond happy when I walked into the apartment. Unfortunately, I was too tired to play or even to talk, and all I could do, was to give him one long hug. I went straight to the sofa where I stayed for the rest of the day. It was a good thing Russia had universal healthcare because my long hospital stay was free. I am sure my dad brought those doctors some presents for taking good care of me and saving my life; presents like chocolate or a good bottle of an Armenian Cognac that everyone in Russia loves. It was a tradition that people gave presents to show their extra appreciation. If that long stay in the hospital had not been free, my mother would have hated me even more.

The next day my dad went to his 24-hour shift. I was still super weak and couldn't even stand straight for too long. I had a list of prescriptions I had to take, but didn't feel like getting up and following the schedule doctors put in place for me. All I could taste in my mouth was the medicine and old food. By that time, I hadn't brushed my teeth in over a year.

After my dad went to work, my brother sneaked into the living room to say hi, and as soon as he did, I heard my mother scream from the kitchen, "Tigran, get away from her, she is infectious!"

"No, I am not. Come here Tigran and give me another hug. Vera missed you," I whispered to him to counter my mother's words.

He looked back to see if my mother was coming, and when he didn't see her, he ran over to me and gave me a quick hug. When he left, I closed my eyes and tried to fall asleep again. I wasn't as sleepy as I was earlier, so I grabbed one of my dad's anatomy books and started to read it, taking my time with those very long, Latin words, some of which took half of a line.

About an hour later, I heard the front door open and Uncle Armen's voice saying hello to my mother. He didn't come to the living room to check on me, but instead went straight to the kitchen. I didn't want any of his attention anyway. I hoped he had some bit of humanity left in him and would at least leave me alone. Unfortunately, I underestimated his need to see me hurt, and after about ten more minutes, I heard him call my name.

"Veeeeraaaa, come over here and bring a couple of thick books with you," he shouted from the kitchen.

I was so tired I barely had the energy to even get up. I really wished that I didn't have to, but I knew that I had no choice. I was deeply annoyed that he couldn't let me relax and get well, even after the doctors explained to my dad that it was vital for me to get rest. I was sure my mother already told Armen about it and he knew that I had been in the hospital for the whole month. For a moment I wished I was back in that square plastic room instead of being here.

I slowly got off of the couch and looked around to see which books were the biggest. I wasn't really sure why he needed them, but I figured he was just too lazy to come and get them himself.

I grabbed two big, heavy anatomy books and slowly started to walk over to the kitchen barely holding them in my hands. Although I only had to walk twenty feet, I think it took me at least a couple of minutes to get there. I wasn't even picking my feet fully off the floor, which I knew would probably get everyone quite angry.

"Here are the two heaviest books I could find, Uncle," I whispered as I struggled to lift both of them onto the table. My brother was sitting on the middle chair and my mom was practicing her perfect "cat" eye makeup and was staring into a magnifying mini-mirror. As soon as both books were on the table, I turned around to head back to the living room.

"Waaaaaait a minute, Vera, come back here! I have to check something," Armen said to me with a strange yet optimistic voice. "I need to see if you have any physical strength left in you, so come and pick these books back up."

"I don't understand what you are trying to make me do, Uncle," I mumbled back at him as I turned and came back to the table.

"Oh I forgot that you are stupid! It's OK, I'll say it slooooo-weerrrr. I neeed youuu tooo taaake theeeese booooks aaaand hooold themmm uuuup iiinn frooont ooof youuu... do understand now?" He made me feel like I was two or three years old.

"I understood that part Uncle, but was I confused about why you want to check to see if I have any energy left, because I don't," I said a little afraid.

"PICK THESE STUPID BOOKS UP AND HOLD THEM IN FRONT OF YOU, OR I WILL SMASH THEM IN YOUR FACE!" he screamed at me as his triangle-shaped eyebrows became even sharper, forming two incomplete letter" A's" on his forehead.

Without saying anything and with both hands I grabbed the books off of the table. They were heavy and uncomfortable to hold and each of them was at least a thousand pages thick. As soon as I grabbed them, I fell forward a little from weakness, but I quickly straightened back up so as not to get him angrier.

"Hold them in front of you with straight arms and without touching your body."

I held them in front of me for just a few moments and then they started to drop down lower, little by little, until it became obvious to him that I couldn't do what he wanted.

"Wow, you are completely retarded," he said as he pushed the books back up to an even level. "Now you better keep them there until I tell you to put them down! Do you understand?" he shouted into my face.

"Yes Uncle, I do," I answered as my tears started to flow fast and heavy. It was as if that was the only time they were allowed to show themselves. I held the books for a little longer and then really started to struggle as my arms became stiff and started to hurt even worse than before.

"Uncle, I can't hold them anymore, my arms hurt badly and I don't feel good in my belly", I said as my salty tears poured into my mouth.

"OK fine, I will help you then!" he said as he rose from his chair and smiled with sarcasm.

For a split second I thought he was going to show some sort of kindness and understanding, something that was perhaps buried somewhere deep in his soul. I was very wrong. He snatched the books from my hands and slammed both of them very hard right down on top of my head.

"How about that: now you can hold them on your head! You can use your hands but just so the books don't fall off! You got that?" As he spoke, he spit small tea grains from his onion infused mouth right onto my face.

I didn't answer anything back because I thought I was going to lose consciousness at any second. My head started to pound with an instant migraine, my eyes were blurry and I started to feel very lightheaded. All I could think about was why I was foolish enough to bring the heaviest books from that room. What he had planned to do didn't cross my mind. He was just too creative.

I stood there in that condition for about fifteen minutes, balancing the books by switching them from one arm to the other. Meanwhile, he finished his food, drank his tea, cleaned up after himself and went to the bathroom. My mother finished her dinner as well and went to her bedroom, walking right by me without even looking or saying a word. My brother sat there and watched me for a while like a baby robot, without any emotion, and then he ran out of the kitchen when he heard my mom call his name.

Then Armen said, "I am booooored! Get out of my face!"

I stood there terrified in the same exact position without moving for another minute until he started to laugh hysterically in my face. "You are definitely and completely stupid, and this is perfect proof of that. I said you were boring me, now get out of here," he repeated as he shoved me with both of his hands.

I flew a few feet away from that spot and the books fell down with me loudly. It took every grain of energy I had left to pick up myself, the books, and then walk into the living room, quietly shutting the door behind me.

"Why didn't I end this ridiculous existence? Why?" I said to myself in complete frustration, burying my face in a pillow on the couch. "This should have ended in the hospital, right there and then, but again I was too weak to do it," I whispered while wiping the tears off my face.

I fell asleep that night, repeating the same sentence over and over again, both out loud and then in my head. *"I don't want to wake up. I don't want to wake up. I don't want to wake up. I don't want to wake up..."*

I spent most of the next couple of weeks in the house either doing choirs or sleeping. My baby brother was very well behaved for me, and clearly understood that I wasn't feeling well. We started to become like best friends and did more and more things together. When he napped, I tried doing the same. When I read, he asked me to read out loud and sat there for hours listening to me until it was time to eat or he got tired and fell asleep. If he woke up before me, he would lie there and stay quiet until I got up on my own. When it was a little chilly, he would cover me from my toes to my neck with the thin blanket from the sofa. He told me a few times that he heard me talk and cry in my sleep. I believed him. It made sense because I hadn't dreamed of anything good, if I dreamed at all.

I started to teach him letters, colors, animals, songs, how to draw and other stuff. He used to love anything that had to do with different colors. He remembered every single one and knew which ones he could mix to make new colors. He was a very smart little boy and super understanding at the same time, even though he was still only little over three years old.

At the end of July, I started to feel better and was able to have more energy, not only for the baby and my household chores, but for other things as well.

One day I was practicing playing piano when my dad decided to be nice to me and told me that I should stop and go outside to play with my friends. Between the hospital and the weeks of recovery, I really hadn't even enjoyed any of that summer, not that I thought I deserved it anyway after the academic year I'd had. Although not really in the mood, I felt I really should go out and play with my friends for at least a little while. I got dressed and quickly left the house just as my brother started his long, early afternoon nap, and just in case my dad changed his mind. When I first arrived in the yard, I could see all the children playing ahead in the distance, so I started to slowly make my way to them.

There was a big bird house at the front of the last entrance to our building. One of the neighbors built it and put at least a hundred different birds in it to live and to give him fresh eggs. He was very anti-social and didn't like it when kids from the building got too close, so he built a tall metal fence around it. He owned some very rare and unusual breeds which I had never seen before.

On this day he wasn't around, so the kids were hanging out by his bird house. I came up and said hello to everyone. There were a couple of new kids, but most of the rest knew who I was. A couple of my old friends ran up and hugged me. They didn't really ask me where I had been because they already knew that my appearances in the yard were always very sporadic. I talked about my time in the hospital for a while and then went up to the fence to look at the birds and chit chat.

The two birds that I loved the most were beautiful peacocks, a male and a female. They were absolutely gorgeous, with colors that I had only seen in children's books. The female peacock always behaved like she was the most beautiful bird on earth, which she probably was, and the male always followed her around. If I waited long enough, they both would come out of the birdhouse. The female used to always walk slowly with her head up like she was the Queen of England or something. In many ways she reminded me of my mother and the way she carried herself, in and outside of the house.

I will never forget the first time I saw these two birds from about twenty feet away. The female peacock showed up and the male slowly followed her around. After about ten minutes the most amazing thing happened. The male peacock opened his incredibly colorful, breathtaking tail, which was decorated with dozens upon dozens of big and round eye-shaped spots. It was like he had hundreds of eyes and they were staring right at me. That was the most amazing thing I had ever seen. It was really overwhelming and made me feel warm and hopeful for better days, for a better life, and for a real hope that one day all my pain and suffering would end. I believed beautiful Mother Nature would find a way to take care of me and to put me on the right path, guiding me away from the pain and unfair world that I was in.

I sat there for a while just staring and admiring their unforgettable beauty, when all of a sudden I heard a couple of kids that were playing on the side of the building start to scream in our direction.

"Watermelons! Run to the river! Everyone quickly, quickly! They are coming!"

Of course the last thing I wanted to do was to get in trouble for leaving the yard especially since I'd had such bad luck with that whole river thing. But as in the past, my curiosity took over, and I started to run toward the river right along with everyone else.

I was the last one to make it to the riverbank and as I got closer and closer, I became more confused. It was the strangest sight! There were literally dozens of huge, bright-green watermelons floating in the water, making their way toward us and some even making their way all the way to the sea. There were so many it made the river look like it was covered in a green polka dot blanket.

Just when I arrived at the edge, everyone started to run toward the opening which the kids used to cross the river. I had a very bad memory of that spot, because that's where — because of me — my baby brother almost drowned. But of course, my curiosity got the better of me as it always did, and I had to see what was happening up close and alongside my friends.

All the kids were standing on the edge of the opening when I arrived and they were trying to grab the watermelons as they passed. The level of the water was actually quite high and no one dared to go into the river itself. Even the edge where we were all standing was submerged in the water by at least a foot. To make it even harder for us, most of the watermelons were not passing by close enough to grab and everyone was becoming aggravated.

I don't know if it was because I cared about my friends that much, or just because I used to take charge of the situations and find a way out, but I made an announcement. "OK everyone, I am going to go into the river. I will try to grab the watermelons and will push them toward the shore so you can pull them out," I said with a brave voice.

Everyone paused for a second and then screamed with excitement. There must have been fifteen of us, so I had to make sure I was able to get a watermelon for everyone.

Once I waded into the water, I found it to be quite deep and I was quickly in all the way up to my waist. The water was cold, too, even though it was the hottest time of the summer. Within the next ten minutes I pushed at least a dozen of the larger watermelons toward the shore, where two kids at the same time would snatch them out and keep count by screaming the numbers to me. Everyone was so thrilled and their happiness kept me going.

"This is AMAZING! Oh My God, look at that one! Vera, grab that big oval-shaped one. Those are the sweetest!" my friends screamed in true pleasure, cheering me on at the same time.

Although the whole experience was something so magical that even I couldn't believe it was real, the current was really strong and I was becoming more tired by the minute. Maybe it was because I was still weak and didn't have the stamina for physical activity, or maybe it was because I was just a little girl going against a more powerful Mother Nature. I suppose it didn't really matter.

The important thing was that those watermelons still had their long stems attached to them, which made them easy to catch and to push toward my friends; otherwise they were mostly round and slippery. I was lucky that there weren't any sticks or other debris mixed in with them because I would have definitely been hurt.

Right before I reached the last one, which was actually the one for me, I started to hear all of my friends screaming their hearts out, as loudly as they could.

"VERONIKA, GET OUT OF THE WATER! NOWWWWW! A HUGE BUNCH OF WATERMELONS IS COMING! YOU WILL GET PUSHED RIGHT INTO THE BLACK SEA! HURRY! HURRY!" one friend screamed after the other, and then all at the same time.

A second later, I looked up and saw one of the scariest and coolest things I had ever seen. The water ahead in the river had become completely green by making it appear that there was really no water there at all. In fact, I couldn't even see the river ahead of me because many thousands of watermelons were covering the water like a thick, green blanket. I started to run toward the shore. I was instantly reminded of the time I had to run to it to save my baby brother.

As I reached the shore, a few of the kids grabbed me and pulled me out of the water. I stood up and turned toward the river to see what I escaped from just as a flat but powerful mountain of watermelons rushed by us. We couldn't even see the end of it and had to move up higher on the walkway because some of the watermelons were hitting the shore with quite a force and cracking and breaking open. I have never seen such a sight in my whole life, nor will I ever forget it. Yet again, Mother Nature didn't fail to amaze me.

I heard from my friends that all of the watermelons came from a huge watermelon farm somewhere up in the mountains. I guess the heavy rainfalls up there washed them off the fields just as they were ready to be harvested. Then they must have made their way into the nearest stream. From there they passed right through the city into the main river which was carrying them all the way into the Back Sea.

I made my way to the front of the building and said goodbye to everyone. I was soaking wet and in need of a good, long, deep nap. Everyone thanked me and it felt super good that I had made their day better and filled up their bellies at the same time. They gave me the biggest watermelon of all, and I slowly carried it up the stairs to the fifth floor.

When I walked into the hallway, my dad wasn't home and the baby was already up. My mother was having coffee in the kitchen and Uncle Armen was making himself his green tea that he had at least once per hour. I didn't realize it, but I had been gone for over

119

two hours. Bringing the watermelon home and making the floor all wet as the water dripped from my clothes didn't make anyone too happy either.

"I am NOT even going to ask you where you went! I told your father that you didn't deserve to go outside to play, but no, he thought you should get some fresh air. I guess living on the top floor of the building doesn't give you enough of that," my mother said in an annoyed and angry manner.

"I told you that we should start the Monday, Wednesday, Friday schedule as soon as possible and see I was right," added Armen.

I had no clue what I had done wrong other than staying out for two hours and coming home wet. My dad never told me how much time I could spend outside and I was the one who would get to clean up the wet floor anyway.

"Well, well, well," said Armen. "I guess it's time, and it is Monday, so why don't you go to the balcony and prepare yourself."

"But Uncle, I am totally wet, tired, and haven't eaten anything; plus, didn't you say the punishment was supposed to be during the school day and from 4:00 to 4:30 in the afternoon?" I asked hoping he would change his mind.

"I don't know exactly what I said, or didn't say, but I do know that you have one minute to go to the balcony, take off your dress, and lie face down. I will be there soon," he answered in a cold tone and unbuckled his leather belt.

Nervous and scared, I slowly walked out of the kitchen and into my parents' bedroom and then out onto the balcony. I really disliked that part of the house, because other than watching my friends play outside, nothing good ever happened in there. I put the blanket over the mini-sofa, took off my wet dress, and laid it down on my belly. I was wearing only my underwear which was also completely wet and now transparent. I was freezing and shaking from being both cold and afraid of what was going to happen next. I wondered how many times he was going to whip me. I also felt very uncomfortable wearing only my underwear. Since I had turned nine a few months earlier, my upper body was showing signs of growth and I was already going to ask my mother to buy me my first bra.

A few minutes later, I heard Armen walk into my parents' bedroom and close the door. First he shut it, and then he locked it. I'm not sure why he thought he had to lock it, but maybe it was to keep my brother out in case he wanted to check up on me.

Armen started to make his way toward the balcony while making a sharp snapping sound with the belt which he knew scared me to the deepest parts of my body. He walked up to me and said, "Are you trying to get me to whip you on top of your underwear? Are you trying to use it as a cover? You are actually quite stupid, because it will hurt more since the material is completely wet." he laughed out loud.

"I know, but I'd rather keep them on. It makes me feel better," I answered him, my voice shaking. The last thing I wanted was to be completely naked. It was already bad enough that I was wearing so little.

That afternoon was the first "just in case" beating that I ever received from him. It was the beginning of what would become a three-times-per-week entertainment session that Armen had created for himself. He never gave me only the fifteen lashes he had originally promised if I don't make any sounds. Sometimes he gave me more. In fact, he did everything possible to make sure that his belt landed on the same exact spots, multiple times, to make it hurt even more. After each of these sessions, I had bloody bruises all over the back side of my body, starting from my upper legs above my knees and extending all the way up to the beginning of my neck. The weekends gave me a two-day break between beatings and were the only time that I had for the wounds to partially heal.

From that time on, and until the first day of school, I gave no reason for him to hit me at all, never mind in such a brutal manner. He said the punishments were "just in case."

What I came to realize was that though I was getting beat up on a more consistent basis, I was living the same life as I had been for years: no fun; no entertainment; no appreciation; no understanding; no praises; no complements and no love. So I made the decision and a promise to myself that summer that once school started, I would behave however I wanted. If I thought of something bad to do, then it should be OK because it didn't really matter if I was a good little girl or a bad one, I was still going to get disciplined. I really saw no point to following rules or behaving, so why not have fun for a change. After all, it was quite boring to be a good girl all the time without my family seeing that I, in fact, really was one.

When I started the 4th grade at the new school, I honestly didn't care if I was going to get good grades or bad ones, and just tried to pass the classes with just enough effort so I would be to be able to go back to my old school. Two days into the school year, I balked and didn't even go to the first period.

I really missed little Maria from the hospital, and other than missing a day from school, there was no other way I would be able to go and see her. The children's hospital was very far from where I was, and it took at least two hours to travel each way between walking and taking multiple busses. For some reason, even though Maria was only five, I really became attached to her and felt a special connection and understanding when I was in her company. It was almost like she knew the pain I was living through and she didn't judge me on anything. I could definitely say that I spent more time talking to her while in the hospital than I could remember even talking to my own parents.

On my way to the hospital, I bought some day-old tulips from an old lady who was selling the flowers from her garden. My dad always did that, too, and he would get into arguments with my mother because she would be mad at him for buying barely-alive flowers just to help out the old ladies. But I kind of liked that about my dad; he was kind and helpful and knew that older people also had to eat and survive.

When I showed up at the hospital I could hardly contain my excitement! While still catching my breath, I ran up to the secretary in the front foyer.

"Good Afternoon, Miss! I am here to see Maria! She is five years old and has been here for a few months now, and she should be on the second floor where all the kids are. She is very nice, kind, funny, and happy! I love her! We are best friends, and she knows I am coming. I told her a few weeks ago that I would come and visit her before she went home to her mommy for the holidays!" I said in a loud, excited voice without taking a breath.

"Sweetheart, I knew you were talking about Maria as soon as you said her name. Only Maria would have another child come to visit her, especially alone," she answered with a calm and monotonic sound to her voice, almost like she was half asleep.

"I didn't go to school today so I could come here. I brought her favorite flowers: white baby tulips!"

The lady slowly got up, went around her tall desk, came up to me and hugged me tightly. Then she whispered in my ear, "I am so, so sorry sweetie. Maria is gone. She didn't make it to her mommy or to the holidays. I am sure she loved you very much and still does, but she is a beautiful little angel now."

I was in shock. I hugged and squeezed the woman as hard as I could and I could feel the pain and sadness rapidly fill my body. Before I let her go, I quietly answered her back, "It's OK, but I won't break my promise to my best friend. I am still going to see her before the holidays."

CHAPTER 7
Banging My Head Against the Wall

From the day my brother was born, my mother always treated him in a strange girl-like manner. She let his hair grow long right from birth, and when it was all the way to the bottom of his ears, she made little pony tails out of his hair.. She would also dress him up in dresses and let him play with some old and weird dolls. She treated him like he was her daughter, not a son. It really made me feel strange and out of place. It was almost like I was a boy and he was a girl.

Because of this, and because of the way she was treating me, I started to question many things. It bothered me that although she already had a daughter, she was in search of another one. I was fighting all the unknowns in my head that told me she didn't see me as her child. I was trying not to blame myself but, it still felt like I might have been just not good enough for her. When she looked at me, all I saw in her eyes was pure disgust and hate. When she looked at my brother, all I saw in her eyes was pure and unconditional love.

Not getting much love or attention from her or my father while at home, I started to look for it elsewhere. That, mixed with my decision to turn my life from boring to fun, drove me to change. I wasn't going to stay away from excitement or other kids anymore, even if whatever they were doing was bad or dangerous. It's not like I was not going to be disciplined if I behaved, so why bother trying.

The new school was actually not as bad as I thought, because I didn't know most of the kids, and even if I misbehaved, well, it's not like I was staying there for a long time anyway. As soon as my grades were high enough to go back to my original school, I was out of there.

The whole month of September I dedicated myself to getting my grades in most of the classes up to at least a "B" level. I didn't really have any distractions at first, though I was noticing what other kids were wearing to school every day. The students at this school were all dressed much nicer than at my other school. This school was right in the center of the city so most of the kids here were from wealthy families; although their personalities weren't that rich, at least in my opinion.

The kids were quite stuck-up and didn't really give me or other kids who didn't dress nicely the time of day. The stuck-up kids would even make disgusted faces and look me over, up and down, when walking by me in the hallway or in the classroom. They probably didn't like my "backpack" that much either, which was still just a plastic grocery bag.

Sure it would have been nice to wear pretty dresses and nice shoes, but at that point I wasn't too concerned with it. I just wanted to somehow survive for the next few years and then run away to live with my grandpa until I was well-off enough to move out and live on my own.

The school itself was actually very big with two buildings right across from each other. A glass bridge connected them through the second floor.

Out of all the kids who did talk to me, I became close to only two of them. Ironically, let's just say they were not the best two of the bunch. It didn't really matter that the kids and teachers did not like them, because to me, it meant they were probably a lot of fun and most likely different, like me.

I appreciated that. Although they were from the "better" school, they still didn't mind being my friends; therefore, I actually really started to like them. Their names were Anastasia and Victoria. Anastasia was a very pretty girl who had long brown hair and big blue eyes. Victoria was also pretty, but had a short, shoulder-length blond haircut that she wore in a ponytail most of the time. Unlike the girly Anastasia, who usually wore fancy but pretty dresses, Victoria wore pants and a shirt almost every time I saw her. I heard that the girls were so bad in some subjects their teachers gave the girls passing grades just so they wouldn't come back to the teachers' classes at all. I thought that was quite clever and really humorous, but also knew that with my luck if I were to do something like that, I would get bad grades and then get thrown out of this school, too.

They were both from rich families, and their fathers were longtime friends who worked for the city of Sochi. My friends always had money with them which I bet must have been an awesome feeling. I remember telling them that if I had all that money, I would give it to old or homeless people, and the girls just laughed at me. Anastasia would say, "They should have worked smarter, not harder when they were young." Maybe she had a point.

Despite their views on the poor, I still liked them and I wasn't going to judge anyone based on his or her beliefs as long as they treated me right, which they did. Most of the time when they went to get food for themselves they would always bring me something yummy.

When I thought about our friendship, I couldn't really figure out why they liked me so much. We were definitely from two completely different households, and other than our age and our attitude about not caring what other students in school thought of us, we didn't have very much in common. All I knew was they gave me what I didn't get at home and that was a feeling of being appreciated, needed, and cherished. They never made me feel like they were better than I was or had more money than I did. I was always comfortable and happy in their company.

We definitely got into a little more trouble than I anticipated, but at that point in my life, it didn't really matter as long as I was having fun. I wasn't doing anything to hurt others, at least not in the beginning. The worse thing I did was skip different periods and classes that bored me or that I didn't like. I already had solid "B's" in them, so attending every single class was not that vital. Of course, when I didn't show up to a specific class, it was because all three of us had left school to go for a walk or to get some snacks. Luckily the school was never locked, so I was able to get right back in and attend the classes I did enjoy like biology, computers, art and music.

Unfortunately, I didn't stay off the radar for too long. Both of my friends were very creative and fearless; that was quite a dangerous mix. One day they came up with the idea for the three of us to write a bunch of bad words in all the girls' bathrooms. I'm not sure why they decided to do that, but I think they thought it was exciting to do something improper in such an uptight and proper school.

"OK girls, let's do this! Let's go into the bathrooms throughout the school and write all the bad words you ever heard someone call you!" said Anastasia. "NOT aaaaaaalll the bad words you know, ONLY the ones someone has ever said to you directly, no matter who said it," she clarified.

"OK, I'll go to the second floor and Veronika, you can do the other side of the school. Anastasia, you can do the first floor," Victoria said.

We had a group hug and decided to do it a few hours later at a specific time, after school was out. It took us about an hour and a half to write the bad words inside each of the stalls. Then we went into each other's territories to read them. Their stalls were first since they were both on the same side of the school.

When I read what they wrote, it was quite vulgar, but nothing that I hadn't heard; however, when they read what I wrote, they had a very surprising reaction.

"Who said those words to you?" Anastasia asked with a stunned and disturbed look in her eyes. "We clearly know you don't hang out with the other bad kids like we do, so who said all that to you?"

"Weeeell, it was my uncle and my mom, mostly. On rare occasions my dad, but in general he isn't too mean," I answered.

"So, you are trying to tell me that your mother and uncle called you a thief, a piece of shit, a scumbag, ugly, a demon, a bitch, a stupid retard and a lazy fat pig"? she asked.

"Aaaaah, yes... why?"

"Hmmm. Is there anything else you left out?"

"Yes, there are many other things, but they are mostly sentences or phrases so I didn't write them down. For example, my mother always says, "I gave you your life and I will take it back," and "I delivered you, so I can kill you." I answered somewhat carefully. It was hard to read her or to see where she was going with all of this information. Her girly appearance really didn't match her strong, masculine personality.

"Do you know that not ONE of the words I wrote down was said to me by any of my family members?!" She put her hands on her waist like she was very angry.

"No, I didn't know that, but now I do. What are you trying to say? I am confused."

"What I am trying to say is that it's insane and crazy to be treated like this by the people who are supposed to say the opposite of these words to you! You know what? I am pissed off now, and I am going to tell my dad about this! No one is going to treat my friend that way, especially when she is at home!" Anastasia said staring right at me. She was the bravest and most outspoken out of the three of us, and actually, I would say out of the whole school; probably out of any of the girls I had ever met.

"Here is what we are going to do," said Victoria, jumping into our discussion right where Anastasia left off. "I am going to talk to my parents tonight and you are going to come and live with us! You can give me your address, and my dad will come pick you up. He is very powerful and no one will mess with him, I guarantee you that! Besides, we always stay at each other's houses sometimes for as much as a few weeks and no one minds," she added.

"That is a great idea V," said Anastasia, "and if Victoria's dad has a problem with it, I am sure my dad will let you stay with us."

I looked at them a little confusedly, but deep inside it felt so good to see them both stick up for me and try to help me the best way they could. I knew that it was a common thing for normal kids to invite their close friends or cousins to live with them for a week, a month, or even for the whole summer, but I wasn't a normal kid. I didn't have any friends visit or even stay over at my house at all, not even for a day.

Right before I was able to answer, the regular cleaning crew showed up. We ran away and out of the school quickly so no one could see us. That would be the last thing we needed. Of course it was too late and they turned us in to the principal the next day, along with a written list of words that they found scrolled in the girls' bathrooms all over the school.

I only wish we knew about that at the beginning of the day because we wouldn't have followed through with another "bad girls" plan we had hatched. We were definitely pushing our last bit of luck.

Half an hour before the first period, Anastasia decided to have fun and have one of us sound the recess bell about ten minutes early before lunch. To fairly select which one of us was going to do it, we found three thick sticks all very similar in length. Whoever picked the longest one was to be the one to pull the bell. I held the sticks in my hand with only an inch of each stick visible. Since the luck was never on my side, both Anastasia and Victoria picked the shortest ones and I ended up being the girl to do it.

I left the classroom about fifteen minutes before the end of class and sneaked into a small room next to the secretary's office. My heart was beating superfast but I was kind of excited to do it. There wasn't anyone in that office, so I ran right in, pushed the big red button and ran out. I was too happy to think of the consequences of my action at that particular moment. The bell rang super loud and echoed throughout the whole school. All of a sudden, hundreds of students poured out of their classrooms and into the hallway. I wasn't in the same class as my friends, so I had to get back quickly to grab my stuff before someone noticed that I wasn't back yet.

I guess we really underestimated how smart the faculty members were. After they held a quick meeting during lunch, they figured out that apparently I was the only student who left the classroom right before the bell sounded.

From that time on, I was proclaimed to be another one of the troubled kids in the school and almost everyone, including every teacher was told to watch out for me. The principal, who was a conservative older man, was beyond angry and called my parents to have them come to the school the next day. Needless to say, I was in deep trouble for ringing that bell, for the bad words I wrote in the bathrooms and for all the skipped classes and whole days of school that I had taken off.

I really didn't even want to think about what punishment Uncle Armen was going to come up with this time. It seemed to me that every time I got in some kind of trouble, he was happy and excited to create or think up some new sadistic method of torture that he called a "discipline."

I still was getting my Monday, Wednesday, and Friday beatings, so I knew that my punishment wouldn't be connected with the belt. I was pretty sure that he and my parents were going to take away my food and liquids, including water, but I was not sure about the rest. I don't know if the people from the school called my parents early Friday morning or exactly when they contacted them, but my parents went to talk to the principal while I was in one of my classes. I didn't know what was discussed. I guess my presence wasn't required and that was not a good sign.

When I got home that day, my dad wasn't talking to me, which was quite alarming. He looked really disappointed and I think I knew the reason. All the other times I got into trouble, it wasn't directly related to my behavior, but this time it was.

Neither my mother nor my father talked to me for the whole afternoon and evening, which was the first time I could remember both of them together giving me the cold shoulder. I was actually more worried about my dad not talking to me then my mom because he was the only reasonable and somewhat understanding adult in the house.

I didn't eat anything that night because I was too afraid to come out of the living room. I finished a bag of gummy bears that Anastasia had given me that morning and I stayed in the same room until I had to go to the bathroom later that night.

The next day, Armen came to our house in the early morning just after my dad left for his 24-hour shift. I was playing in the living room with my brother when Armen called out my name.

"Veeeraaa! Come heeeree!" he screamed from the kitchen.

My brother looked at me with scared eyes and I just shook my head from side to side. I didn't really want to deal with Armen at that moment, but I knew that I had no choice. I stood up and told my brother to go to our parents' bedroom and watch TV. I didn't want him to hear me scream and cry, in case I was going to be disciplined by Armen in the living room. He only used the balcony for those useless three-per-week prophylactic sessions, but not for the rest of the punishments. That was done in the living room and in other places around the house.

I walked into the kitchen and saw Armen drinking his usual green tea while my mother was drinking her coffee and eating assorted chocolate candy from a small plate. She didn't look up, which didn't surprise me, but what did surprise me was that Armen seemed to be in a good mood. He actually had a smile on his face when I walked in, which didn't appear to be sarcastic.

"You must be wondering why I am so happy, aren't you?" he asked me.

"No. Not really." I answered unemotionally. "I wasn't wondering that at all. I didn't even realize that you were."

"Well, in case you WERE curious, I am just so very amused at how stupid you still are, even at your new school. I am also amused at how much you don't learn or understand what it means to be a normal human," he added without a smile.

"As you already may have suspected, you will have to be punished, and as you also probably know, you are still going to stay on the three-times-per week schedule. What you don't know is that in addition to those punishments, you are not allowed to eat or drink until Monday morning which is almost 48 hours away. You can't play the piano either or even do your homework from the music school. Oh, and you can't play with your brother either, or watch any TV, go outside, or read. And you are definitely NOT going to get any new clothes or boots for the winter, so I would suggest you practice wrapping your feet in plastic bags so they don't get wet from those holes in your shoes."

"Is that it?" I asked with a hint of sarcasm that I felt like I couldn't control. For a split second, it felt like it was Anastasia who was saying these words to Armen, and not me.

"Is that it? You are asking me if that is it?" asked Armen as his eyebrows shifted into the familiar angry triangular letter "A" shape. "No, that wasn't it at all! I have another new punishment that should make your brain think better," he added.

I stood there tired but curious, just wondering what sick, new, torture this strange man had come up with this time. For a moment, I even found my question to him kind of funny. It was as if there was no punishment that was going to break me.

"What you going to do is face the cement wall right next to you and start to hit your forehead on it, non-stop, until I see the first trickle of blood. I read somewhere that this is supposed to promote brain activities," he said with a smirk.

"You want me to do what?"

"I know it's too difficult for you to understand because you are stupid, but I need you to simply hit your forehead onto the wall, as hard as you need to, until blood first shows itself, most likely from your nose," he explained further.

I clearly understood his instructions the first time, but I didn't think that this man was so sick that he actually wanted to give me a head injury and make me bleed from my nose. That was taking his games to a whole new level of sadistic discipline. Since talking to him was a waste of time, I just turned to the right and stood very close to the wall. A second later, I started to carefully tap the wall with my forehead. It was a strange scene, almost like something I would see in a movie about crazy people who lived in an asylum.

I did that for few minutes, doing it harder and harder, but my nose was fine, and no blood was coming out. I actually wasn't one to get a bloody nose so easily, so I wasn't sure if this was going to take me a few more minutes or another half an hour. At this point it wasn't really that painful and I just felt a lot of pressure and the start of a headache.

After about ten minutes like that, I got lightheaded and uncomfortable. It seemed like my nose wasn't going to bleed any time soon, though it was more likely I would lose consciousness from this activity. My head was sore and my headache was getting worse.

My mother sat at the kitchen table, not more than three feet away from me, just drinking her coffee. After a while, Armen started to make strange and annoying noises as if he were bored or tired from sitting there and watching me. Without saying anything, he abruptly got up out of his chair and took a large step in my direction. He grabbed my pony tail and smashed my forehead right onto the wall with great force.

I felt my whole brain shake inside my skull and then a sharp feeling of pressure went throughout the rest of my body. It was completely black in front of my eyes. I couldn't see anything except some gold lines on a black background, almost like out of control electric waves.

I couldn't keep my balance and took a couple of steps backwards. The hallway was only four feet wide, so I ended up hitting the wall behind me with the back of my head; at least I didn't fall down.

I felt blood gush out of my nose, but I was still confused about my physical state and what had just happened. My eyesight came back, but just a little, and my vision was still blurry. I was able to see lots of bloody spots all over the bottom part of the wall and the floor. I grabbed my nose and squeezed it hard.

"NOW your brain woke the hell up!" Armen said. "You see what I was talking about? That is how you properly hit your head on the wall and it is the fastest and easiest way to get the blood to come out, too!" he said as he walked back to his seat.

Without responding, I took a few very slow steps to make it to the bathroom which was only few feet away and on the same side of the hallway. When he saw me walking away he screamed out, "Wait a minute! We have to test if it worked! What is one plus one? Tell me."

I stopped and barely turned toward him. My left hand held my nose and my right hand held the wall so I wouldn't fall. I was groggy, confused and in a fog. I didn't know what he wanted me to say.

"Threeee," I said, not loud, but enough for him to hear me.

"One plus one is three?" HAHAHAHAHAHA! Can you believe that? The answer is three! HAHAHAHAHA!" He laughed overly loudly to intimidate me and make me feel stupid. "Wow, I guess we have to repeat this session a few more times until you get smarter! Your brain really is not much smarter than that of a pig! Now go clean up and then take care of this mess you made, ugly slob!"

I barely made it into the bathroom, closed the door behind me, and turned on the cold water. My head was pounding uncontrollably and I felt like I was going to throw up. I was lightheaded, dizzy, and still wasn't able to see clearly. My bright red blood was all over the sink and my beige t-shirt. I slowly cleaned the sink with a small, wet towel, then soaked it in cold water and placed it on my forehead. While I was in the bathroom, I could still hear Armen laughing and making fun of me and my answer.

I eventually came out and made my way back to the kitchen to clean up the blood from the wall and the floor. Neither Armen nor my mother said anything to me and talked about something else at that point.

After I was done, I slowly made my way to the living room. My brother was still in my parents' bedroom, probably napping.

It was a good thing I drank some water from the faucet while I was in the bathroom, because Armen also grounded me from drinking and I didn't know when I would be able to get my hands on it again. I planned to keep sneaking out to the bathroom to wash my hands and sneak a drink from the faucet so no one would get suspicious and accuse me of disobeying my punishment.

I sat down on the chair and put my head back to let the cold towel calm my headache. I realized that I had not yet cried since Armen started with me in the kitchen. That thought made me feel kind of sad for myself. Any normal human being would either cry from the pain or from the abuse, but I didn't. It was like I had already gotten used to it. It was just another punishment. I didn't even try to stand up for myself and I was acting like a punching bag. I let him harm me in whatever sadistic way he wanted. I could have told him that I wouldn't do it. I could have run out of the house, but I didn't. I didn't even try to fight it, and instead, quietly did what I was told. I had no courage or any will to protect myself.

A few minutes later, without even trying, tears started to slowly come out of my eyes and slid down both sides of my face. "I am completely useless and only good for the abuse and sadistic fun of that man. I am like an animal, with cruel owners who hurt me just because they feel like it. I can't help myself, and therefore can't help anyone else," I whispered to myself. A few minutes later, without realizing it, I closed my eyes and drifted into a deep sleep.

I don't know how long I was out, but it must have been at least a few hours. I was awakened by my brother's hands carefully moving my face back and forth. I opened my eyes. I still had a heavy headache, and realized that it was quite late.

"It's already seven o'clock Vera," he said happily now that I was awake. "Go eat so we can play! Uncle already left!"

A minute or so later, I was completely awake but stayed in the same position trying to figure out what was real and what was just a dream. Usually, I wasn't able to take a nap during the day and even when I did, I never remembered any of my dreams. Dreams only happened at night.

Then a memory suddenly came back to me. I remembered a very clear and vivid image of my now dead best friend Maria. She looked the same age as when I first met her in that hospital. But now, her dress was white, and her hair was light and wavy all the way to her waist. This time it looked like it was her real hair, and not a wig. She wasn't wearing any shoes and her feet weren't touching the floor either. She appeared to be floating in the air, but not more than an inch off the ground. She was smiling and happy just like I remembered she was. I couldn't see anything around us or behind her other than a bright light which made me able to see right through her. She moved very close to me and put her hands on my shoulders. I don't remember feeling her hands on my body, but I felt their warmth all over my skin and my face. She even spoke to me.

"I know you came to the hospital to see me. I know you kept your promise. And I really tried my hardest to stay there and wait for you. I also really wanted to go home to my mommy for holidays, but I couldn't. They were waiting for me over here and I had to go, but I am still happy. Now I have powers to protect and watch over my family and all of my friends, even the doctors who cried a lot when I left. But out of everyone, I am watching over you the most. I know you want to play with me, and trust me, I really miss you and wish we could, but I can't bring you here, not yet. You have to wait and you have to stay where you are and help others. They all need you. Many people need you. You are very strong, much more than you think! I will wait for you as long as needed, but you have to show everyone that you are a fighter and that no one can bring you down! You have to go on, even when it feels like every single person is against you! You have to prove to the world and to yourself that you are stronger than all the others. Show them that they can beat up your body, but not your soul. When you are ready, I will be here waiting for you."

Everything she said to me was clear in my mind and I felt a strange boost of some unusual physical energy. I got out of my depressed state of mind and looked around. My baby brother was sitting on the sofa, staring at me with his usual big smile.

"OK sweetie, we will play something. Just give me a few minutes to get my thoughts together," I said to him. He was so patient that I felt bad making him wait any longer and I decided to spend time with him right away, although my stomach was growling and I was very thirsty.

We played for over an hour building a house made of playing cards. My brother loved that game and could play it for hours. We would use a few cards to build a triangle on top of the rest of the card deck and then we would take turns pulling cards out from underneath the house, one after another, until the house fell. Whoever caused it to fall was the one who lost the game.

While we sat there, many thoughts started to fill my head, mainly about Maria's words and what would happen if I suddenly wasn't alive anymore. Watching my brother, I thought about how much more self-sufficient he was now, and my mother loved him way too much not to take care of him. She would never let Uncle Armen touch him again, that's for sure, especially not after he ripped the baby's ear off his neck. My grandpa and grandma were both amazing people, but I also knew that they were all set and had other relatives to watch over them if there was a need. My friends in school were awesome, but I knew that the school I was in was only temporary, and I would most likely lose the connection I made with them when I was sent back to my original school. I didn't believe I was as smart as I thought, between getting barely passing grades and not even being able to answer a kindergarten question like, "What's one plus one?"

In addition to all that, my mother completely hated me, and if I were never to see her again, I doubt she would care one bit. I knew my father loved me, but between working nonstop and hardly seeing me, I thought he probably wouldn't care much either.

When it came to my music, because of my wounds and not having any time to heal between the prophylactic sessions, I couldn't even normally sit at a piano to practice. I remember that during the piano lessons, my teacher would put her hand on my upper back to help me feel the music and show my emotions. She didn't know that my back was very sore and I was in pain. When she touched those spots, the pain was terrible and agonizing so even my piano performance suffered like never before.

The only person that I knew who loved me and really needed me was Maria, so I believed I should be there for her, not here unhappy and in pain. It just made no sense and although I respected and loved her, I decided not to listen to what she told me in my dream. I was older so I knew better, and I decided it was up to me to make better choices for myself.

I didn't think she really understood how my life had turned out since I left the hospital. I wish I could tell her that it got worse and that I was being subjected to Monday, Wednesday, and Friday beatings that made wounds that never healed. I just could not see any reason important enough for me to stay here and endure this never-ending pain.

It wasn't easy for me to come up with a way of ending my own life. I really wanted something painless, because I had been through way too much of it and just couldn't inflict it upon myself; plus, it seemed like I wasn't as brave as I used to be.

On many occasions I overheard my dad telling my mom about different cases he had seen in the ER with people who had tried to commit suicide. Most of the things I heard him say were too scary for me to do and they seemed to be extremely painful. There were a couple of things that I remembered hearing about that sounded easy for me to accomplish.

I spent the next couple of weeks going to the big library, a street away from our building, to research two different methods that I had chosen. One method was to poison myself with a mix of chemicals from around the house which sounded like it could take longer than anticipated and could possibly not even be fatal, leaving me blind or paralyzed.

The second method was to overdose on pain or sleeping pills which we had plenty of at the house. Being in the family of a doctor, we had lots of different medications available. My dad kept them on hand in case he had to go to an emergency call nearby before an ambulance was able to get there. Most of it was stored in his hard covered, rectangular medical suitcase with all his other first aid supplies. But he also stored some medicine in a plastic bag in the fridge, and in his bedroom; I think my mother used them when she couldn't sleep.

The easiest medications for me to get my hands on without being caught were the ones they had in their bedroom. To be completely sure no one would see me take it, I had to do it right after the prophylactic beating from Armen. He would always leave me alone on the balcony to recover after he was done.

Two days later on Monday when I prepared myself for my scheduled beating, I felt somewhat free. I was set and determined to make this beating my last one, and as Maria said, it was only my body that was getting abused, not my soul; that was still untouched.

I really had to make this session the last one because I noticed that my body was really starting to change and mature. My breast size was already a size "A" and it was very uncomfortable to be almost naked in front of Armen. He was a grown man and I was just a little girl. It just didn't feel right. I shouldn't have to be forced to get undressed, to lie there, and then to pray that he wouldn't make me take off my underwear. Even my father shouldn't see me naked, unless it's some sort of an emergency. Armen never touched my naked body with his bare hands, but it still felt shameful to be beaten while almost naked. It's not like I could turn around, otherwise he would see my breasts. So I had to take the beatings on the same spots over and over again. My skin became discolored and sore since wounds didn't even have time to heal.

Lying there on the sofa for that one last time, all I could think of was how to find and take those pills without being caught. Just as

I expected, after he was done with me, he left the balcony and the room.

After I heard him go into the kitchen, I got up, put on my clothes, and stepped into the bedroom. I looked in the dresser, under the bed, inside the nightstands and even inside the flower vases, but I couldn't find anything. Still determined, I decided to look in their tall armoire which was locked most of the time. I was lucky and I found the keys which were hanging right inside of the left door. I opened one side and found the bag with the medicine right away, hidden under the hanging coats. I didn't see any pain pills but found the sleeping pills easily. There were two packages with at least two sheets of ten in each. I knew those were the sleeping pills because my dad used to always write on top of the medication boxes what they were to be used for. I only grabbed one package and quietly closed that door making sure that the key was in the exact same position as I found it.

My heart was beating very fast and I was praying I would not get caught. My brother was in the living room, and even though the new beating schedule had been in progress for a while now, he still didn't know about it. I was able to keep all the pain to myself every time I was subjected to it, and just whimpered, moaned, or cried into the pillow.

When I went into the living room, my brother was coloring at the table and was, as usual, happy to see me. He always showed love and affection every chance he got. I never turned him down, because I knew how that would make him feel. The times that he hugged me after I got the beatings were incredibly painful and hurt so bad sometimes that I wanted to scream and push him away.

Sure enough, this time he ran right up to me and hugged me. His little hands felt like someone was pressing on my fresh wounds with their boots. The pain was so terrible and sharp that I could barely keep myself from screaming out loud and I felt like a wounded animal in agony. Strangely, that pain was somehow balanced out by his little body pressing against me. I felt his care and unconditional love pour from his heart right into mine.

I knew I had to prepare him and also say my goodbyes, but I honestly didn't know how. I just wanted him to remember me and the things I always said to him just in case anyone ever asked, "What were the last words your sister said to you?"

I sat him down right next to me, and while facing him, I addressed him by his cute nickname that I used to call him most of the time.

"Tiko, do you know what people call 'freedom'?"

"Yes! It's like when you can do what you want."

"Yes it's kind of like that, but there is more to it."

"I know it's also kind of like birds that fly outside."

"Yes. That is very good. That is the perfect way to see it."

"And it's also like when we can play when we want!"

"Yes, and we can laugh, sing and even run around the house."

"And go outside and come home when we want, even late."

"Yes sweetie, all that is what freedom is! You are smart."

"Oh, oh and also when Uncle Armen doesn't come here."

"Yes that is definitely a huge part of our freedom, especially for me! If you can't have a carefree feeling inside your heart and if you are scared to come home every day, it's just not worth it. It's a terrible way to live! I can't do ANYTHING that I want without getting in trouble for it. And you know that Uncle Armen beats me all the time because you probably heard me scream and cry. Do you agree with me?"

"Yes, Vera I think I agree with you, but I'm not sure."

"OK, Tiko.If we switched places with each other, would you stay here or would you go away to be free"?

"I... I... would leave I think, and go to be free, so I could play with kids and not see Uncle Armen."

"OK! I hope you fully understand me and will one day remember this conversation without being mad at me. I want you to understand why I did what I had to do, and I don't want you to judge me for giving up and choosing freedom over everything else."

He smiled and shook his head like he was giving me an OK. I wanted to hug him but I didn't want his hands touching my wounds again. I didn't want to cry in front of him either so he wouldn't get confused about what was going on. I just held my pain in, tried to smile, and made it look like everything was OK.

That evening, I told him to sleep in my parents' room with my mom. I already had it all planned out, and having him wake up next to his dead sister in the morning was not part of my plan. Other than him falling asleep on their bed, all that was left was for my mother to go to sleep, too. I was just hoping she wasn't going to stay up very late.

It was a quarter past eleven when my mother finally left the kitchen and went into her bedroom. I needed to get a large glass of water to help me swallow all twenty of the pills I had found.

I waited for another fifteen to twenty minutes just to make sure she was asleep, and then I quietly and carefully made my way into the kitchen. I grabbed the biggest glass I could find and filled it up almost to the top. I just wanted to make sure I had enough.

I returned to the living room, put the glass on the table and took all the pills from the package. I really disliked taking any medication, and I wasn't sure how I would swallow all twenty of them at once without throwing up.

I put them all in a little pile and decided to stop thinking about it and just do it. I grabbed all the pills at one time and jammed them into my mouth. I immediately tasted the disgusting chemical flavor of the medicine and I gulped down the glass of water to flush them faster into my stomach. It was making me feel sick, trying to swallow pills and water against my body's needs. As soon as I felt the last pill hit my stomach, I lay down and closed my eyes to prepare my body and mind for my long awaited departure.

A few minutes later, I felt very warm and sleepy and with a smile on my face and a free spirit in my heart, I drifted away.

CHAPTER 8
Karma Does Exist

"Veraaaa, Veraaaa, get up! Geeeet uuuup! Mom is already up!" I heard my brother's voice somewhere in the distance like it was in a fog. I felt his hands pushing my face from one side to the other and he tried to physically pry open my eyes with his small fingers.

I tried to understand what was going on but I couldn't think clearly or even open my eyes. I tried moving my arms and legs and found I had no control over my body whatsoever. I didn't have enough air and felt like I was choking, yet I couldn't take a deep enough breath. I was scared and paranoid.

The last thing I remembered was taking a bunch of pills and falling asleep. I also remembered that I took them to end my life and to reunite with Maria in heaven. The physical and emotional state I was in at that moment did not look or feel like I was with her in heaven at all. I could still sense the smell of the room which smelled like the bouquet of flowers that my dad brought to my mother a couple of days back.

I was confused about why I couldn't move and why my brother was screaming at me to get up. After a minute or so, he ran out of the room and started to call my mother.

A moment later, I saw her silhouette in front of me, moving closer and closer. As she approached the sofa I was laying on, she started to act out of her character.

I'm not sure if she saw the empty pill box or if she just got scared, but she started to panic and ordered my brother to call our dad at work to see if he was still there or already on his way home. The next thing I recall was that she started to call me all kinds of names, right in my face, as she tried pull my eye lids up.

"You are such a stupid fool! Why? Why! Why would you do this!? Throw up right now!" she demanded as she pulled me up into a sitting position.

I felt a plate or a bowl touching my chest but had no strength to stay up or to fully open my eyes. I still didn't understand what was going on. The only sense that seemed to be working well was my hearing.

She grabbed my right hand and pushed two of my fingers together. Then she stuck them into my throat.

"If you don't throw up right now, you may die! DO YOU understand me or not?"

I really wanted to cooperate, but I just couldn't control any part of my body including my speech. I tried telling her that I was OK, but all I heard coming out of my mouth were incoherent mumbling sounds.

A few moments later, she grabbed me under my arms and carried me into the bathroom. My legs were lifelessly dragging behind my body, and I could see my brother's silhouette following us. As soon as we made it to the bathroom, she put my head right over the toilet and again stuck my fingers into my throat. This time a big amount of a liquid came out and splashed into the toilet bowl. The mess went everywhere and lots of it ended up on the seat and the floor. I wasn't even sure what I was throwing up since I hadn't eaten anything since lunch in the cafeteria at school the day before. Still, I was throwing up something: maybe just very small amounts of stomach acid. I had no idea.

"You are crazy! You are psychotic! You are selfish! You only ever think of yourself! Why would you do this to me? Did you think about your brother or who would raise him when I am working? No!" My mother kept screaming at me while my body convulsed over the toilet bowl.

After a few minutes of emptying my stomach, and my mother splashing my face with cold water, some of my upper body strength started to come back. I could see a bit clearer, too. I pushed away from the toilet bowl to try to take a deep breath. She was still standing above me and screaming in anger. As crazy as it may sound, this was the most attention I had received from her in years. A minute later I heard the front door open. It was my dad.

"What happened here? What is wrong with her? Why is she throwing up?" My dad asked.

"I don't know what happened exactly, but I think I saw an empty box of sleeping pills on the table. Most likely she took all twenty of them! Tigran called me because she wouldn't wake up and she is always up before all of us.

Without asking anything else, my dad moved her out of the way, picked me up, and brought me back into the living room. He laid me down and started to clean my face with a wet towel. He told my brother to bring him his medical suitcase from the hallway and I heard his little feet running out to get it. When my dad received his case, he immediately took all the different things out of it. He measured my blood pressure and my pulse, then filled a syringe and injected me with some kind of white liquid.

"I don't know why you took these pills, but when you feel better we need to talk! You can't do this and think it's OK! I don't know what is going on with you, but I don't think that killing yourself is the right choice. You are almost eleven years old!"

He told my brother to stay with me and if I moved or talked to come and get him. Then he and my mother left the living room and went into the kitchen. I couldn't make out what they were talking about, but I did know that they were disagreeing or arguing about something and that their voices were louder than usual. I started to feel very sleepy again and my eyes closed without my control.

I woke up many hours later. It was almost midnight. There was no one in the living room, and although I was very thirsty, I had no strength to get up and do anything about it. I closed my eyes and went back to sleep.

The conversation that my dad insisted we were going to have about what I did, never happened. He must have either forgotten that he said we were going to talk or got too busy to make time for it. I understood that and was not surprised. It wasn't the first time he said we will talk and then never did. It was OK with me, though. After all, I figured he was just very busy saving other peoples' lives.

I went back to school a few days later and I didn't tell anyone, not even my friends, about what had happened. I just said I was sick. It wasn't a lie either; I was definitely not well.

* * *

Eating lunch in school was never enough to satisfy my hunger because I didn't have breakfast every day, and most of the time I didn't have dinner the night before, either. My stomach would growl and the pain would interfere with my concentration. Besides that, Armen had started to add extra "hungry days" to my punishments. I had to think of something and think fast. Eating out of the garbage and off of the trees was not an option as it had already landed me in the hospital and near death, so I came up with another alternative, not any less disgusting or shameful, by any means.

I started to pick up used bubble gum off of the ground, first the gum my friends spit out, and then from everyone else. I looked for it everywhere — on the river walkway to and from school -- on the stairs of the building entrance and anywhere on the ground in general. The first time I did that, I felt disgusted, but hunger overpowered my feelings of repulsion. I forced myself to chew and often just swallow it.

As the days passed, I realized that chewing the gum was helping me not feel so hungry as much and made my belly hurt much less. And if I was really hungry, I could just eat the gum instead. The bigger the gum ball the less pain I was in. Most of the gum I found had no flavor left. Some of them were clean but most were very dirty, and had sand, hair, or even bits of food stuck in them. I would just clean the stuff up and then combine them together. I wasn't proud of it and it was a big secret, but I did what I had to do.

For the next few weeks at school, I stayed low key and tried to stay out of trouble. I didn't want any negative attention from the faculty or the principal. I was already marked as a "bad girl," so I expected they were all keeping a closer eye on me. I still skipped some periods here and there, but not as many as I had in the past.

My grades got a little higher and I even got an "A" in one of my classes. In fact, I had found a new favorite subject, something I enjoyed even more than piano lessons; it was biology.

I always loved Mother Nature, but learning how it actually works on a cellular level gave me a whole new perspective on all the living organisms and plants around me.

I will never forget the day I saw plant cells under a microscope for the first time. That day, my regular teacher was actually sick and we had a substitute. In my city there was no such thing as a substitute teaching position. When a faculty member was sick for a day or even two, another teacher from the same school would do the lesson by combining the students into one classroom. On very rare occasions, even the principal would handle the lessons. As we all sat there waiting to see which teacher and class we were getting mixed into, we received an unexpected surprise. The faculty member who walked in was our school principal. I almost slipped off my chair and hid under the table. It was a good thing I was sitting all the way in the back of the room out of his view. He didn't notice me until the middle of the class when the laboratory part was about to start.

We were separated into small groups of three, and had to view a small piece of leaf through the microscope. Then we had to write a quick report on our observations. I was the last one from our group to get to do it and there were only about ten minutes left in the class.

The principal walked around from table to table and checked on what everyone was doing. I bent down and pressed my left eye firmly into the microscope. At first, I couldn't see what I was supposed to look for, but after I adjusted the focus, I froze in place. What I saw took my breath away. It was the most amazing phenomenon; even more than the watermelon river during the previous summer. There were thousands upon thousands of little green circles moving around, almost like a busy metro station filled with millions of people. The little green circles were called the chloroplasts, and I knew all about them from reading the textbooks. (I already had an "A" in this class.) I had never seen the chloroplasts in action or in real life, and there they were right in front of my eyes. Not having cell phones or internet back then made it hard, so the only other place I could see this happen was in the biology textbooks and that just wasn't the same.

Watching actual life taking place right in front of me took my mind into another world and away from the everyday struggles I had to survive. I started to say "WOW" out loud, over and over, without moving my eye away from the microscope.

"Are you OK? You have been saying "WOW" for a couple of minutes now," the principal asked from somewhere behind me.

"WOW," I said again. "I have never ever seeing ANYTHING like this. This is so amazing and overwhelming that I just cannot move away from it or stop saying "WOW"! I answered without moving my head or eyes away.

"Well, yes, this is surely an amazing phenomenon, and I am glad you see it as that! Class, has anyone else had any other thoughts, after seeing the actual movement of the chloroplasts?"

"It was cool." It was OK." "Yeah, it's nice to see." "It's just a cell, what is the big deal?" "I didn't see anything interesting about it." the disinterested students answered one after another.

"OK, kids, the report is due tomorrow, so I hope you got a good look at what you needed. You can go now. The bell will ring any minute," he said, disappointed that he didn't get a more enthusiastic reaction. I wasn't sure why his tone changed from optimistic and loud to low and disappointed, but I wasn't concentrating on that.

The live action that I had just witnessed would be forever imbedded in my mind and because of that, I have developed a deeper love and appreciation for Mother Nature and all her beauty. From that day on, I became involved in the Green Peace organization we had in the city and I took an active role to help plant the trees in our central park which was named "Riviera." I was assigned a nickname — "Tree Hugger" — and I could pinpoint this lab in biology class as the exact moment I saw life in each of those leaves. When the bell rang, the principal told me that I had to go, so I moved away reluctantly from the microscope and looked up at him with disappointment.

"Are you OK?" he asked me with a wide smile across his face that I had never seen him have before.

I just shook my head up and down and put my books into my plastic bag I was still staring at him as if he had three eyes instead of two. He slowly took a step towards me, as other students started to come in, and said, "You know something? I haven't had any interaction with you other than when you have misbehaved. I have only seen the 'troublemaker' part of you, but I have to say I was wrong about you. You are not how I thought you would be. I don't know why you were trying to have a bit of dangerous fun, but inside, I can see you are very smart and a different person. Remember that, and keep what I just said between us."

I was surprised that he would say anything like that to me because it was a known thing that school principals never gave compliments to students, even to those who deserved to be recognized. Amazed or not, I didn't reply, and left the classroom in a rush.

I spent the rest of the day in some sort of a daydream state and could not shake what I had seen out of my head. I tried telling both of my friends about it at lunch break, but they thought I was going crazy and just laughed at me. Anastasia told me that I needed to come down to planet earth, implying I was not from here and was possibly an alien.

After classes, I went straight to the music school because it was Thursday and I didn't have to go home to get my "prophylactic" punishment. That day I played piano with much better speed and with proper technique.

"Did you have too much sugar or something today? Because you are playing the same part you played yesterday at twice the tempo," my music teacher asked surprised and satisfied at my performance.

"No, I didn't have any sugar today, but I saw this insane thing through the microscope in biology class and now it won't leave my head. When I play faster, I feel like the little green circles I saw inside the plant cells under the microscope move faster. I try playing at a higher speed, so they move along faster in order to keep up. It's kind of fun and sounds like a game, but it's all in my head!" I paused without taking my hands off of the keys.

"Wow. That is a very interesting point of view you have there! I didn't realize you were that creative, but I guess I should have known better!" she answered me with a kind and warm smile. I couldn't wait to tell my grandpa about it when he picked me up on Sunday to go to the cemetery. He always understood.

That night I wrote my report on what I saw and I drew pictures of the plant cells and everything inside them. I described it the best I could and wrote a few paragraphs on my personal feelings about it all. The next day I proudly turned it in and found out on the following Monday, that my report earned an "A+". It was the best report in the whole school.

When there were only a few days left before winter break and the end of the second quarter, I was told that my grades were good enough to go back to my original school. I knew I would miss both of my new friends as well as the principal who thought well of me, but it just didn't feel right being in that school. I wanted to go back to where most of my old friends and the kids from my building were. My parents needed to do some sort of paperwork for me to move back in time for the third quarter.

Near the end of the second quarter, before I left for my old school, my friends and I were sitting together in the cafeteria when I noticed that some boys were watching, talking and smiling at us. I was not sure if this was something unusual because I had never noticed it before, but that day I must have paid closer attention. Both of my friends were very pretty, so I expected the boys to stare at them.

"Why are they staring at us like we have two heads?" I asked my friends. I had my head turned so the boys couldn't read my lips.

"They are staring at us because we are very BEAUTIFUL," said Anastasia with a big smile as she fluffed her thick, beautiful hair back so it looked fuller and longer. Victoria shook her head and took a bite of her ham sandwich. Then she looked at me and said, "Those boys always stare at us, but I think they are giggling now because your nipples are showing through your shirt today."

My eyes widened in surprise and I covered my chest immediately by crossing both of my arms like I was trying to hug myself. "I didn't even realize it! Oh my God, why didn't you tell me that before?" I demanded to know.

"I never paid any attention or noticed until just now when you said those boys were acting like that. They are just immature, that's all, so don't pay them any attention. You do need to ask your mother to buy you a bra, because you are kind of showing boobs already." She delivered the news gently, the way an older sister would say something to her sibling.

I spent the rest of the afternoon walking around with my chest covered. I even walked home in that same exact manner just so no one could notice anything inappropriate. When I got home, the first thing I did was walk straight up to my mother.

"Mom, I really need you to get me a bra as soon as possible like this evening, because my boobs are showing and boys in school can see my nipples!" I nervously addressed her.

She looked at the front of my t-shirt for a split second and said, "You still have a long way to go before I buy you one of those."

"But mother, others can see them and I feel shy and uncomfortable about it. Please, I will massage your feet for an hour if you just get me the cheapest bra there is! Please!" I begged her, hoping she would change her mind.

"I said no. I don't have money for useless things like that right now. Go do something useful and leave me alone."

From that day on, I came up with my own solution to the problem. I started to fold two pairs of my underwear together and put them up under my shirt. It looked and felt quite strange, but it was better than nothing.

The next day was the last day of the school for that quarter and I was happy to get my report card, with only a few "C's" on it.

It was a big difference from just a few months ago when I was kicked out of school for failing three different subjects. It was the last day at my music school as well, and I had to perform a few classical pieces for my end of the quarter practical. I had to rush home, warm up my fingers, and prepare for my performance later that day. Unfortunately, that didn't mean much to Uncle Armen. It was just another Friday for him and he was there at the apartment, waiting.

"Let me see your report card!" He shouted the second I walked through the door.

"OK, here it is Uncle. It is not too bad." I answered as I took off my old, secondhand rain boots before walking into the kitchen. It took me a bit longer to take them off than usual because I had to wear them with plastic bags over my feet. The bags kept the rain from getting inside through the holes I had worn through the soles.

I came up to the kitchen table where he was sitting and gave him the report card. My mother must have been in the bathroom because I could see a bunch of candy wrappers on the table by her half-full coffee cup.

"Well, you are lucky you have the prophylactic session today, otherwise I would have had to use the whip or other things on you. These grades are terrible. Go to the balcony and get ready. I will be right there."

"Can we not do it today, Uncle? Please! I have my final music performance in two hours and still have to warm up and catch two buses," I begged him.

"NO! I AM NOT CHANGING OUR SCHEDULE FOR ANYTHING! GO! I WILL BE RIGHT THERE!" he screamed back at me.

It was no use. I walked away and headed toward my parents' bedroom, then out onto the balcony. My baby brother was sleeping in the living room as he took a mid-day nap almost every afternoon. I felt like I had not been giving him enough attention the past couple of months, and I worried that I wasn't only becoming a bad girl in school, but I was also not being a good sister or mother.

I walked onto the balcony. It was very chilly, but I started to take off my clothes anyway. When I took off my top, both of my folded underwear fell out and I realized that my breasts were much bigger than I thought. I covered them up with my hands and firmly locked them under my armpits.

I lay face down, turned my head towards the wall, and just waited for Armen to walk in. A minute later I heard the familiar slapping sound of his leather belt as he made his way toward me. It sounded like the belt was floating in the air all on its own, without Armen holding it or helping it make those threatening sounds. It was a weird feeling because the sounds were so rhythmic and consistent that they almost felt like my own heartbeat.

Out of nowhere, I suddenly saw those plant cells under the microscope and I started to visualize that I was one of them. I just wanted to use that beautiful image to live through this one beating. Strangely, my body felt like it was much more sensitive than it was just a couple of days ago. Maybe it was because I was emotionally tired or maybe because I was just sore. All I knew is that every single stoke of the whip I received that day felt sharper and burned much more than it had ever before. It was almost like he knew how sensitive I was at that moment so he hit me on those same spots more than once.

I remember writing into my little mini-diary about that session, and how I felt more physical pain than I had ever felt before. I wrote about the strange and new thoughts that came into my head while I lay there; thoughts I never had toward anyone in the past. For the first time in my life, I wished that Armen would die or be killed by someone. It was something I had wished for my own self before, but for some reason, my anger and hate moved from me and onto him.

I realized that I didn't deserve any of this, and he was just taking advantage of me because there was no one to protect me or stop him. He could pretty much do whatever he wanted to me and I was too scared to tell my grandpa or anyone else.

That terrible hope of death that I developed for him started to also grow toward my mother. I realized that she let all these things happen, and in many cases, was the one who asked Armen to beat me. I felt that she actually enjoyed me screaming and crying and liked listening to my moaning sounds, all a by-product of Armen's sadism.

* * *

About a week later, on New Year's Eve 1991, my life changed forever. I remember it was a Tuesday and I was in the kitchen peeling potatoes with a knife. I was probably the best in the world when it came to peeling potatoes because I was trained by Uncle Armen to remove as little skin as possible. He would sit in the kitchen and watch me peel the potatoes and if I took too much skin off, he would smack me on my face and on the back of my head. By the age of 9, I was able to peel the potatoes with my eyes fully closed, which I found to be a disturbing yet strangely entertaining thing to do.

It was about six o'clock in the evening and the rest of my family was in the living room watching the annual New Year's Eve concert on TV. I got up to take a quick bathroom break because I had been holding it in for over an hour and my belly started to hurt. I hadn't felt well for a few days as it was.

When I was finished going to the bathroom, I grabbed a small piece of toilet paper, cleaned myself up quickly and got up, putting my underwear back on. I suddenly felt something very weird on the inside of my legs. I looked down and saw bright red blood slowly trickling down my thighs. I got so scared that I started to cry uncontrollably. I had no idea where the blood was coming from or why it was happening. I had never heard any of my girlfriends say anything about bleeding between their legs, and I did not know what to do. I recalled hearing my mother talk to her friends about how I had to stay a virgin and that I must not have any physical encounter until I got married. I also knew that being a virgin meant that my "legs had to stay closed." The only reason I put those two things together was because I overheard my mother say, "She has to keep her legs closed so she can stay a virgin until we marry her off." All kinds of thoughts were racing through my mind. I didn't know what to do next.

Because my mother was the only other female in the house, I decided to call her over. I opened the bathroom door, just enough for her to be able to hear me. I felt desperate.

"Mom, Mom! Please come here right away! It's very, very important! Something is very wrong with me!"

I then closed the door and moved a couple of feet away from it so it wouldn't hit me when she walked in. Our bathroom must have been not more than six feet wide and eight feet long, so there was not much room to move around.

My mom didn't come right away, but someone else did.

"Open the door, Vera! What's wrong with you"? my brother shouted through the door, knocking on it with his little fists.

"Nothing is wrong, Tiko. I just don't feel well. No worries! Where is mom? Is she coming?"

"Yes she is, but she is watching some singer on TV right now, so she sent me to see what you need!" he added.

"Tiko, just go back to the living room and tell her that I will wait for her."

I wasn't feeling well, but didn't want to sit down on the edge of the bathtub and get it dirty. I was also afraid to take off my underwear without knowing where exactly this blood was coming from.

About ten minutes later, my mother came into the bathroom and looked me up and down. She saw the blood all over my legs. To my shock, she did not look surprised at all and just closed the door behind her so no one else could walk in. When I looked at her I felt scared and guilty, like I had done something terribly wrong. I had no idea what was going on or what reaction I was going to get from her.

"Well, I can congratulate you now, for you have become a woman," she said as she folded both her arms together in front of her.

"I am now a what? I'm a woman? What do you mean I am a woman? Wasn't I a woman before? I don't understand."

"Yes, you are a woman now. You are not a little girl anymore! You can now have children of your own. So from now on, you can't talk to any boys or be in their company, even if that was OK in the past. I expect you also may start to feel attraction towards them, or even like them; but it's all bad and not a normal thing to feel at your age. Only very bad girls feel that way about the boys and show it. Also don't tell anyone that you got blood today. It is a secret!"

"So you are saying that I am not a child anymore and now I can have my own kids? Like you had Tigran and me? And I am a grown woman now?" I kept asking the same questions to make sure I understood her correctly.

"Yes that is correct," she answered back, very short and to the point.

"But where is the blood coming from Mom and how long will it last? How do I stop it? I can't go anywhere looking like this and my belly and my back also hurt today!"

"I don't know how long it will last, maybe a week or ten days, and yes you may have pains and be much more sensitive. Some women have a little pain; some have a lot. You need to use cotton balls or your old underwear to prevent the blood from getting on your clothes. Clean and wash them regularly, and keep putting them between your legs while you have the blood. And do NOT let me ever find out that you spoke to or were near any boys, other than your brother or your father."

"What about Uncle Armen? He is a boy, no?" I asked hoping that he would be included into this new "male" category I had to avoid.

"He is an exception, because he is our best friend and your uncle. Now I am going back to finish watching the concert and then finish cooking a couple of dishes for the table."

"Wait Mom, you didn't answer my question on why the blood came now and where is it coming from?" I asked as she left, poking my head through the door. I was just trying to make sure I knew everything I had to know about my new predicament. She didn't stop or turn around to answer.

I felt a little better about the whole thing, and figured I would find the answers I needed in one of the medical books or the dictionary. I cleaned myself up and felt more at ease knowing that it was a normal thing that happens to all girls at one point or another. She also said I wasn't a child anymore. I was a woman now; therefore, I won't get disciplined or abused. That was only for kids, or so I assumed at that moment.

I cleaned up and came out of the bathroom to continue peeling potatoes. I was happy and full of hope that my abuse was not going to continue now that this special moment had arrived, which changed me from a little girl into becoming a woman.

A few hours later, when it was time to write down our yearly New Year's wishes, mine had a totally different theme. I didn't wish to die, to be killed, or to kill myself. I wished for a little kitten, for new clothes, to go on vacation, to go back to my original school, and for fun times. I did have one "bad girl" wish though, and that was for Armen to fall or get hurt in front of me, just for my own entertainment. I thought he surely deserved it.

The first three days of the New Year I spent in dramatic pains from my first period. I cried, I screamed, I moaned, and I tried all kinds of positions to make my lower belly and my back feel less painful. Nothing helped until my dad gave me some pain medication. I wasn't too happy that I would be in this condition now every month for a whole week straight. But, as long as I wasn't going to get abused anymore, I believed it was well worth it.

On the following Monday, the sixth of January, I was home alone with my brother when Uncle Armen arrived at our house. He had been away on vacation for a week and had just gotten back. He always behaved like it was his own house when he came over, and the only thing that was different from my parents was that he literally didn't have the key. And that was the only difference.

"Veraaaa, come here and bring me my slippers!" He screamed as I could hear him drop himself into the kitchen chair. I immediately grabbed them and ran up to slip them onto his feet.

"Now go make me my green tea in that round cup that I like, the one without any handles."

I gave him what he needed and turned around to walk away. "Now go put your brother down to take his nap, and then go to the balcony for your prophylactic session," he said in the same routine tone he used to ask for his slippers and tea.

When I heard him say that, I almost choked on my own saliva. I turned around with my eyes wide open and looked right at him in total surprise.

"What is your problem? Why are you looking at me in such a strange manner"? He asked.

"My mother didn't tell you about what happened?"

"No, Tell me. What happened?"

"I am not a girl anymore, nor a child. I am a woman now," I announced in a low voice with bits of bravery seeping through.

"Oh good for you!" he answered back, "but that doesn't change a thing about your discipline Vera, not while you are living here, eating our food, and sleeping under our roof." he added.

"Why do you say our roof? Don't you mean my parents' roof?"

He didn't like my last question and jumped off of his chair.

"Do NOT make me beat you up right here where your brother can see it! Go out onto the balcony right now or I will show you how I discipline a woman versus a child."

I got really scared and quickly left the kitchen thinking about what he just said. I didn't want my brother to know what was going on. God forbid he should see this. But as I was leaving the kitchen, I asked myself how he would know how to discipline a child versus a woman. He must have beaten a woman up before. I had to assume that's the only way he would know the difference.

On my way to the balcony, I peeked in to the living room and told my brother that Armen and I had to talk and that he should stay right where he was until I came to get him. As always, he listened.

I walked onto the balcony and started to get undressed. I felt so disgusted and unhuman, and thought that if I could jump off that balcony right there and then, I would. If my mother had been home I probably would have considered it, but at that moment it wasn't an option. There was no way I was going to leave my baby brother alone with a monster like Armen.

I took everything off but my underwear with my t-shirt rolled into a ball stuffed inside. It looked like I had a small cantaloupe stuck between my legs.

I got undressed and lay down, trying to position myself so I would be in as little pain and discomfort as possible. Deep and serious thoughts ran through my mind. I decided that before my next prophylactic session, I would tell my mother that if Armen touches me again, I would run away from home. If that didn't work, I would threaten to take my baby brother late in the night and leave. I figured I could go to one of the churches or maybe just to my grandpa's house for a day, just to show them all I mean what I say.

A few minutes later, I heard Armen walk into my parents' bedroom and lock the door. Then I heard the usual sound of his belt, which he so loved to create, and I got scared.

As he walked up to me, he started to laugh. "Did you poop yourself or something? What is that in your underwear: a small volleyball? Hahahahahahaha!"

"It's an old t-shirt. My mom told me to use it."

"I don't even believe you. You aren't even eleven yet. You probably made this all up to try and get out of your well-earned prophylactic sessions."

I stayed quiet and tried to concentrate on deep breathing and stopping my tears, which started to flow onto the pillow. Within a few seconds, I felt the metal buckle land on my upper thigh. I screamed out loud, which was way out of character for me, especially on the first hit. It was just so painful and so unexpected. He had never used a buckle on me during these specific sessions before and my skin was extremely sensitive.

"Shut your ugly mouth, bitch," he said to me as he pushed my face into the pillow with his large hand. He was mad that I screamed out loud. I wasn't supposed to.

"I'm sorry. I'm sorry. I didn't mean to. I didn't expect the buckle, Uncle. Please don't use that on me now!

"Ok fine! Just shut your mouth! I don't even believe you are having a period in the first place!"

The sharp pain from the buckle didn't fade and stayed excruciating for many seconds. I guess my mother was right when she said that things would be different and I would be much more sensitive during this time.

Before giving me a second whip, Armen said, "I want proof that you aren't lying and do in fact have a period!"

A second later, I felt his hands grab my underwear and pull them down. "You are a nasty and dirty liar! You are a little bitch! A dirty lying pig!" he screamed like he just learned a top secret from me or something.

I don't know if it was because I had cleaned myself up just before he came to the house, or maybe it was because I was lying down, but there was no blood on the t-shirt between my legs.

"I am not lying, Uncle. I just cleaned up and that's why you may not see anything. I am sure if I get up and walk around for a minute, some of it will show up again and I can prove it to you." I really wanted to get up and run out of that balcony if he saw me fully naked, but I couldn't. If I did he would see the front of my body also, so I stayed put.

"I am keeping your underwear down and will be beating you on your bare skin! If you don't like it, you can turn over and I will whip the front of your body instead."

"No, no, not on the front, please! I will stay just like this! You can leave my underwear down if that's what you want! Just please don't make me turn around!" I begged him and cried.

He started to whip me with his belt all over my back, my butt and my legs. The blows were non-stop, coming as fast and as strong as he could throw them. I wasn't screaming, just making noises like an animal would make when its back legs got stuck in a man-made trap. I didn't know if it was my sensitive skin or if he was hitting harder than in the past, but with each and every hit, I felt unbearable pain.

I didn't say anything else and I was desperately hoping it would end as soon as possible. The realization that my girl to woman transformation didn't make any difference in my life was devastating.

A few minutes later he stopped and said, "Oh look! I guess you weren't lying! I see some blood coming out. I will stop for now. I think you got more than thirty today, anyway."

At that point I just lay there like a piece of raw flesh, like meat that my dad used to buy at the meat market and my mother would beat with a kitchen hammer before cooking.

Armen walked out of the balcony and into my parents' bedroom. A second later I heard a loud noise as if something large had fallen to the floor.

BOOM!

I couldn't fully get up because I was naked and had no strength left in me, but I did turn my head to the right and peeked out a little. As usual my curiosity took over. What I saw was like a scene from a comedy TV show, and it somehow made me laugh, even if the laughter was just inside of me.

I saw Armen lying on the floor of the bedroom with his belt behind him like it was his tail. He was grabbing his toes with one hand and his forehead with the other, almost like he was some funny looking creature that was magically frozen by a fairy. He was very angry and swearing up a storm using words I had never even heard before. He was calling the bed itself all sorts of bad names, which I thought was funny since the bed couldn't really hear him. It looked like he might have hit his toes on the bed's leg while walking out of the balcony. And then he must have somehow hit his head and fallen when he bent over to grab his hurting toes. He reminded me of Tom from my favorite cartoon "Tom and Jerry" after he unsuccessfully attacked poor little Jerry Mouse.

I couldn't laugh out loud or make any noise and I was barely containing a completely insane laugh. I realized that I was witnessing one of my wishes come true from New Year's Eve and it was really happening. It was almost like this thing called Karma that I had heard my friends talk about.   I assumed by its name, it was a female. She had hurt the man who was hurting someone else weaker than she was .Karma does exist.

CHAPTER 9
The Edge of the Blade

I went back to my original school at the beginning of the fourth quarter. Although my grades were good enough to go back earlier, my parents didn't submit the transfer request to the principal in time.

Unlike other countries, in Russia the schools have all grades housed under the same roof. We had first graders in the same building as fifth graders, and even tenth graders were there. Our country was not like other countries, we only had ten years of schooling and not eleven or twelve; however, the school days were longer and stretched from 7 a.m. to 3 p.m. for all ages.

I noticed many changes in the faculty and children in general. Maybe things were the same as they were before. I just never noticed them, due to missing many days, or maybe I was seeing the world with more seriousness than before. One of the things I noticed right away was the amount of bullying that was going on every day. It was mostly by the older kids bullying the younger ones. It was kind of strange because I was under the impression that older people should always be the protectors.

During the first few weeks I was back, I saw all kinds of unfairness. Older kids would take lunch money and food from the younger students. They would even spit in their food as they walked by them. They would steal their personal items, like elastics, coin purses, or snacks and commit many other outrageous and ridiculous acts. I also saw an older student empty out the contents of another student's backpack right onto the floor. Then the older student would smack the younger one in the face or head with the backpack.

To my amazement, most of the bullies were teenage girls, which I thought was odd. I figured females would be kinder, nicer, and more motherly then the guys would be. I guess I was wrong.

After seeing this unfairness all over the school, I decided I couldn't tolerate it anymore and stepped in to help at least a few first graders. In the beginning, when I got involved, I would get pushed around as well, but the bullies underestimated my patience and determination. Their punches and hits were nothing in comparison to what Armen did to me, so I had no reason to back down from what I believed in.

I realized that if I wanted to be more useful to the little kids at the school, I needed to learn a few good moves, so I decided to sign up for karate. The lessons were held in a nearby school, and even though I didn't have any free time, I was able to convince my dad to let me sign up anyway. I told him that I wanted to learn a few things so I would be able to protect myself.

I was a good student and earned stripes on my karate belt very fast. Practicing the moves I learned there was very easy since all I had to do was to fight the bullies when they attacked the weaker and smaller kids.

There were times when I got in trouble at home because my clothes would be ripped or I would have scratches and bruises all over my face or hands. It was all worth it though, because the kids I protected truly appreciated my help and were always thankful. They said they didn't fear school anymore knowing I was around.

One time I got into a fight with a sixteen year-old bully and found out after the fact that she was a daughter of a Sochi Police Department captain. Although she was winning at the beginning of the fight, I was not giving up. I remember her saying, "Look at her! She is unstoppable and won't stay down! No matter how many times we hit her and push her, she just keeps coming back at us, more and more!"

At the end I head-butted her, and she got a bloody nose ending the fight. I guess in their minds whoever bled first lost. I probably won because my forehead was well-trained from those times Armen made me hit it on the wall in the kitchen.

I was afraid that I was going to get in big trouble because I made her bleed, but to my relief, she didn't tell her father. I also noticed that she had started to respect me more, and the days I was there she didn't bully any students.

While showing that I could fight and protect others was a great idea, I was very well aware that I was still a child and a female; therefore, I was expected to act appropriately and be more feminine. As my grandpa used to say, "Not everything can be resolved with the fists."

I actually told him about that fight during our birthday celebration about a week later. I was turning 11 and he was turning 66, which I thought was funny because if you add those two up it makes 77 and seven was always his favorite number.

"You remind me so much of myself and how I was during World War II," he said to me after hearing about my fight.

"Really, Grandpa! That's a huge compliment! I wish I had been in that war with you!"

"Oh! Noooo! You would NOT want to be in that war. Trust me on that! There was way too much horror. I am sure you read about it in the books from my library."

"OK Deda, but can you at least tell me some good things about the war? Or interesting stories? Pleeeeease?"

"OK! I will tell you a couple of stories, but just a couple!" He put his arms on the table and crossed his hands together.

His mother looked like she already knew he was going to say something interesting, so she smiled at me and pulled up her own chair in preparation. She was one of those rare mothers who never got tired of her son's company even though she had lived with him since the day he was born. She always took care of him first, before anything or anyone else. To me, she represented the perfect mother, kind of like I tried to be with my baby brother.

A few moments later, my grandpa asked me, his mom, and the other guests who were visiting if we were all ready for a quick war detail from his past. We all shook our heads "yes" and he went on.

"So when someone would ask me, what was the hardest battle that you were part of during World War II, I would always tell them it was the Battle of Stalingrad. It was the hardest yet the most important, because if we had given that city up to our enemies, most likely, the whole war would have been lost!"

"Wow, Deda. Really? I mean were you right there with all those solders?" I asked with wide-open eyes.

"Yes, with all of my "brothers." It was negative twenty-five degrees Celsius at times, and people were freezing to death all around us. We had no supplies and lived days without sleep. I was there for the entire battle, from the very first day up until we raised the red flag of our victory!"

"I can't believe it! You never told me you were there, Deda!"

"It's OK, as you grow older, I will tell you more and more. Here is another important battle that I was part of, which you might have heard of: The Battle of Berlin," he said with pride.

"WHAT?" I screamed out in amazement. "Why wouldn't you tell me that also? That's so important! I could have told all the kids in my history class. They would have been so impressed!"

"Do you want to know the best part about that battle?" he asked me as he raised his eyebrows.

"YESSSSSSS! Tell me!"

"Berlin surrendered on our birthday, May 2nd. Ha, ha, ha!"

I smiled, got up, and hugged my grandpa as tightly as I could. I was yet again very proud of him. I kissed his smooth forehead and said, "I am sooooo proud of you Deda! You are the best! I love you more than anything and everyone in this whole wide world -- and then that times a thousand -- AND THEN to the moon and back!"

"I love you more," he said back to me with the smile. "You are my one and only granddaughter and everything I have is yours! Soon I will show you my military jacket with all of my medals. You can count them and tell me how many there are," he said as he kissed the top of my head.

The guests were all smiling and talking about what he had just said and my great-grandma sat there and looked at her son with amazement. I am sure she had heard hundreds of his war stories, but she never grew tired of them. She was actually very family- oriented and loved the gatherings at their house. It was really cool to have a great grandmother, especially since she was as healthy as I was, even though we were born over 75 years apart.

Her name was Siranush, which in Armenian means a "Sweet Heart." It was the perfect name for her because she truly was the sweetest little old lady I had ever met. She was just as nice to me as she was to my grandpa. I remembered many funny moments with her. She used to make me laugh when she washed my hair with a fresh cold egg from the fridge. She would crack it on the edge of the sink, and pour it right onto the top of my hair. That was just one of many cute memories of her that I keep to this day.

When summertime came, I was actually looking forward to it, because my parents had another vacation all planned out and couldn't wait to go. They left in the middle of July, this time on a cruise ship that took them to different countries all around the Black Sea. This time my grandma and a couple of my aunts, all from my father's side, stayed at our house to watch after us. One thing I can say for sure is that those two weeks were the best of my entire childhood.

I played outside with my friends every single day. I ate yummy food that my grandma and aunts prepared. I played with my brother whenever I wanted to and I didn't when I was too tired. I stayed up late at night and slept in every morning. I wore cute girly clothes that I borrowed from my older cousin Rita who was also visiting. To top it all off, I didn't have to do anything other than play all day because my relatives did the housework for me.

My favorite aunt, out of my dad's three sisters, was Marina. She was his youngest sister and had two kids: a boy named Tigran and a daughter named Rita who was the youngest cousin I had. My cousin Tigran wasn't there, but Rita was, and that made my days even better. I felt like I was the one on vacation for those two weeks.

Right before my parents returned, Aunt Marina and my grandma rented out an apartment because they decided they wanted to stay in Sochi for a bit longer. The place was about forty-five minutes away from where we lived. I went to visit them at least a couple of times per week. My dad didn't mind, as long as I was home before the street lights were turned off. The city was still financially bankrupt and had to use electricity and other resources very efficiently. Either way, I really enjoyed the company of my relatives from my father's side. I was never forced to do anything I didn't want to do. I ate yummy things, played with my cousin and laughed my heart out with my aunt and grandma.

My mother wasn't too happy about me going there because it took me away from my responsibilities at home, but we didn't really argue about it. When my dad was home I was able to go; when he wasn't, most of the time I couldn't. It was as simple as that.

One Saturday, at the end of September while visiting them, I got carried away having non-stop fun. I lost track of time and didn't realize that I was running late.

I honestly liked not having electricity. Uncle Armen never stayed late at our house because he wanted to make it home before all the streets got dark. My baby brother never minded because we would do all kinds of fun things like: playing games, bingo, cards, making funny drawings and animal shapes out of coins and even just naming cities and places that we knew. We were even allowed to play hide and seek, which was super fun in the dark.

The area where my relatives rented their apartment was considered to be on the outskirts of the city, and other than residential buildings of different heights, there weren't many other things around. There were no stores, supermarkets, restaurants, or even gas stations within at least a fifteen-minute drive. There was just one large four-lane street in the middle of that whole area, and a couple of dozen five to ten story high apartment buildings. The buildings were either next to one another or across from each other. They looked like bodyguards protecting the main road.

In general, I would always be home by the time the street lights went off, just because I heard way too many scary and horrifying stories about things that happened after dark. I heard about people getting beat up, robbed and kidnapped, so I tried my best to stay off the streets at night.

This time I wasn't doing a good job of that. After a ten-minute walk from my aunt's apartment to the bus stop, it was already almost dark. Usually the buses ran on time, so I sat down on the bench and waited. The bus stop was a regular half-open structure, with one long

bench inside it. During the day, there could be dozens of people waiting, but because it was so late in the evening, I was the only one who
was waiting for a ride.

A few minutes later, I saw the headlights of the bus coming
toward me from far away. This bus was in the second lane, not in the
lane near me and it wasn't slowing down. I thought that maybe the
driver could not see me waiting for him, so I got off of the bench and
started to wave at him. I was wrong, and a few seconds later, the bus
flew right by me with a big neon sign on the front that read, "OUT
OF SERVICE."

If I say I wasn't scared I would be lying. I was petrified and
shaking. Now I was in complete darkness with not one car on the
road and no street lights. The only thing I could see were random
candles shining in the windows of the buildings. It was getting chilly
and I was severely late getting home. Not getting on that bus meant
that I would miss the connecting one, which meant I was pretty much
assured of a few hours of walking in the dark.

Without knowing when the next bus was going to show up,
or if there was even going to be a next one, I was lost on what to do.
If I chose to find my way back to my aunt's apartment, I might not
make it home at all and be in big trouble, plus I was afraid to walk
back through the small paths and roads in the dark to get to their
apartment. Unlike the open road I was on at the moment, those small
paths were shrouded in complete darkness, so I decided to do what
made me feel the safest and I started to walk toward the next bus
stop.

I was very thankful for the moon which was big and bright.
It was just what I needed at that moment. It gave the road nice light-
ing and brightened up my way while making me feel less scared.

Sure enough, just as I feared, I could hear different kids
screaming in the dark alleys between the buildings. The screams
sounded almost demonic as if they were intentionally trying to scare
people or animals away. Along with the screams, there were random

barks from homeless dogs and the high-pitched cries of hungry cats. None of the sounds were too close to me, so I felt OK for the moment and continued walking.

But just as I began to feel at ease, I heard someone's footsteps coming up behind me from the bus stop which I had just left. I quickly turned around, but didn't see anything or anyone. It seemed like the moon was only brightening the road in front of me and not the road behind me. I continued to walk, with my anxiety growing with every step I took. I naturally sped up and my stride became almost twice as big as it had been a minute before. All of a sudden, I heard those same steps getting louder. I turned around and saw the silhouette of a tall, broad-shouldered man, dressed in dark clothes from top to bottom.

At first he was walking right on the side walk, and when he saw me speed up, he moved to the middle of the road. I was so scared I started to walk faster and faster, hoping that he was just a random person walking to the next bus stop like I was. I was wrong. When I walked faster, he did the same. It was clear to me that this was not a coincidence and he wasn't just going somewhere. This man was coming to harm me unless I acted fast and ran away from him at that exact moment.

I started to run. He ran right after me. I could hear his heavy footsteps getting closer and closer, almost like his boots were purposely trying to make me scared.

A few seconds later I turned around and saw that he was only about fifty feet away from me. I started to run for my life. My heart was beating so hard I could hear it through my chest; it felt like it was trying to break through my rib cage and run away without me, saving its own life.

I moved to the other side of the road, which was the lane with oncoming traffic. It didn't matter.

A minute later, he was so close that I could almost see his face. The moon light shone right on us. He looked like he was about fifty years-old with a mustache and a beard, wearing a black hat, a black leather jacket, dark colored jeans and tall black boots. He had no emotion in his face at all. I screamed.

"HELP! SOMEONE HELP ME! PLEASE WHOEVER YOU ARE, STAY AWAY FROM ME! MY DAD IS WAITING FOR ME A FEW MINUTES FROM HERE! WHAT DO YOU WANT FROM ME! I DON'T HAVE ANYTHING TO GIVE!" I screamed everything I could think of hoping someone would hear my pleas.

He didn't say a word or react in any kind of way. I felt my legs giving up on me. As I turned around one last time, the man grabbed me by my jacket and the back of my neck. He lifted me off the ground for a split second as he wrapped his left arm around my waist pulling me toward him.

"HELP, SOMEONE HELP!" I screamed into the dark, empty road, but other than my own voice, there was nothing but total silence. I tried fighting him off, but he was far stronger than I was. After a few seconds of struggling, I stopped. I felt the energy fully leave my body.

Out of nowhere, by some absolute miracle, bright headlights from an approaching car shone right into our faces. The man let go of me and I dropped down to the ground. A second later, he ran away from the road, first toward the curb, and then into the trees on the side.

I was in shock and stayed on the ground to catch my breath. I was petrified and I didn't even know what exactly had just happened.

I heard the car's brakes make a squeaking sound and then the car came to a loud and abrupt stop only a few feet away from me.

From the position I was lying on the ground, all I could see was a pair of shiny black men's shoes coming out of the car and running in my direction. I still didn't move.

"Are you OK? What happened to you? I thought I saw someone else here. Do you need help?" a manly but nervous voice asked.

I still wasn't moving. My head was fully on the ground, turned to the left, and I just stared into space.

Without touching or picking me up, the man waved his hand in front of my eyes from one side to the other. He got down on his knees and looked at my face up close.

"Oh! My God! I know your father! I recognize you! I have seen you a few times in the ER, waiting for your dad! His name is Gegam, right?"

I was exhausted, but immediately felt safe. I was so lucky my father was so well known throughout the city. I turned my head towards him and whispered, "Yes, that is my dad."

"Oh My God, I am so glad! Can I please help you get up?"

"Yes," I answered, then reached out and grabbed his warm hand.

"You don't have to talk right now. Do not worry about anything. You can tell me whatever you want to tell me later. I will bring you home right now. You are safe," he said as we walked toward his car.

For no reason at all, I felt a sudden wave of paranoia. I stopped abruptly and maneuvered my body away from him. I ran a few steps, stopped, and looked back. He appeared completely calm and collected like he knew that I was afraid and unsure of what to do.

"I don't know what you are doing out on this dark road at this hour, but you cannot stay out here alone. I will bring you home and if you don't trust me, you should take this and keep it in your hands for the whole ride." He took something from his pocket and handed it to me. It was a pocket knife.

I looked at it, then at him, and then back at the knife. I decided to go for it. I ran up and snatched it out of his hand. I then ran toward his car and jumped into the back seat locking the door behind me.

He walked slowly back to his car and got in the driver's seat. "You are a smart girl, just like your dad. If you feel safer, keep the knife pointed at me the whole time I drive. I don't mind that at all."

I didn't point the knife at him, but I did sit with the knife open and ready. I felt like I could trust him even though I wasn't at complete ease.

He turned the car around and went back in the direction he came from. A minute later we passed by the second bus stop which I was originally running toward. As we got closer and closer to the center of the city, I saw more cars on the roads. When I looked down, I realized that I was not pointing the knife at him any longer. I put it down on the seat next to me and looked at him in the rearview mirror. He had saved me.

"There was a man who ran after me, grabbed me, and was going to hurt or kill me!" I said breaking the silence.

"What? Where? Was he the man who I thought was with you when I first saw you? Oh my God! Why are you out here in the dark anyway? Does your father know you are not home? Is he working in the ER tonight?" He asked question after question.

I didn't answer any of them. I think I actually blocked them all out. All I said back was one sentence, "I hope you know that you just saved my life!"

To my surprise he didn't answer and just continued driving. All he did was shake his head from one side to the other, almost like he was in disbelief. He turned up the sound on his cassette car player, and classical music filled the car. It was "The Four Seasons" by Vivaldi one of my favorite musical selections.

Within seconds I felt at peace, and when he stopped the car in front of the entrance to my building, I folded his knife and carefully tossed it onto the front passenger seat. He turned his head to see what it was, smiled, and said, "Please wave at me from the window when you make it home."

"Thank you." I answered him with true appreciation in my voice and opened the car's door.

I ran into the building as quickly as I could. It was completely dark and hard to navigate. I had already memorized the set up and size of the stairs since I would often use them in the dark. I felt the wall with my right hand and made my way up, floor after floor.

I was still scared and confused about what happened in the past hour. Getting home late was the last thing on my mind, not that I wasn't worried that I would get in trouble; but it was not as scary as what I had just gone through. Besides, I figured my dad was at work and Armen most likely went home when it was still light out. It surely didn't mean that I wouldn't get in trouble the next day, though. All my mother would have to do was tell Uncle Armen that I was late and if he wasn't available, she would demand that my dad discipline me. He would feel that he had to do it.

When I made it to the top floor, I rang the doorbell and knocked on the door as loudly as I could. A few seconds later, I heard my mother's steps approach.

"Who is it?" she asked with an annoyed and sarcastic tone.

"It's me, Mom. Please open the door!"

"Oh, look who decided to show up! I thought you were going to stay with your father's relatives WITHOUT my permission," she said as she unlocked the door before slowly opening it all the way. She held a small plate with a short burning candle on it.

"Mother, you don't even know what just happened! It was terrible! I left there in time. I was at the bus stop on time, but the bus was out of service. The bus was broken so I started to walk to the next bus stop when some guy started to follow me and ran after me; then he grabbed me! By some miracle he was interrupted by a car. The bad guy ran away and the man in the car brought me home. He even knows dad from work." I told my mother the whole story without taking a break or inhaling any air.

She stared at me for a moment, then turned around and walked away. "You are totally crazy," she said without even turning her head.

"Mom, you don't believe me? I swear to you. It's true! I am not lying," I answered trying to be as convincing as I could.

All of a sudden I remembered that my dad's friend, whose name I didn't even ask for, told me to wave to him when I got in the house. I ran to the kitchen window and quickly opened it up. He was still there, sitting in his car, and I waved to him hoping he could see me. With the help of the bright moon that shone right on my face, he saw me and waved back. After a few more seconds, he drove away.

"Mom, look outside at the white car that is leaving now. He was the man who saved me and brought me home tonight." I screamed at her hoping she would look down from the window to prove that what I told her had really happened.

"It's all good. These ridiculous visits are ending very soon! Your grandmother is moving, finally and permanently! You will not be able to visit her anymore anyway, so I hope you have enjoyed every minute of it so far," she added.

"Leaving? What do you mean leaving?"

"Oh, your loving grandma didn't tell you that she is leaving you?" she said with a smile. "She is moving to America to live with her daughter Varvara and your other cousin Lusine," she explained, then fully disappeared into her bedroom.

I was confused and wasn't sure what I just heard. I was also a bit surprised that no one had said anything to me and it was my mother who told me about these surprising plans. If it were true, my grandmother probably didn't want to upset me, but my dad should have told me knowing that she's the only grandma I have. Without getting myself more upset than I already was, I decided to ask my father for details in the morning. As soon as I decided that, something else popped into my mind. Since I came home so late, why wasn't my mother worried about my whereabouts? It appeared she did not even care.

The first thing I asked my dad when he got home the next morning was why grandma was leaving Russia and moving to America. I also told him that it's surprising that she didn't want to stay here with him, her only son, or even me her favorite grand-daughter. He didn't approve of me asking such a direct question, and refused to answer it. He seemed annoyed that I had asked about it and made me feel like he was hiding the truth from me. I decided to take a chance and to continue to bother him until he told me something.

A few minutes later, before walking away from me, he conceded and said, "She does want to stay here with us, but under no circumstances will your mother let her do so. Now leave me alone!"

I was upset, but not that surprised, to learn my mother did not want my gram to stay to with us. I was amazed, however, that my dad didn't put his foot down and say to my mother that it is his mother and he wants her to live with him. But, as it has always been, my mother was the boss in the family and whatever she said, was done.

My grandmother moved to America at the beginning of November and I was left with only my grandpa around. He was surely my favorite person in the world, but still, a grandma is a grandma. I just hoped that I would be able to visit her soon, although going to America probably wasn't ever going to happen. It wasn't remotely on my wish list. I was just sad because year after year, all the people I cared about seemed to leave or die.

Two weeks after my grandma left, my mother pleasantly surprised me.

"Your dad and I are going away for two weeks. We have to attend training sessions, one week in one city and one week in Paris, France."

"OK, no problem," I answered her hiding my excitement.

They decided they would open a body care salon for my mother to run, and they needed to be trained on the machines and products that they were going to use there. They were set to leave right after school broke for winter vacation, ten days into December. Needless to say, I was counting the days until they were leaving. It was going to be yet another vacation for me.

Then another surprise! My parents didn't mention who was going to watch after us. I knew that Uncle Armen was away for a few weeks so it wasn't going to do it. Thank God. All of my aunts were either in Armenia or with my grandma in America. I decided to ask my mother directly, not because I was worried or anything, but just because I was curious.

"Mom, who will be staying with us while you are gone"?

"Staying with you? No one! You are already eleven and don't need anyone to babysit you. Your brother is already four and is self-sufficient," she answered, surprised that I had even asked.

I didn't say a word and just turned around to go about my business. It sounded like a very good thing, plus, if I needed anything important, I could just visit or call my grandpa.

"Oh, and make sure that no one knows that you are alone here with the baby for two weeks just in case someone would think of robbing us, or something like that," she added sounding guilty. I just nodded my head "yes" and left the kitchen. I was surprised that she would trust me with her baby for two whole weeks. I wondered if I had finally earned her trust.

Once they left, I felt like I was as happy as I was when they went on their last vacation a few months earlier. I didn't even care that they didn't leave any money for us, or very much food. That wasn't new to me. I was just happy that I had freedom and could relax and not worry about anything.

At first my brother and I were fine, but a week later we ran out of food. This time I didn't have to work and make money because I knew my grandpa was home. Without calling him, since I promised my mother I wouldn't, I took my baby brother by the hand and we walked to his house. The funny thing was that my grandpa and his mom didn't even suspect that we had been left alone for two weeks. I often took my brother for a walk and went to grandpa's house to visit in the past, so he just figured I was coming for another one of those routine dinners together. They didn't even ask about my parents. My grandpa and my mother still didn't talk that much, so he didn't think to ask about her anyway. We hung out with them, ate dinner and went home before dark with a bag full of goodies. Even though it was cold outside, my baby brother and I didn't mind walking a few miles. Anywhere we went was OK with him as long as we were together.

Things were going very well and no one came to visit. When someone called, I didn't answer because my mother told me not to. When I went out of the house for any reason, I took my brother with me. No one really had cause to question anything since most of the time when I went outside, he was with me anyway.

One afternoon when there were only a few days left before my parents were to return, my brother and I were playing in the living room. Suddenly, I heard the doorbell ring. I wasn't sure who it could be, but I figured maybe a neighbor or one of my friends from the building was dropping by. I ran up to the door and looked into the peep hole which was just low enough for me to barely see through. What I saw frightened me. It was Uncle Armen.

I decided not to open the door and tried to make it look like there was nobody home. I stayed completely quiet and sat down on the floor right next to the door. The doorbell only rang a few more times and then stopped. I got up, looked through the hole one last time, and saw him turning around to leave.

Out of nowhere, and with the worst possible timing, my brother ran out of the living room and screamed out loud.

"Here you are Vera! I found you!"

"OH, MY GOD, TIGRAN! BE QUIET!" I whispered while gently covering his mouth with my hand, but it was too late. Armen heard him through the door.

The doorbell rang again and this time he didn't let the button go, making it sound like it got stuck. A few seconds later, he banged on the door with his fist.

I had to think quickly.

"I'm coming! Hold on one minute please! I'll be right there."

I came up to the door and pretended to look into the peep hole while asking who was there. Armen screamed at me right through the door.

"Open this damned door NOW!"

I unlocked it quickly and moved a couple of steps back.

"It's open Uncle, please come in."

The door opened fast and with a heavy force, slamming the wall behind it. He walked in screaming.

"Are you trying to fool me you little bitch?"

"No, no, no Uncle, I wasn't fooling you. I opened the door as soon as I heard and saw you! The door in the living room was closed and I didn't hear the bell." I answered with my head and eyes pointed down.

"Do you think I am a stupid man? I heard Tigran scream out that he found you. You were not in the living room!"

"No, I don't think you are stupid and I didn't hear the door-bell, maybe because the TV was too loud in the living room. But I did hear you knocking on it, so that's when I came up and opened it." It was the most logical lie I could think of.

"Where are your parents? You are getting punished for lying to me, RIGHT NOW!" He grabbed my hand as he screamed, pulling me into the kitchen.

"My parents... my parents... are not home." I said nervously, not knowing how to explain their absence.

"That is even better. I don't need them here. They trust me enough to know that I am working on you. I am turning you from an animal — an absolutely nothing "it" — into a good human being," he said as he forced me into a chair.

I was afraid that he was going to get angrier if he figured out I was withholding details, so I mumbled at him under my breath. "I mean to say that they are not here — not in Sochi – because they are on vacation for two weeks. They will be back a few days from now."

"What? Wow. That is strange. They left you alone; just you two, for two weeks?" He sounded sincerely surprised.

"Yes Uncle, they did and it's OK. I don't mind."

"That's very interesting! I wish I had known about it when they left. Well, they won't be back for a few days as you said, so we have plenty of time," he said in a calm and happy voice.

My brother was alone in the living room. He ran there as soon as he heard Armen banging on our door, but at least I wasn't worried about him at the moment.

Armen sat down in his usual chair and started to rub his chin like he was thinking, and making "hmmmmm" sounds.

"OK... so you did lie to me about not knowing that I was the one ringing the doorbell. I see some dishes in the sink. You left lots of dirty clothes in the bathroom that you should have hand-washed, squeezed and hung on the lines outside the window to dry. I see that none of that is done, so you are in trouble." I realized the mess wasn't very bad. He was just looking for reasons to torture me and to satisfy his sadistic needs. I didn't say anything back. It wouldn't have made any difference anyway. I was just waiting to hear what inhumane method of torturing me he was going to use this time.

About a minute later he got up and went to the end of the hallway. Then I heard him close the door, which separated the front foyer, bathroom, and kitchen from the rest of the apartment. Then he went into the bathroom and came back to the kitchen table holding our first aid kit and a small towel. He placed them right in front of me on the table without saying a word. I was confused, but didn't dare ask him what they were for.

He stood by the table humming a melody that didn't sound familiar to me. The atmosphere the song created creeped me out, and for a minute it seemed like it was the soundtrack from a scene in a horror movie.

A few moments later he began to look through all our kitchen cabinets. I still wasn't saying anything but I was definitely anxious about what was coming next. Then not even a minute later, he slammed a thick glass jar onto the table in front of me. It didn't look familiar to me and I didn't see any labels on it. It was half full with some white substance that looked like salt but had much larger grains. I figured it was some kind of sugar.

"All right now. I think I have everything I need! Hopefully you will appreciate my creativity."

I looked up to see what he was talking about but I still didn't understand what he was planning to do. He jumped up suddenly and ran into the bathroom. He returned just as fast and dropped back into his chair.

"NOW I have everything I need!"

He handed me the towel, opened up the first aid kit, and took the lid off of the glass jar. He started to unwrap something very small and flat; it was the thing that he almost forgot and ran at the last minute to get. At first, I couldn't make out what it was, but then it started to look very familiar. It was the flat spare blade from my father's safety razor which he used to shave his face and neck.

"OK! So what we are going to do is a method of punishment that was used many centuries ago, often on someone who was hiding the truth or lying. What I will be doing is cutting your inner arm with this thin, sharp blade. I will cut you slowly so it won't leave big scars." he explained patiently like a teacher explaining something new to his students.

I didn't understand what I was hearing, because when he said he was going to cut me, it didn't sink in that he was literally going to cut into my flesh. I was scared!

"I am very confused Uncle. You are saying that you will cut my arm open?" I asked in a shaky voice.

"Yes I am and you deserve every second of it! You are a terrible person, a horrible daughter and not even a complete human being."

"But Uncle, I took care of my baby brother day and night, cleaned the house, didn't get into any trouble and always did everything you asked me to do." I tried to reason with him.

"Your brother is fully your responsibility, so don't make out like you are doing your parents a favor by watching him! Put the towel in your mouth and bite down on it, because I don't want to hear your animal-like noises! The longer you wait, the longer I will take, so give me your right hand now!" he said as he grabbed the top part of the thin blade with his fingertips.

Many thoughts ran through my head at that moment. I wanted to get up and run out of the kitchen and apartment, grabbing my baby brother along the way. I thought of screaming out loud for help, but all the windows were closed and no one ever came to help anyway. The last thought I had was to grab something nearby, like a knife to throw it at him, just to buy myself a little time to get out of the apartment.

All of those things also meant that as soon as I left the kitchen, I had to run to the living room to get the baby, and by the time that happened, Armen would most certainly catch up to me. Then my brother would be beyond scared, and who knows what Armen might do to me in front of Tigran. My brother could be emotionally damaged from this experience for the rest of his life. On the other hand, leaving the apartment without my baby brother would save me for that moment, but who knows what Armen would do to him there alone. It's not like my mother was home to stop him. Knowing how horrible a person Armen was, he could hurt the baby anyway he liked and then tell everyone that I did it.

All those thoughts left my mind within a few seconds and I decided to simply deal with it, the same way I had dealt with the pain and suffering for so many years now.

"OK, Uncle, go ahead. I will just bite down on the towel," I said as I stuffed the corner of it into my mouth.

He smiled and looked right into my eyes with sadistic anticipation. He looked like a vampire who was about to bite his victim on the neck. I closed my eyes and inhaled a deep breath through my nose.

A few seconds later, I felt the edge of the sharp blade slowly cutting into my skin and the trickle of warm blood flowing down my arm. It took a second for me to grasp this type of pain because I had never felt anything quite like it before. When I realized how sharp the pain was, I screamed into the towel while sounding like an animal right before it dies in a fight against a more powerful rival.

The pain was inexplicably sharp and intense, kind of like when the whip hit the same exact spot more than twice. I started to shake as the razor cut through my flesh in a slow and steady manner. I was not prepared for this type of pain and none of the pain relieving techniques I had taught myself helped me at that moment. In fact, I couldn't even concentrate. If I didn't know any better, I would think I was in hell.

He was taking his time, slowly cutting through my skin, deeper at the beginning of each cut, and less deep at the end of it. If I didn't know I was being cut alive, I might think he was a famous painter who was painting a portrait of someone important to him. He cut with great care almost like he cared for me and loved me.

This torture and agony lasted for what felt like at least ten minutes. I was convulsing in my seat and my moaning sounds became rhythmic.

"OK, you did very well. It's all cut and now you can look."

I opened my eyes and looked down at my arm. What I saw was so disturbing. I had six straight lines, each about two inches long, sliced into the inside of my right arm, each spaced perfectly about half an inch from each other. The cuts bled from their lower part right onto a plastic table cloth which was, ironically, red. I looked up at Armen and saw him looking at my cuts with pure pride, like he had just finished a unique and permanent artistic creation. He didn't say anything. He just stared at my wounds like I wasn't in any pain.

About a minute later, when it was becoming harder for me to breath, I took the soaking wet towel out of my mouth and placed it on my lap. I knew that the worst was now behind me, and I was working hard to calm myself down. I tried inhaling to balance my breathing.

"If I were you, I would leave that towel in your mouth."

"Why? Are you going to cut my left arm too?" I asked him with a voice full of pain and agony.

"Oh! No. No more cutting. I don't think it affects you that much. This was only the first part of the procedure," he said as he cleaned my blood from the blade and placed it carefully back into its protective paper.

"It didn't affect me? It was the most painful thing I ever felt!" I was crying through hiccups and could barely talk.

"Whatever, just put the towel back in your mouth and be quiet! I have to continue," he said as he grabbed the glass jar.

I quickly stuffed the towel back into my mouth. If, up until now I thought of him as a mentally sick and disturbed human being, after today I could not consider him to be a human any longer. No human could do this to a powerless little child; only a devil could.

He poured some of the contents of the glass jar onto the table. He grabbed a few grains with one hand and spread the first cut on my arm open as wide as he could with the other hand. I screamed into the towel which made the sound muted and scary, like I was a war captive who was being tortured by soldiers.

When the cut was open wide enough, he pushed the white grains right into them, one after the other like pearl beads, until there was no more room. Then he closed the skin back together with his fingers. The tops of those grains were still visible from the outside.

I was making more and more animal-like sounds, which even through the towel, sounded louder than before. My whole body was shaking from the excruciating pain. It was worse than anything that I had felt before and it was so bad that I wouldn't wish that upon anyone. I realized right away that those grains weren't made of sugar. They were made of salt!

The worst part of the torture was that it wasn't going to be a quick sharp pain. It was purposely created to be a long-lasting agony, hours upon hours of excruciating pain from inside out. It became an unbearable feeling of wanting to die, but that wasn't going to end until the last bit of each of those large salt grains melted away into my flesh.

"Stop shaking, it is only salt! The faster you let me place the grains inside every cut, the faster you'll be done."

When he was done stuffing my open wounds with salt, he grabbed a large roll of white medical bandage and started to wrap my arms from the wrist up. Every time he circled my forearm, the pain intensified. I could feel the larger grains being pushed deeper and deeper right into my flesh.

"See it wasn't that bad, was it? Now you will have a few hours, maybe the rest of the day, to think about fooling me again," he said with a sarcastic smile.

My whole body was shaking and the sounds I made were starting to scare even me. I didn't sound like a human at all. The sounds were petrifying and chilling and it felt like something evil and demonic was taking over my mind and my body.

I couldn't think clearly or control myself. All I felt was deep anger, hate, frustration, and the urge to hurt him somehow, in whatever way I could. I felt like a monster had taken over my mind and I was turning into a beast from hell. I felt like I should kill him at that moment, and in my mind, it would be totally justifiable.

"Oh my, I didn't even realize I have been at it for over an hour," Armen said as he rushed to clean up the mess he made. "Actually, why don't you get up and wash these dishes in the sink and then boil me some fresh water for my tea. After all, I am your guest."

I couldn't move. I continued to do nothing except shake and moan. It didn't even feel like I was in the present moment. I wondered if I was in some crazy and unexplainable dream.

After a few minutes with zero reaction from me, Armen grabbed the back of my chair and pulled it right out from underneath me. I fell to the floor and my freshly-wrapped arm hit the edge of the table. I screamed.

The pain was so intense that it became impossible for me to control the sounds I was making. Armen was becoming even angrier. He bent over and pushed down on my mouth with his large hand.

"Shut your ugly mouth, you useless pig! Don't make me squeeze your right arm, because trust me, I will!" he stared into my eyes.

A split second later, the doorbell rang and three knocks followed.

CHAPTER 10
Surviving By the Skin of My Teeth

A rmen was getting nervous. As the doorbell was ringing off the hook, someone's strong fists were also pounding on the door. "Go into your parents' bedroom, close the door, and pretend you are sleeping! You better not make a sound until I come and get you! If you do, you will regret it for the rest of your worthless life!" Still shaking, I walked out of the kitchen and into my parents' bedroom as I was ordered.

"I'm coming! I'll be right there!" Armen shouted.

Then I heard the front door unlock and heard Armen say, "Oh hello! How are you?"

The next sound I heard was the voice of my favorite person in the whole world!

Hi! I am fine. What are YOU doing opening the door?" my grandpa asked Armen with a short and suspicious tone to his voice.

"I came by to check on the kids, while your daughter and son-in-law are on vacation," he answered nervously.

I always thought that Armen might be fearful of my grandpa, but I never heard the two of them ever talk to each other. My grandpa surely carried a military presence everywhere he went. Armen, on the other hand, was thin and out of shape, certainly no match for my strong grandfather.

"Where are Veronika and Tigran?" he asked Armen as he strolled into the kitchen.

"Tigran is taking a nap in the living room, and Vera is sleeping in the bedroom. I wasn't going to wake her up because it looked like she had been cleaning the house all day."

"Hmmmm, that's strange. She's always told me she is never able to take naps at home during the day, and what do you mean my daughter is on vacation? Do you mean they went on a day trip?"

"No, I guess they went away for two weeks."

"WHAT! WHAT DO YOU MEAN TWO WEEKS? ARE THEY CRAZY? THEY LEFT TWO LITTLE KIDS ALONE? Oh my God. I didn't even know. When Vera came by the house with Tigran the other day, I assumed they were just visiting."

I was so eager to come out of that bedroom knowing that my one and only savior was standing just a few feet away, but I didn't. I was too terrified of Armen and of the possible consequences I would face if I did that.

Grandpa left a few minutes later and told Armen to have me call him when I woke up. I watched through the balcony window and saw my grandpa walk out of the building and then disappear around the corner. Tears of sorrow wanted to fill my eyes, but I pulled myself together and went back to the bedroom. I guess there was still a human being inside of me, even if just a few minutes earlier I was convinced I had become a demon from hell.

Armen opened the bedroom door and then told me to finish the dishes and make him some hot tea. I obeyed and did it all through unbearable pain and non-stop tears.

The burning and excruciating pain lasted the rest of the day, the whole night and into the early afternoon the next day. After that, it started to burn less and became more of a steady pain, like a more typical deep cut, but with lots of sharp and pulsing sensations.

I never told anyone what happened and just switched the bandages when needed. When my parents came home and asked me what was under the bandages, I just told them that Tigran and I were playing around and I got a few deep scratches. Those cuts never did heal completely and left permanent thin, white scars as a reminder of the inhumane and sadistic torture that man had inflicted upon me that day.

After my parents came back from their trip, they noticed that I was acting differently. They saw some things that I did which were very strange to them. I stopped watching TV which I was usually begging them to let me do. I purposely did not eat at the table with them and my brother, something that I had enjoyed in the past. And in general, my drive and mood toward everything I used to like had changed. I noticed that in myself as well, including bigger things like not enjoying the piano any longer and even spending less time with my baby brother.

That gruesome day and the torture that Armen subjected me to brought out a very dark side of me. I no longer thought the same way about life and others around me anymore. I didn't look at other kids as my friends, or even in a friendly manner. I saw them all as spoiled brats who didn't know how good they had it, and who didn't appreciate the pain-free life they enjoyed.

When I was in school, I spent more time daydreaming and zoning out than I did paying attention to the material or my teachers. My grades were just "good enough" not to get kicked out of the school again, but I didn't put in any extra efforts to get high "B's" or "A's".

Sports that I was involved in at the school were also not that enjoyable anymore, but I didn't stop going to them. I noticed that they helped me release my inner anger and negative mindset. I guess the old saying: "A healthy body means a healthy mind" had some truth to it.

I did gymnastics, track, karate, tennis, volleyball, swimming, and a few others. Even if I only went to each once per week, I still managed to participate and was actually quite good at all of them.

I started to get stronger and stronger and more mature, as well as more serious. I didn't let any kids, no matter their age, hurt me or even say bad things to me. I noticed that, unlike in the past, I was much more aggressive toward them. Before, I would have to be attacked or hit first to respond, but now if anyone started to talk down to me, I would get physical right away, with my fists and without any warning.

These same behaviors started to show at home, too; not toward my baby brother of course, but toward just about everyone else. I started to talk back. I put minimal effort in my chores and didn't care if the house was still dirty when I was done. I even segregated myself from everybody as much as I could, because I learned that if I was alone no one could hurt me.

Outside of the house, the only people I didn't push away were my grandpa and his mom. Everyone else was too annoying and too needy in my eyes: some less, some more. After I turned twelve, I started to isolate myself from others even more and I didn't go outside to play even when my dad offered me the chance. I would say no and stay inside.

When it came to my punishments, they still happened as often as my parents or Armen felt they had to be executed; but there was a change that was taking place. I had started to fight back, and that resistance was both verbal and physical. It never worked out to my advantage, but I still fought every single time and every single minute. It felt good in a way because I realized that someone weaker than I was would have given up after so much torture and abuse. But that was not who I was. I was stronger than that, physically and emotionally. I was becoming many things, but I was not a quitter.

Neither my parents nor Armen liked my new attitude at all, because now I was quite strong and also fast. My mother had to avoid disciplining me when my brother was home or was awake; she didn't want to scare him or upset him with my reactions. The few times my brother did see me being abused, he tried to get involved and cried very loudly. He would shout things at my parents and Armen, saying things that my mother didn't like. After all, what mother would like a 5 year-old telling her that "she is a bad person."

In addition to fighting to protect myself, I started to become more outspoken and fearless. I would grab the belt from Armen's hands when he would hit me on the face or head. I would run away from him, going through different rooms of the house, like the kitchen or the bathroom, with him in pursuit. I also started to scream out loud for help to anyone who could hear me. I knew that most likely no one would help, but I saw no reason to hold back any longer. These disobedient ways of protecting myself, seemed to shorten the physical part of the ever-increasing punishment I was getting.

Sometimes I would even fight Armen back, pushing him away with my arms or legs. I never hit or pushed my dad hard when he was disciplining me, but I did try to grab the belt out of his hands. It wasn't really a common thing for my dad to beat me anyway; my mother would only make him do it when Armen was away. I was quite thankful that my dad only used the belt and nothing else. It wasn't that I liked it, but it was better than the brutal beatings and torture methods Armen inflicted on me year after year. It seemed to me that my dad didn't want to hit me and only did it because my mother told him to. Some days he would find an excuse why he couldn't, and he would tell her that he had to run out on an important errand. When he did use the belt on me, he would beat me with it very quickly and not with his full strength.

Fighting back also turned into: locking myself in different rooms, running out of the apartment if I could, or even trying to bite Armen. These were just the defense mechanisms I developed, though I knew they made me look like an animal.

Another benefit was that Armen really had to watch out for me now, and he had to work much harder at abusing me. It was not like in the past when I just lay there helplessly and took whatever sadistic and sick things he came up with.

Once I started to scream and cause a ruckus, my abuse became a known fact to our neighbors. It was hard to miss it and people started to talk about it. Soon enough, news got to some of my other relatives who lived in Sochi. They started to call and ask my parents about what was going on in our house and why they were hearing stories about my constant heartbreaking screams. Of course, neither they nor our neighbors knew to what extent I was abused and brutalized.

One thing that did change, because of all my screaming, was our neighbors' reaction to it. As soon as I would get too loud, they would start knocking on our door or banging on the walls to make us stop. It usually did stop the beating, at least for the moment. It wasn't much, but it was progress.

Armen started to dislike my active fighting and decided to ask my parents for help. He told my mother that if she wanted him to continue disciplining me, then he needed them both to hold me down and cover my mouth. My mother agreed and so did my dad, since he wouldn't ever go against his wife's wishes.

It started with my mother holding me down, while Armen used sticks, belts, shoes, or the whip to beat me. Then when my dad came home, all three of them would hold me down and cover my mouth so I couldn't scream, while Armen would try to whip me on any spot he could find on my wiggling body. I started to get wounds and bruises pretty much all over and even on my face. Those times when it was all three of them against me, my mother would order my brother to stay in the kitchen or the bathroom. As long as he couldn't hear me scream, he didn't come out. But the moment he was able to hear me cry, then he would run out and try to stop them. He was a brave little man.

The best thing about fighting back was that my physical punishments became less frequent. Although Armen tried different approaches with me, and on some occasions would even offer me a deal, they still all involved physical beatings of some sort. In exchange for my co-operation, he would hit me less.

I once expected big trouble when I received bad grades on two important tests at the same time. My mother and father had gone away for a weekend, and they took my brother with them. That kind of scared me. I knew that if I were home alone, Armen would have no reason not to come over and whip me. I had to think creatively and I made the decision to use his approach. I was going to offer him something in exchange for his leniency.

When he arrived at our house that Saturday, he already knew about my grades. Without wasting any time, he said, "Vera, it's very simple. If you put up a fight, I will give you twenty-five whips with the instrument of my choice. If you cooperate, then I will only use my belt on you, ten times with a leather end and five times with the metal buckle."

"Uncle, thank you for the offer, but I also have one for you. If you don't touch me at all today, I will go to your house and clean it, shop for your groceries, cook you a few dishes of food, and even massage your feet! You know from my parents that I am very good at massage. I massage my parents' feet and bodies a few times every week."

"HA, HA, HA, HA, HA, you are way too funny and definitely desperate. I don't need your help with anything."

I realized that I had to offer him something much more desirable and appealing. Maybe I could offer something that a grown man would be more interested in, something that carried more weight than a desire to physically abuse me.

"OK Uncle, there is one last thing I would like to offer you. Would you please accept sex in exchange for the beating? I promise I won't tell anyone about it, and I will tell my parents that you did beat me after all."

I delivered the offer in complete desperation believing that I had no other options in place. I had heard older girls talk about sex and how their boyfriends would buy gifts and treat the girls well as long as they were willing to have sex. I really didn't understand much about sex or even how it was done, but it didn't sound like it would be as dangerous as getting beaten, especially since some girls I know said they had sex all the time.

"Wow! Look at you being a street girl and offering me sex. I can't believe how weak and scared you are!"

He paused for a moment and then he laughed very loudly while grabbing his belly at the same time. He reminded me of one of those bullies at school who would laugh at kids after the bullies made them cry.

All of a sudden I realized what I had just done and how much trouble I would be in if my mother ever found out. I also felt ashamed that I had to stoop to that after he declined all other offers I made him.

When he stopped laughing, he said, "OK wow, that was very funny. You are a comedian! For making me laugh so hard, here is my new counter offer! It is up to you to choose your physical punishment and what you would like me to use on you." After I stood there for few moments in silence, he gave me a quick list of choices. Maybe he was trying to be helpful in his own sick way.

The whip was not a good choice because my back and legs were still very sore and my active wounds were way too sensitive.

My butt was actually bright red and blue and did not have a single spot that was the normal color. The cuttings, hand-twisting, kneeling on beans, pressure points, and other tortures sounded agonizing and I couldn't bring myself to pick them. The only one that sounded OK at that moment was a method that he had not yet used on me: a whipping with a cane on the bottoms of my bare feet.

He had used both the cane and the switch on me in the past, but never on my feet. And considering the other options, it did not sound that bad at all.

Well, it turned out that I was right, it wasn't bad; it was unendurable, agonizing, and brutal. It was literally the most misleading description for any punishment I have ever heard. He knew exactly how and where to whip me to make it most painful. He beat me right in the middle of my feet where they arch. I was only able to sit and let him do it for about a minute, and after a few hits on each foot I decided I couldn't take it, so I got up and ran into the bathroom.

"Get back here now or I will get a whip and you will feel it all over your body," he screamed after me.

I closed the bathroom door and leaned against it. It didn't have a lock. The pain was still pulsating from the bottom of my feet and throughout my whole body in a rhythmic manner, and I couldn't think clearly or even concentrate.

A second later, he pushed the door in with his weight and I ended up sprawled across the floor. He was furious, and his eyes were shining like he was some strange monster or demon. He was caning me all over my body, and even struck my neck and face. He was merciless and was hitting me fast and hard. All the while I lay on the floor in the corner by the tub near the sink and I was unable to get up or even move. I looked like a small animal that had been caught in a trap and had no way to escape, while some of the neighborhood hooligans were beating it with their sticks for fun.

After a while he got tired and stuck his head out of the bathroom door to catch his breath and to get a little extra air since our bathroom didn't have any windows. As soon as he did that, I saw my opportunity to escape.

His legs were blocking my way out, so I grabbed them both, and then bit him on one of his calves as hard as I could. He howled in pain.

"YOU ARE A WORTHLESS PIECE OF SHIT! YOU WILL RE-GRET THIS FOR THE REST OF YOUR LIFE!"

I didn't hear the rest of his rant, because after I ran out of the bathroom, I ran out of the apartment. I spent the rest of the afternoon and night hiding in the woods next to the building. I didn't go to my grandpa because he would have seen my bruises and marks and would have started World War III with my parents. I am pretty sure he would have done something to Armen, too.

Biting him was the worst thing I could have done, because his threat would become a reality within the next few days. The punishment I got for biting Armen was going to last me a lifetime.

A few days later, I overheard a very strange conversation between Armen and my mother; they were discussing my teeth and how bad they were. He told her that because I hadn't brushed them for over two years, he was afraid that after I bit him, he would get an infection. I thought he was exaggerating about that because I didn't think I even punctured his skin at all. Either way, it was just odd to hear him, out of everyone in the family, having such concern about my hygiene. He then went on to tell my mother that he noticed my bite was wrong and uneven, and offered to take me to the dentist to have it checked out. He said they'd take care of my cavities, too.

He was technically right about my mouth. I did have cavities and my bite was off; but the only time anyone would notice was if I flexed my lower jaw or opened my mouth wide while screaming in pain during the beatings. Otherwise, my jaw appeared to close properly and looked fine. He told my mother that my lower jaw stuck out too far and made me look like a monkey.

A week after this conversation between my mother and Armen, I got an unpleasant and unexpected surprise. Armen picked me up in his car without telling me why. My mother was the one who told me to go downstairs because Armen was taking me somewhere important, so I couldn't really disobey. I already guessed he was most likely taking me to the dentist to get checked, so there was no point arguing with him or my mother about it. After few minutes of driving, Armen broke the silence.

"Do you remember how hard you bit me on my leg?"

"Yes Uncle, I am very sorry. I was just trying to escape from the pain. I really didn't mean it, and I won't ever do that again. "He laughed for few seconds and then stayed quiet for the rest of our ride.

When we pulled into the parking lot, it looked like we were at a small private practice and not the regular children's clinic I had visited in the past. There was only one black car in front and I guessed it belonged to the dentist. I was getting anxious, but I knew that on the first visit, you usually just get an x-ray. That couldn't be too terrible.

When we walked inside, a middle aged well-kept man came out to greet us. He looked Armenian and almost reminded me of my dad. He and Uncle Armen shook hands and we all went into his examining room. The smell of different medicines made me feel like I was in the hospital again. The scary-looking metal machines that circled the room reminded me of the buzzing noises they make when the dentist drills children's teeth. I started to feel more nervous. The patient's chair was very old and looked super uncomfortable as it had more metal on it than material. It also looked very large, like it was only meant for an adult to sit in. There were a few windows on the wall in front of the chair, but they were all covered with dark-colored blinds. It was eerie and spooky.

Armen told me to get into the chair and to open my mouth for the doctor. I listened, but was already shaking. This was my first dentist visit in a very long time and the first without my dad. The dentist started to poke at my teeth one by on and shook his head.

He turned to Armen and said, "Her teeth are some of the worst I have seen in a long time, especially for someone as young as she is. Terrible!"

"Check her bite-down Doc, she looks ridiculous when her mouth is closed," Armen said, not listening to what the dentist just said.

"I see it. I see it. But that's not the main issue. All those cavities in her mouth are the real problem. Many of her baby teeth are rotting and will soon start to infect the new set that is growing in."

"I have an idea on how you can fix her bite-down," Armen said as he stepped toward us like he was a colleague. "Let's go into your office and discuss it."

The doctor put down the instruments and they left the room together. I don't know exactly how long they were gone, but it felt like forever and it was certainly enough time for me to get more edgy and tense. A moment later, they came back in and the doctor started to get out a different set of instruments. I was starting to freak out, and could feel panic setting in.

Before I could ask the doctor about what he was doing, Armen said in a very sarcastic way, "After today you will look better and you will feel better, too!"

A thought rushed into my mind. I wondered if this procedure had something to do with the threats Armen hurled at me. I decided to ask the doctor myself.

"Excuse me. What exactly are you planning to do? Don't you have to do X-rays to see which teeth are bad?" I asked him politely.

"We have to correct the way you bite down, and for that we need to pull out a few of your teeth." he said calmly, though I wasn't convinced by the tone of his voice. I wish I could have seen his full face to read his expression better, but he had a mask on already.

"Pull my teeth? Why? The only bad ones I have are the baby teeth and they are falling out one by one anyway. Please don't hurt me!" I said back to him nervously and sat right up in the chair.

"We have to pull some of the permanent teeth to make your jaws close correctly," he answered as he prepared a needle to inject my gums with a pain killer.

"But I can close my mouth perfectly, doctor. Look! Look!" I pointed at my mouth and showed him how my teeth were fine. "I won't bite on them wrong ever again, I promise!"

For a moment it appeared my pleas might be working, and the doctor hesitated then looked over at Armen.

"Are you sure you don't want me to just grind down her canines? She will be all set with her bite-down," the doctor asked him quickly.

"No. Just do what we agreed to and she will be fine," Armen responded. "She needs to learn how to listen to adults."

After that moment, everything happened quickly like you would see in a vivid nightmare or a horror movie. The doctor stuck me with the needle and I felt my gums fill up with the sour medicine which was also dripping onto my tongue. Then he stuck the needle directly into my hard palate. That hurt so bad that I started to fidget around and closed my mouth. The doctor got nervous and instructed Armen to hold my forehead to stop me from moving.

When that didn't help, Armen said, "Doc, go ahead and put the metal mouth prop in. That's the only way we we're going to be able to keep her mouth open."

The dentist grabbed the steel device from the drawer next to him and stuck it into my mouth. It was big, painful and uncomfortable, like it was meant to be used on an adult, not on a child. Then the doctor finished giving me the rest of the shots under my tongue and all over the inside of my gums. He wiped the sweat from his forehead and stormed out of the room like he was aggravated and annoyed by what he was doing. Armen chased after him, and I was left there sitting alone in that uncomfortable chair with the metal device protruding from my mouth.

Before I was even able to catch my breath and calm down a bit, they both came back. The medicine had not even started working yet and the only things that were numb so far were my tongue and lips. The large metal surgical device was hurting my jaw more and more and saliva was dripping out of my mouth. I couldn't even swallow because of that terrible thing. I felt like a lab animal that was being used for tests. Yet again, I was helpless and alone.

The doctor grabbed his forceps off of the table and looked at Armen like he was signaling him to do something. A second later I felt a strong arm grab my forehead and press it down into the chair.

The next thing I felt was the dentist opening up the gums around my teeth. The medicine wasn't blocking the sensation and I could feel every single movement he was making.

Armen held me down as firmly as he could as the doctor pulled out my teeth, one after another. The taste of blood filled my mouth and mixed with saliva and the medicine. I started to cough and choke but it seemed to me that they didn't care. After a few minutes, the doctor stuffed cotton rolls into my mouth and that made it even harder for me to breath. I thought I was going to die right then and there. I became light-headed and I was overcome with crazy thoughts like they were purposely trying to kill me using this teeth-pulling as their excuse.

The doctor pulled two teeth from each side of my mouth from both the upper and the lower jaws. By then I had just given into the pain and stopped fighting them. I moaned and sat lifelessly in that chair.

I felt like I was dying and it felt like less and less oxygen was reaching my lungs. If I died at that moment, I wouldn't even have cared, because it didn't seem like my life could get any worse, other than maybe living with the memories of this horror for the rest of my life.

When I thought I couldn't handle any more pain and couldn't really breathe, something strange and bizarre happened. All of a sudden, all the pain stopped. I also stopped moaning and I felt like I had physically separated from my body. It was a very odd and scary feeling. Within seconds I somehow sensed I was floating above the dentist's chair, looking down at my own body and both of those monsters standing over it. I actually saw myself lying there with Armen holding my forehead down and the dentist pulling my teeth and placing them next to him on a blue piece of plastic. My physical body wasn't moving or making any sounds. It looked like another strange scene from a scary movie, but this time a more familiar little girl was being tortured in a very brutal way.

I felt light and free and I believed I was able to fly away at that exact moment without being hurt or held back. But at the same time, watching this brutal torture of my own body stopped me from leaving. It felt like if I was going to leave at that moment, I was somehow betraying my body and leaving it behind in brutal agony.

The moment the doctor was done, he removed the metal device from my mouth and Armen let go of my head.

"Bite down on all this cotton, now," I heard the doctor say, but my physical body didn't respond. A moment later, something that I couldn't control started to pull me back down and into my body.

That's when I started to cough up blood and gasp for air while making awful loud and scary sounds. My whole body was shaking. The agonizing pain took over again. I was back. My soul, which had been free just a moment earlier, had made the difficult decision to stay.

I saw blood everywhere, even on the dentist's face mask. At least now the medicine was finally working, even if it was too late, and it dulled some of the pain. I was in complete shock and I was breathing heavily and fast. The doctor wiped the sweat off of his forehead and looked down at the teeth he had just pulled. Then he looked up at Armen.

"I hope you understand that this was unnecessary."

"No Doc, you helped her to look normal."

"Buddy, those were her permanent molars and she won't have anything back there to chew food with now or for the rest of her life. That will likely cause her to use her other teeth which will wear them out faster and eventually break. The front teeth are not meant for chewing like that." I could tell from the tone of his voice that he was regretting his actions.

"She is fine, doc! At least she will think twice before biting someone again," Armen said sarcastically.

I looked down and saw eight perfectly white teeth laid out lifelessly on the blue paper. I looked up at the doctor with pain in my eyes and covered my face with my hands. Big tears started to flow down my face and I felt an emotional pain somewhere deep above my belly.

The doctor walked out of the room and slammed the door without even saying goodbye to us. Armen told me to get up and get in the car. I felt lightheaded but listened to him, and slowly walked out of that office and out of the building.

On the ride back home, Armen blasted the radio and sang along happily despite what had just transpired. When we got home, he told me not to eat anything for the rest of the day and told my mother that he was in a rush. She never even asked him what was done to me and why I came home in the condition I was in.

I hadn't eaten since early that morning, but food was the last thing on my mind. All I could think about was why this monster didn't get terminally ill, or why someone didn't just kill him. If there was a God, why was he allowing this man to harm me? I was just a little girl. Why wasn't God protecting me from this demon and from all the pain he inflicted day after day.

The next day Armen came over to have dinner with my parents. I overheard him telling them that the dentist said there was no other choice but to pull out all eight molars, to correct the way I was closing my jaw. My dad wasn't too happy with that explanation and questioned him, but Armen told him that his dentist-friend had been in practice for over twenty years and he knew better than anyone.

I stayed in the living room laying on the sofa for almost two days without eating a thing. All I did was drink a little water from the faucet whenever I went to the bathroom. I had lots of time to think about what happened and no matter what scenario or reason I came up with, nothing made sense. I had never heard of anything like this happening to a child before. The only time I read about these types of tortures was in those heartbreaking books about the Jewish and Armenian genocides, when their enemies kept their gold fillings.

What happened that day made me feel like I was a worthless piece of garbage at best. I became even more distant from everyone except my grandpa. It had also become more difficult to keep my pain hidden from him, but I had to. I didn't want him to be stressed nor did I want him to stop talking to my parents either. I started to spend much more time at his house and made sure that I was home as little as possible.

Meanwhile, I noticed that many of my physical punishments were going away and were being replaced by emotional and verbal ones. It was mostly my mother who took on the practice of this type of abuse. She would attempt to hurt me by exploiting the most insecure areas of my mind and my body. She knew what would affect me the most and she used it to inflict her own style of abuse.

It began when she put me down and compared me to my brother. She would call Tigran and me into the kitchen and tell us to stand across from each other, or next to one another. It didn't matter.

"Go ahead Tiko, show Vera your beautiful long fingers, your long neck, straight legs, smooth shoulders and thick black hair. Put your index fingers together to show her how straight they are!"

My brother, still naive, would follow her instructions not knowing what a big impact it was having on me. I also think he was afraid, like I was of our mother and Armen, but he didn't show it as much. He wasn't stupid and was well-aware of what I had been going through.

Then she would say, "Now look at him, Vera. Do you see how beautiful he is compared to you? Do you see how straight and long his fingers are, unlike your short and curved ones? Just look at his long, straight legs that look like bottles. THAT is how women's legs should look! They are perfect, with the calf muscles touching each other. His are just like mine; but not yours! You look like you've been riding a horse for the past two years; plus you don't have a neck. There's hair all over your body and you have a big round face with a short forehead, which means by the way, that you aren't too smart. You have a terrible manly body type. I feel bad for you because you definitely inherited that from your father. It's OK for a man to look like that; but NOT for a woman."

At that point I would usually just run into the living room and cry. I knew I couldn't change the way I looked, no matter how much I hated my body or the different parts of it. I didn't understand yet that it would all change as I grew older.

She often liked to tell me that her blood was "blue" and her relatives were descendants of the Counts, who a few centuries earlier sat next to the king and queen. She would brag about it constantly. She would also point out how beautiful all the other girls my age were, including the pampered young female actresses on TV.

After she was through attacking my physical flaws, she would jump on the perceived negative things in my personality and focus on how bad I was as a person.

"You definitely took after your father and his mother or maybe one of his sisters when it comes to your manners and character. You are useless and stupid as well as selfish and lazy. Oh and you can't even get a single "A" in school."

My dad didn't like her putting me down like that; but he wasn't around much and he didn't really know how badly she would ride me. When he was home and she would start up with that type of verbal abuse, he would cut her off.

"Well, maybe some of those physical characteristics are true because she does look just like me, but that doesn't mean it's a bad thing! It's not known yet if our son's feminine features are a good thing or a bad thing, so we shouldn't talk about the physical appearances of our kids at such a young age. They are too little for us to tell what they will look like later on in life."

At that point my mother would usually stop. It seemed like she was overpowered by my dad's quick and sharp answers to her negativity. It didn't take him long to come up with some truthful and humorous barbs of his own.

"At least, among all the other great things she inherited from me, is the most important one: her brains and how smart she is!" I used to smile at that and my dad would wink back at me.

Although he and my mother never told me that they loved me, I could say for sure that I was loved by my dad and I always loved him. How could I not, when this man's job was to save peoples' lives every day? I know he didn't have much time for me and let Armen get away with terrible and brutal things. I know he also gave me beatings with his belt under pressure from my mother; (He wasn't around much and didn't know about the worst things Armen was doing.), but at least he was out helping others day and night in any weather and under any conditions. I admired him for that! I also felt bad for him. He worked so many hours every week and then had to do stuff around the house. When I wasn't around, he went shopping for the groceries. Even when he had free time, which was a rare phenomenon, he would spend it with my brother and would take him out to the park for some fresh air. He was simply always doing something for someone, somewhere.

Things for me continued to worsen. The only things that were getting better and stronger were my anger and my aggressiveness toward almost everyone around me. I was miserable and unhappy and I disliked people of every age.

I was turning into a terrible and rude human being, and I knew it, but I couldn't help it. I didn't try to stop or change the negative world I was stuck in, but at least I understood that it wasn't a good thing for me to be part of it.

Occasionally there were small things that happened in my life that were positive and heartwarming. For example, there were times when I didn't mind staying home, such as when my parents had two of my dad's friends, Hachik and Sergey, over to visit.
They would come over once every few Saturday nights to play cards when my dad wasn't working. Sometimes they would play from seven in the evening until one or two the next morning. I liked that because my brother and I could watch TV in the living room and stay up late. Armen never came when they were in the house.

My brother cherished those evenings even more than I did, because he hadn't been seeing me as much lately. Armen's sadistic punishments and abusive ways took a toll on me personally, and I think it also helped separate Tigran and I in many ways. Of course there were still many good moments and days that kept our bond strong.

It seemed to me that when everything looked the darkest and the most hopeless, something bright and good would happen to make me realize that positive and hopeful things were still possible in my life. It kept a slight glimmer of hope alive deep in my heart for better days and it made me smile at the simplest things I felt or saw. I think I was always able to see these slivers of positive light because I was always looking for them.

In December of 1993, my parents opened a beauty salon which offered different services to their customers -- from facials to machines that did different kinds of body massages — everything to

210

keep people looking beautiful and young. I was extremely happy because my mother was now rarely home and I surely didn't mind that. It also looked like they were bringing in more money and our fridge was always half full, which was a great thing compared to the last few years when it was almost always empty. My dad only worked his 24 hour shifts at the ER and stopped taking on extra hours even though they were available. My mother only taught music to the minimum that was required by the school and started to spend mornings and weekends at her salon.

I remember starting to see new and yummy things show up on our kitchen table, but of course I wasn't always allowed to taste them. There were times when my mother let me try some things here and there, but I would have had to be a very good girl for a few days prior to that and have only "A's" and "B's" for a few weeks straight.

I will never forget the day my dad brought home what I thought was a Snickers Bar. At first I noticed it looked a little strange, but then I realized that it wasn't a candy bar at all; it had ice cream inside of it. My brother and I were so excited we couldn't wait to try it. My dad grabbed the knife and cut it into four pieces. Of course I was given the smallest piece which was probably not more than an inch wide, but I will never forget how good it tasted. That was just one of the many new yummies that my dad surprised us with. As we started to have more money, the fridge became fuller and fuller.

There wasn't much making me happy back in those days and it felt like I was only existing, and not actually living. The only times when I felt that my life was worth more than usual was when my grandpa came by to pick me up and we would go off and do things together. We might walk to the Black Sea, go shopping, or even do some fishing together from the seaport's shore. He would always catch a cool-looking fish and then his mom would cook it for us later on in the day. I would sit and watch her clean it, dip it into egg and flour and then fry it in a scalding hot pan.

The week before I turned fourteen, I received a pleasant surprise that made me feel like a normal kid for a change. One night, when I was home alone, the doorbell rang. I went to open it and when I looked through the peep hole, I saw the miniature white face of a little baby kitten. I opened the door as fast as I could, in complete disbelief, and saw my mother, with my brother standing next to her, holding a cute Persian baby kitten in her palms. He must have been at most three weeks old, but he already had long and fluffy fur. He looked like a doll and just stared at me. I grabbed him right out of her hands and kissed his little head and face all over.

I have never seen anything that cute in my entire life. His name was Bormon and he came with his own passport; even I didn't have one yet! His passport listed three generations of relatives from both sides of his family to show that he was purebred. Bormon's family came from Germany and his name was given to him at birth. My mother didn't like the name so we just called him Brulik, which is short for "brilliant." The name was perfect for him, because he was not just a regular cat. He acted like a human being who was stuck in a cat's body. He was as smart as any adult that I knew and he had better manners than most of the people in my circle.

Brulik loved me the most, and almost never left my side. He would sleep with me on the sofa for the whole night. He would lie on top of my fresh wounds after my beatings. He would not eat his food unless he saw me in the kitchen eating mine. We were the best of friends. I took care of him as much as I could. He became like a second son.

Although my birthday wasn't something I always looked forward to, getting a little family kitten for the house was the best present I could have asked for. Things seemed to be looking up.

That summer was the first one I remembered that we had more food than we needed. I couldn't eat anything sweet or expensive when I was in trouble, but I was allowed to eat specific portions of regular food. I felt like we actually had much more then we needed and it started to bother me deeply. That is when I decided that it was time for me to keep my promise I had made a few years ago to those poor, elderly people.

Every time I was home alone, I would take small amounts of food from the fridge and bring it over to the poor people begging at the churches. Doing that made me feel like I was still worth something to others and to life in general. It made me feel like I was useful and like I was fulfilling some specific purpose that I was meant for. I started to believe that the reason I had survived was to help others: those in need. Also, I wanted to always keep my promises.

When I brought the food to the same church where I had begged before, there was no one there whom I recognized. I hoped they had gotten money somewhere else, or maybe their relatives and children had finally decided to help them out. Still, I gave what I had to the people who were there. They were all hungry and thankful.

In the beginning my mother didn't realize that food was missing, because I was taking such small portions, but that changed as the weeks went on. Each time I went, it seemed like I was seeing more and more hungry or homeless people than before. I started to take more and more food from the house, although I always left plenty for our family.

I don't know how, but my mother noticed that something was going on. She asked me where all the food was going, to which I usually answered that I ate it. But then she realized that I couldn't possibly be eating that much food every day, so she started to keep careful track of everything we bought.

By the end of that same summer, she had enough evidence of missing food that she asked Armen to step in. And as always, the only way he knew how to communicate was with physical abuse. He simply beat me with the whip and didn't even care to know what I had to say about it.

That day was the first time I had ever run away from home. I went to my grandfather's which was the only place I felt safe and I stayed there for the rest of that night.

I didn't tell him why I came over but he knew that something was wrong just from the way I was acting. I wished I could have told him everything I was going through, but I didn't feel that it was the right time. Maybe one day I would.

* * *

When the new school year started, my baby brother went into first grade. He was actually accepted into a special school for very smart kids, but my parents decided not to enroll him there because they couldn't commit to bringing him or picking him up every day. I thought it was quite sad and I believed that they should have found a way, because I firmly believed that's what dedicated parents are supposed to do. I was proud of him and I felt that I did a good job teaching him different things that made him be accepted there.

He ended up going to school number eight, which was the same school where I spent the first three quarters of the fourth grade. I was still in school number seven but I wasn't worried about him being there alone; he fit right in quite well. He was very well dressed, well-kept, and well fed, so I knew that the kids there would accept him without a problem.

On the first day, he was so handsome and so excited that he smiled the whole morning. He had a new outfit, a brand new backpack and nicely combed hair. I hugged and kissed him, but inside I felt like he was now all grown up and didn't need me anymore. It was a very unusual feeling, but I did my best not to show any emotion. From that day on, I helped him with his homework and projects, and always found the time even when I was busy with my own duties, school, or activities.

Meanwhile, because of all the food I was taking from the house, I earned a new nickname from my mother. It was "thief." She used it every time something wasn't in its place. I finally decided to tell her why and where I was taking the food, but she just got mad and called me all kinds of terrible things. She even threatened me with an extra visit from Armen. From then on, she kept the stock of food in our house to an absolute minimum.

I had to think of something else. I couldn't let those people go completely hungry especially after they were now counting on me. I knew how it really felt not be able to eat anything normal for days at a time. I was sure they were waiting for me to bring something, so I just couldn't stop now. If I could get even a simple loaf of bread it would feed a few people.

Since my parents' business was booming, there was always a little extra cash around the house. I knew that it was really a terrible thing to do and that I could get badly punished if anyone found out, but I still decided to go for it. The thought of hungry people waiting for me and hoping for food overpowered my fear. At the end of November, for the first time in my life, I took money from my mother without asking for it. I felt terrible doing it, but we had so much of it just sitting there while those homeless people had nothing. They didn't even have a stale piece of bread to feed their kids.

From that day on I didn't take any more food; I took only money. I would purchase the most important things, like loaves of bread, milk, cooked chicken, and water. Sometimes I bought chocolate bars because there were a few homeless families who had children of different ages with them.

I didn't get caught for many months, probably because I only needed a little bit of money to buy vital things. I knew I was doing something really bad and that I shouldn't take my parents money at all; but I always found some way to justify it in my mind.

At times I believed that some of that money was rightfully mine because I still wasn't getting supplies or new clothes from them like other teenagers were getting from their parents. Even when my parents brought something rare and yummy home, like pineapples, kiwi, or bananas, I would rarely be allowed to have any. Not being able to eat was a punishment which I was happy to endure compared to the other types of physical discipline I lived through.

Feeling guilty or not, I estimate that I must have fed several hundred people of all ages that year. I even compared myself to my dad, and felt that we were very similar in what we were doing. While he was saving peoples 'physical lives, I was doing the same except I was feeding them. I never got into trouble from him for taking food, but I was sure he would be very upset and angry if he learned that I took the money.

It still felt right to me, but I decided to tell my grandpa about what I was doing. I just needed to hear his opinion and what he would do because I didn't want to get in too much trouble when the truth came out. I was comfortable telling him pretty much anything, even bad things that I did. I was sure that he would somehow understand me, because when I used to tell him that I helped older neighbors, he would hug me and say, "Sweetie, all the good deeds you do will one day come back to you. Something great always happens to kind and generous people. It's a simple circle of life."

He was right because on February 8th, 1995, my life took an unexpected turn. That day was the beginning of one of the most important developments in my life, something that helped define my future. It was a day that gave me the happiest feeling I had ever felt, and the most terrible and heartbreaking one both within a couple of hours of each other.

The night before, my parents had company over to visit and we had lots of leftovers all jammed into our medium-sized fridge. I didn't want it to go to waste, so I grabbed a few plates and decided to bring it to the homeless. Unlike previous trips, something made me go outside my usual route. I took a more direct bus to a different area which was about twenty miles away from my home. I knew that there was a bazaar at which many refugees from nearby countries like Georgia and Abkhazia were selling fruit and vegetables, which they struggled to obtain elsewhere. I also knew that those people were very poor and sometimes two more families lived together in small rooms and apartments.

When I arrived, I saw about fifty to sixty people, mostly middle-aged women, selling different greens, vegetables, fruit, and even homemade pastry. They were screaming different advertisements out loud about the low prices of their product. They had tables set up in front of and next to each another, and were right in front of a small supermarket which appeared to be open only until late afternoon. Each of their tables was not more than three feet long and four feet high. We had a few of these bazaars throughout our city with the main one in the city center, but this one was very small compared to them.

I noticed about a dozen small children playing in a big puddle which was half water and half ice. I figured they were the children of the people selling in the bazaar and the parents were trying to make a little bit of money to feed their families.

I came right up to the kids and told them that I had some food. They were beyond happy and started to shout and clap their hands. I told them to make sure to share the food evenly among all of them. My heart filled with a painful yet fulfilling satisfaction, because I knew exactly how they felt at that moment. I knew the feeling of a hungry stomach. I knew the feeling in their thirsty, dry mouths. I knew the feeling of excitement when food was right there in front of you, ready to dig into it with your bare hands.

One little boy who was not more the three years of age, came up to me and said, "You didn't have to tell us to share our food. We aaaaaalways share it evenly with each other!" That made my eyes watery, and a few happy tears dripped down my cheeks as I unpacked my food containers right there on the ground.

It made me sick to my stomach to know that there are so many people who have so much money and food, yet don't bother sharing it with others. They probably just throw the leftovers right into the garbage can. Yet this little boy, who was not more than three, already knew that food should be shared with others who are also hungry.

With everything unwrapped, the oldest boy who was probably around my age, looked up and said, "Don't worry. I will make sure it's all divided evenly. I always do. We have a good teacher here, who taught us how to be good human beings."

I didn't say anything and just stared while my heart filled with a powerful but strange, warm feeling of pleasure. I was so amazed with the whole scene that I became speechless. I realized that I was with a group of people and kids who were the same as I was. I felt remarkably comfortable and not out of place here. There was just something so unique about.

A moment later the same boy shouted out, "Look she is coming! She is coming! Come here Asmat, have some yummies!"

I immediately turned to see who he was talking about, and I saw a pretty girl with very long hair and an amazingly smooth style of walking, approach our circle. She resembled me in some ways and she was close to my age. She had a smile painted across her face, and her long brown hair, that hung well below her waistline, waved in the cold wind.

"Hi there, my name is Asmat. What is your name?" she asked with a thick accent while looking up and down at me. "My name is Veronika, but you can just call me Vera like everyone else does." I smiled without realizing I was doing it.

"If your name is Veronika, then I will call you Veronika. Why would I call you some other name?"

"OK, you can call me by my full name. You will be the only one to do that."

"You brought these kids some food I see. That is very nice of you. You look like you are not from a wealthy family though, so what is your story?" She glanced down at my old clothes and the plastic bags protruding from the holes in my boots.

"I'm actually not from a poor family, at least not anymore. My mother doesn't buy me much stuff because I always misbehave. We had lots of leftover food from yesterday's party, so I wanted to bring it to someone who was hungry and could use it. I usually don't go this far away from the center of the city, but something told me I should come here today."

"Well it must have been meant to be, because I was thinking this morning about what a nice blessing it would be to have some homemade food for these children. None of them have had anything tasty to eat since New Year's Eve over a month ago, so I am very happy that you have blessed them with your presence. We are all refuges from Abkhazia, but we are Georgian-Christians. There is a war there, and many people are dying, but some families were able to escape and come here to Sochi which is the nearest city to our border."

I had heard on the news about the different wars that were going on in nearby countries and I had seen quite a few refugees in the city over the past few years. I had never talked to any refugees: until now.

"Wow! I am so sorry you had to leave your homes and come to our country. I don't know if I would be able to leave my country. It sounds scary."

"You do what you have to do, when you have to do it, to stay alive." Her smile slowly returned to her face.

"Trust me Asmat, I do know how that feels."

Asmat reached out her right hand and extending it to me she said, "So Veronika, do you want to be my friend?"

"Yes definitely Asmat! I don't have any close girlfriends, so you can be one."

We shook hands and gave each other a hug. She invited me to go with her to meet her mother and her brother. She grabbed my hand and pulled me toward the stand where her mother worked.. It was getting dark, but I was happy to go with her.

"I want you to meet my mom," she said as we approached a skinny woman in her early forties who wore a thick winter jacket with an apron right over the top of it. "Mom, this is Veronika, the girl who brought lots of food for the children today."

"Hello Veronika! Call me Mama," she answered with the same thick accent as Asmat. She smiled as she shook my hand. "Do you want something to eat? I have some vegetables over here, or you can go trade mine with the lady at the other end of the row who is selling fruit." She pointed to some nicely displayed greens that included parsley, kale, broccoli, and cabbage.

"No thank you, I am not hungry."

Although I was smiling on the outside, on the inside I wanted to cry. I didn't remember ever hearing my own mother being so caring and kind toward me.

"You didn't call me Mama. I told you that is the name I want you to call me," she said and laughed.

I looked at Asmat with questionable eyes. I was almost sure that I wouldn't be able to say "mama" to a lady I just met; not to mention the fact that the word mama is a more intimate and personal way of saying mom or mother. After a few seconds I decided to try and say it anyway. I wasn't the kind of girl who was afraid to simply say one word, was I?

"OK Mama, I am not hungry," I shouted out loudly in a brave, almost soldier-like tone. We all paused for a second and then laughed hard because I said it in such a robotic and serious way that it sounded like someone paid me to say it.

Calling another woman mama was much easier than I expected. I didn't feel bad or feel like I was betraying my own biological mother in any way; plus, this woman was making me feel so welcome and warm that I was surprisingly comfortable in her company.

"My son, Aslan, should be arriving here from work any minute," said Mama. "Hopefully you will get to meet him. He is a very good boy and super handsome!"

Time was passing and I needed to take the last direct bus to get home the fastest. As I helped them pack up for the night, I told them that I had to leave and I hugged them both. As soon as I turned to walk away, a boy appeared right in front of me. He was tall, very handsome, had thick black hair, and huge shining eyes. He had a big smile, too, and was staring right into my eyes.

"Asmat, who is this girl?" he asked his sister, careful not to move his eyes away from mine.

"It's my new best friend, Veronika!" she answered. "She is from the center of the city and from a good family."

"Is she? Well, that's good. She looks Armenian," he said to his sister. "Well! Are you?" he asked me.

"Yes I am," I answered but my eyes did not move away from his either, not even for a second.

It seemed as if no one was around us at that moment as the moon brightened his beautiful face. It was freezing outside, but I felt warm. It had become fully dark, yet I felt like we were standing in broad daylight. It felt like I had known him for many years, and that he was somehow my soulmate, the kind that I read about in different books. Maybe it was the way he was standing in front of me, or maybe it was because he was much taller and smiling, but it felt like I was looking at a Greek God from some ancient myth. I felt a strange and calming harmony fill me from within.

"Don't tell your parents you were here. I bet they will tell you not to talk to us. I know how those Armenian fathers are!"

"Yes, my dad doesn't let me be friends or talk to anyone who isn't Armenian, so I won't tell him."

I looked away and saw the big bright headlights of a bus approaching the bus stop. The bazaar was not more than fifty feet away from it. I didn't want to leave, but I knew that I had to.

"I have to run now, but I hope I can see you all again very soon," I said as I hugged Asmat and then Mama. I was too shy to hug Aslan, so I just waved goodbye to him. It was the first time I had ever stood so close to a boy. It made me feel all strange inside my belly, in a good way of course.

"We are here every single day, seven days a week until dark, so come next time and we will go to our house for dinner," Asmat said as I headed away.

As I ran toward the bus, I turned back to look at Aslan every few seconds. I hoped that every time I turned to look at him, he would still be there, watching me and he was. Even when I got on the bus, I noticed he was still looking my way.

All the way home I felt weightless and lightheaded. I knew about these types of things from books and movies, but I never really thought I would experience anything like that in real life. It was love at first sight, and I knew right then and there that it was a love that was meant to be. Maybe this was what made me go to that bazaar that day.

I could hardly wait for the next day when my grandpa was going to pick me up to go to visit my grandma at the cemetery. I couldn't wait to tell him all about the new family I met. He would be the perfect person to talk to about love and feelings because he knows how it feels. I also wanted to tell him how right he was when he told me that good deeds do pay off with blessings, sooner or later.

I was still happy when I arrived home. It was about eight in the evening which wasn't extremely late. My father was at work, Armen was away, and I knew that my mother wasn't going to get into any discussions with me.

As I bounded up the stairs and came to the door, I could hear my mother screaming and arguing with someone. I couldn't really make out what she was saying, but it was odd and alarming.

I rang the doorbell and even knocked but got no answer. I continued ringing and knocking until finally, a few minutes later, I heard my brother behind the door. He unlocked it and slowly opened it while holding a glass of water in his hand.

"Hello Vera, Mom is crying!" he said to me as he ran off toward the bedroom to bring the glass of water to her.

I got really scared, quickly locked the door, and kicked off my shoes. I had never heard her cry before, never mind this hysterically. As soon as she saw me, she hung up the phone and looked right into my eyes. Her face was bright red and her cheeks soaked in tears. Yet strangely, even that visual did not make me feel bad for her.

"What happened, mother?" She didn't answer me right away and just whimpered.

"Please tell me what's wrong. You are scaring me! Did I do something bad to make you cry?" I asked her again as she wiped the tears off of her face with both hands.

"About an hour ago a group of men wearing ski masks broke into grandpa's home. One locked his mother in the bathroom, but she is OK. Another beat up grandpa's sister who was visiting. She was injured and is in the emergency room, but is stable. Grandpa got hurt the worst. He was attacked by at least four men who beat him all over his body, breaking many bones and cracking his head open. He has internal bleeding and is in the ER now undergoing multiple surgeries. The doctors are saying that there is almost no chance that he will survive. He will likely die at any second, right on that operating table."

I froze in place. I did not say a thing. In an instant, the world as I knew it had come to an end. My hopes and dreams disappeared. I dropped to my knees and covered my face with my hands. It was over!

CHAPTER 11

11:11

I was not a religious person when I was growing up. I believed in God and went to church once in a while, but I never read the Bible. I was eleven years old when my brother was baptized at one of our local Christian churches, so my parents figured they might as well get me baptized at the same time.

I did wear a cross, but to pray meant that I would have to fully believe that God did exist. At that point, I highly doubted that, because I had seen way too many homeless and hungry people in my world. Through the abuse, I was more accustomed to finding my own ways to survive, but now I was completely powerless. I came to realize that praying was the only hope I had.

Here I was, on my knees for the first time in my life, asking God to let my grandfather stay with me and not die.

By some miracle, or because God heard my prayer, my grandpa made it through the surgery. He was still in critical condition, but he had already beaten the odds. He would live.

When I saw him in the hospital for the first time, my heart broke. He was unrecognizable and I was truly in shock at how badly they had beaten him. His body was wrapped in different ways and his whole head was swollen. He had stiches everywhere and his eyes had disappeared into his forehead because of the swelling. He was in so much pain that he could only utter agonizing moans. Here he was back in the war, fighting for his life.

I was so angry at whoever did this that I wished those animals harm, pain, death and even hell, and I was prepared to do those things to them myself. I held his hand and whispered to him so he would know I was there.

"Deda, I need you more than ever. You have to fight for yourself, for your mom, and for me. You have to fight the pain and think healthy thoughts so you will get better. You can't go away yet."

He barely moved his fingers but it was enough for me to see that he could hear me. I knew that he would fight and he would win — again!

The doctors said that he had to stay in the hospital for a few weeks until he fully recovered from the broken bones, the cracked skull, and all his other injuries. It was very hard on me because he wasn't just my grandfather, he was everything; my father, my mother, my grandpa, my friend, my teacher, my Guardian Angel and my only break from my abusers.

Even though I went to see my grandpa as much as possible, I also wanted to spend time with Aslan, my new one-and-only love. I went back to see him a week later. His family invited me to their home which made me feel even more connected. I couldn't remember the last time I was so excited about something. (Maybe it was when I saw my little kitty, but that was different.) I couldn't really explain why or how it was possible, I just felt like Asmat was my real sister and Mama was my real mom. I wondered if I could have been born into the wrong family. I met them at the bazaar and we all walked toward their apartment. Aslan was acting strange and almost looked uncomfortable.

"I hope you are not scared off by our apartment, because it's all we were able to afford to rent," he said breaking an uncomfortable silence.

"I don't care about the appearance of your place. I am not that kind of person," I said with a reassuring voice. I surely did know how it felt to be poor.

About ten minutes later we approached a very poor area of the city that I had never visited. The streets were lined with two and three-story high apartment houses.

Asmat pointed to the last door on the building. When we came up to it, I saw that their front door was at least eight feet up off of the ground with five large steps made of rotting wood that led up to it. She told me to step on them carefully and slowly. I went up the steps, one by one, and opened their front door.

Their whole apartment was not more than fifteen feet long and fifteen feet wide. In that small area it had a kitchen, living room, and a small bedroom that Asmat and her mom were sharing. None of that bothered me or made me feel uncomfortable. I still felt like I was in my own cozy home.

When everyone made it into the living room, we all started to laugh at the same time for no particular reason. It was as if we all understood how bad the place was and still found that funny for some strange reason.

To me, this family was simply perfect. I loved Asmat like she was my twin sister. I loved Mama like I should have loved my real mother. And when it came to Aslan, it was love at the first sight. We both assumed quickly that one day we would get married.

That evening, Mama prepared a meal with pasta and some birds that looked like they might be chickens. I was in heaven. I just couldn't wait to tell my grandpa all about these nice people and how happy I finally was.

When he came home from the hospital, he was still in bad shape and his bruises had not yet faded away. My great grandma and I took care of him and his wounds. There was nothing new for me to learn here. I had become quite good and efficient at tending to wounds. His mother spoon fed him every time he was hungry. I will never forget sitting on the floor in his bedroom watching them, and thinking to myself, "Here she is -- the perfect mother, selfless and devoted -- taking care of her baby boy with love and care just like she did seventy years ago when he was a little baby. She reminded me so much of me with my brother. I wish my mother was just a little bit like us."

Once my grandpa was able to talk, he was interviewed by the police, as was his sister and his mom. The police ended up catching the group responsible for what happened and charges were pressed. They assured my grandpa that they were all going to jail and what happened to him would not go unpunished. Come to find out, the same group of thugs had robbed and beaten up many others in Sochi and in nearby cities all in the past year and a half. Crimes like the crimes that they committed, were not a common thing in our area, so it was assumed that this group came from another city, further north.

The police told my grandpa that they had been looking for this group for a while, but were only able to catch them after their attack on him. I guess the design of my grandpa's apartment building provided police with many witnesses who saw the vehicle and offered other vital details. It was so sad to see him in this condition. Up until that attack, he was in amazing health, and now, he was totally consumed by his suffering.

A few months later, at the beginning of July, my grandpa was diagnosed with colon cancer. The doctors attributed the disease and other health issues he developed to the attack, saying that the stress on his body must have awakened all these other problems. They started him on chemotherapy and he was in and out of hospitals for weeks. They also had to perform different surgeries for all the different kinds of problems he developed, including glaucoma procedures in both of his eyes.

It was a very tough time for me and I was losing hope. I had graduated from school, but didn't even go to the prom and eventually just went by the school to pick up my diploma. It wasn't as if anyone was able to buy me a prom dress or new shoes anyway. The only time I felt good and alive was when I spent time with Asmat and Aslan, even if it was only for an hour or two.

When it came time to start my freshmen year at the music college, I was required to perform some very hard musical pieces before September and I should have been practicing for many hours each day all summer. Yet again, I just didn't feel like doing it and couldn't concentrate or play for even a few minutes.

At the beginning of August, when my grandpa had one of his surgeries and had to stay in the hospital for two weeks, something else happened that made me question my own humanity.

One afternoon when my dad was at work and my brother and I were home with my mother, she suddenly became really sick. My brother and I didn't expect it, because while we were playing in the living room, she was dancing in the kitchen to some concert music on TV. The next thing I knew, she was screaming for us to call Dad and to tell him to come and get her. Come to find out she had appendicitis and her appendix had ruptured. All that matter leaked into her abdomen, poisoning her from inside. She underwent emergency surgery and had to stay in the hospital for two weeks.

With both my mother and grandpa in the hospital at the same time, my dad had many responsibilities on his hands. He had to work, take care of the salon, check on my mother and my grandpa and had to watch over the two of us at home.

My brother went to visit our mom as often as our dad was able to bring him. I, on the other hand, refused to go. I couldn't explain why I couldn't bring myself to go to visit my own mother, but I just couldn't make myself do it. I don't know if I just didn't really care enough or because I knew that she would be fine.

I saw my grandpa almost every day, although I never liked the hospital's smell, which was always filled with different scents of medication. I overcame my aversion and went, just for him. Even he told me to go and visit my mother who was two buildings away, but I still didn't.

After about ten days of her hospitalization, she told my brother to relay a message from her to me. She said I was a terrible daughter. She also told him that everyone in the hospital was saying how unthankful and selfish I was and how egoistical it was for me not to visit my own mother when she was sick. I knew they wouldn't think that way if they knew what my mother had done to me and how badly she had betrayed me ever since my brother was born. My brother, being only seven and happy to play the role of the messenger, didn't understand her comments.

With my grandpa back from the hospital and seemingly doing well, I took some time for myself and tried to enjoy what little bit of summer was left. It felt good having him home, and I was able to go back to practicing piano for a few hours every day. I also felt better about spending more time with Aslan's family and building our connection even more.

Together, Aslan, Asmat and I went to the beach, to the city, to the parks, watched funny movies on TV, played bingo, read anecdotes to each other, and cooked meals. For the first time since I was seven years old, I felt like I was part of a happy and loving family. There was no one and nothing that would take this away from me, not this time.

Meanwhile I found out that Aslan and Asmat were both attending the choreography department at the same music college where I had been accepted. They were part of a dance group and were very good at it. They traveled all over the region to participate in different dancing competitions. They performed many different genres, from modern to traditional. It was wonderful. I was in heaven.

My life was changing for the better day after day, and month after month. At college, I found myself surrounded by mature and intelligent people who understood and appreciated the smaller things in life. There were musicians, singers, artists, choreographers, and music writers all under the same roof: an amazing mix of talented professionals. The college was actually in the process of being re-named from just a music college to The Sochi College of Arts and Music. That made more sense.

Because I was very talented and passionate about piano, I was accepted into both the classical and jazz departments. It was considered to be a double major. The workload I had to worry about was doubled, too. But it was all worth it, because I met so many talented people who breathe through their art and see the world in vivid and positive colors.

The college was always filled with different sounds coming from all kinds of instruments. Even if I was in a bad mood, as soon as I stepped into the building, my mood would brighten right up.

My homeroom, where I practiced piano, was on the fifth floor and I would hear all kinds of instruments on my way up there. It would definitely quiet down as it got later in the day, but there were a few students who took their passion seriously and practiced a lot more than was required. I was one of them and would stay at the college all day and into the early evening.

A couple of months into my first year I noticed another dedicated musician who was on the same floor as I was. This person was a violinist who also stayed late to practice a lot. Violin had always been my second favorite instrument, so I had to find out who was playing it. Whoever that was, I could tell that the person was devotedly perfecting a beautiful technique every day.

One evening, when I stayed at school longer than usual, I heard singing coming from the main concert hall. I went closer to hear the voice better, and when I got all the way up to the door, I couldn't believe how amazing it sounded. If I didn't know any better, I would think it was Mariah Carey. When she was finished singing, I quietly opened the door just so I could place a face with the voice. I couldn't see her very well, but I heard one of the teachers say, "OK Victoria, good job, see you tomorrow."

The next day I went to the vocal department to try and find this singing girl named Victoria, but had no luck. They said there was no one in the department with that name.

That same afternoon, while on my way to my homeroom, I heard that amazing violinist again. I recognized the sound right away. I was dying of curiosity, so I decided to knock on the door to see who the person was. A moment later, a girl opened the door with her violin in hand.

"Can I help you?" she asked me with a smile.

"Hi, sorry to bother you, but I just wanted to see who it was who was playing violin all the time after hours. My homeroom is down the hallway and I can hear you play."

"Oh are you the one who practices piano every day and late into the evening?" she replied with surprise.

"Yes, I'm' the one.

"That is amazing! I admire that! What is your name?"

"My name is Veronika, and yours?"

"I am Victoria."

"Victoria? Oh my God! Please tell me you also sing?"

"Yes I do! I sing mostly Mariah Carey's songs. She is my favorite."

I couldn't believe my eyes and ears. This girl was so talented and dedicated, not only with her musical instrument but also with her voice. In an instant I felt a special connection.

"You are absolutely amazing, Victoria. I heard you sing the other day and you sounded just as good as your idol."

"Oh, don't say that. I am not that good! I just love her singing and her voice! My mother is also a singer and my dad is a piano player, so I have a very musical family. I am self-taught."

From that day on, we became great friends. I saw her almost every day and we talked late into the afternoons when most of the other students were already gone. She was my first Russian friend and the only one that my dad approved of. After he met her, he said, "I am OK with your Russian friend Victoria ONLY because she has all "A's", sings, plays violin, dresses conservatively, and doesn't have a drop bit of makeup on her face."

Victoria, who was a little over a year older than I was, became like an older sister. She was someone I could always ask for advice, especially when it came to love. She understood everything about my situation with Aslan and the issues we would face; issues like his nationality, origins, and even the financial status of his family. She could relate to my feelings because she was also in love, ironically, with an Armenian boy and was up against the same roadblocks with his family. He was also in our college and played a saxophone very well. They were a very loving couple and saw each other almost every day, but he was an Armenian and she was Russian. His family only wanted him to marry an Armenian girl, so they were struggling as a couple, very similarly to Aslan and me.

Despite my difficult love situation, Victoria taught me many interesting and important things. One of them was the way I viewed love and the importance of it in my life.

"Veronika, when it comes to loving someone special or liking just a friend, there is one thing you have to remember: it does not matter what nationality that person is or how much money he has.

What is important is how you feel toward each other when you are together. It's important to have the same beliefs and values, the same goals, and the same mindset. The rest will fall into place and harmony will fill your life." I knew exactly what she was talking about but it didn't change the fact that my parents didn't think that way, especially my father, who was very old fashioned.

As time went on, my mother noticed that I was staying at the college much later then I had to and not coming home until late in the evening. Unfortunately for me, the music school she worked at was only fifty feet away from my college's main entrance. She started to take time off between her students and spy on me during the hours she was working, just to see why I was staying late and who was I hanging out with. After about three weeks, she found what she was looking for and reported it to my father. My dad didn't get too mad, but he did tell me that my mom constantly saw me talking to a boy outside of the college after hours. They both knew a few things about Aslan's family, but not about us being any more than just friends.

One Saturday Aslan and I planned our first-ever full day together, just for the two of us. We were going to walk the beach and talk about life and our future plans. I was beyond excited. My heart had been beating twice as fast from the moment I woke up.

I finished all of my household chores, helped my brother with his homework, practiced piano and got ready to go. I didn't want to lie to my dad and was hoping he wouldn't ask me about where I was going. I wasn't that lucky.

"Where are you going and with whom?" he asked.

"Dad, I am going out to walk by the beach."

"Walk with whom? I am asking again! Are they Armenian friends?"

"Dad, please don't ask me those things. I am almost sixteen."

"Tell me right now, or you are not going anywhere."

"No they aren't Armenian. They are Georgian."

"Did you say the Georgians? No you are NOT going any-where with them.

Dad, please! They are Christian just like we are. Please!"

"No! And that's it. You are staying home!" he screamed as he walked to the front door, securing both locks and the metal bolt.

I was so upset and angry. I started to cry and begged him to let me go, even if it was just for an hour. Nothing changed his mind! I knew it wasn't because they were poor, because my dad didn't come from money either. It was because they weren't of Armenian descent. Seeing that he was not going to change his mind got me very angry and something came over me. I shouted a very hurtful phrase at him that I did not mean to say at all.

"I HATE YOU!" I screamed in front of both my mother and brother. Then I ran into the living room slamming the door behind me.

I had no clue where that phrase came from or how I could consider being so disrespectful toward him. All I know is that I did not hate him by far, and now I was worried that he thought I really did.

Needless to say, he was shocked, angry and hurt. And so was my mother, who told him a few hours later that I deserved a beating for it.

The punishment I received for my insolence was far worse. My father chose to not speak to me at all for the next six months; exactly six: not a day less and not a day more. No word, no sound, no gesture: nothing. I must have apologized over a hundred times, tried to be home early almost every day, and kept the house spotless. But nothing I did could make him change his mind.

Not being able to talk to him was terrible. It was like losing the only ally I had in the house. I couldn't ask him a question, ask for a ride, or even ask for ice cream money. I learned my lesson the hard way about respecting people and adults.

Since I was an honor student, I was able to get a small monthly allowance from the college while my dad was ignoring me. It was a good thing they had that type of incentive for students who were able to earn high grades, or I would have had nothing.

When I told my grandpa about what I said to my dad, to my surprise he said that my father's punishment was way too harsh, and he should have given me another chance. After all, that was the first bad thing I had said to him in my entire life.

As my grandfather got a little better, he was able to sit at the table to eat and play backgammon with me. It was his favorite game, and he was the one who taught me how to play it when I was only five years old. I was actually super good at it and he lost to me as many times as I did to him.

With his condition somewhat improving, he was more talkative and in much less pain. He was home most of the time and was only able to sit outside in his garden for no more than an hour. He would just sit and watch me take care of the soil, trees, leaves, and collect the fruit. He was thankful that I still went to the cemetery on Sundays to clean up and to leave fresh flowers for his late wife, my grandma Veronika, although he felt terrible that I had to go there by myself.

On my fifteenth birthday, as usual, I celebrated it with him and a few other people and relatives that came over. He surprised me with something that he promised me a few years earlier.

After we were finished eating, he went into his room and came back with a jacket. At first I was confused because it looked too shiny to wear, but then I realized that it was his military jacket and it was shiny for a very good reason. The whole front of it was completely covered with medals, from one side to the other. I was mesmerized and captivated by it.

There must have been over two hundred different medals of all sizes, shapes, and colors on that jacket. There were so many medals that he ran out of space and had to attach some of them to a separate piece of material.

He held it up and looked at me with total pride. My emotions took over and my eyes became watery.

"Deda, this is unbelievable! You are so incredible, even more than I thought! How did you get all of these medals and why are they from all the different military branches?" I was fascinated and kept touching them all with both of my hands in honest disbelief.

"Well, before World War II started, I was chosen to go through a special training program and I was prepared to serve in all of the military branches. It was four years of training that covered: the Army, the Coast Guard, the Marines, the Airforce, and the Navy and all of the training was crammed into six months. Also I was trained and served in special forces, infantry, tankers, cavalry, scouts, machine gunners, snipers, artillery, pilot bombers, submarine bombers, ship bombers, and lots more," he answered as humbly as he could.

"You are a hero! I am so proud of you!" I told him as I unbuttoned the jacket to try it on.

"It's not a big deal. It was a war, and I am glad I was able to contribute as much as I did. Don't think you are that much different from me. You are just as great a fighter as I am. Trust me."

"What do you mean, Deda?"

"You have been in a long battle for many years. I am not stupid. I see things and I hear things. Even though you are keeping a lot of it from me, I still know that you have had a very hard time for a long while now. You might think that you wasted all that time, but I see it very differently."

"What can you possibly see in my life that is good? There hasn't been anything, other than pain and suffering, at least up until lately. Even with that, you were unexpectedly attacked, so yet again it all became quite bad.

"Sweetheart, you were at war. You survived it and now you are out of it. You can start living a better life, while always being prepared for the worst. Your sufferings were the learning curves that you, sadly, had to experience way too early. But at least now, you can use the strength you developed from enduring that pain to fight for what you want and what you believe in."

"I still don't see anything good in my life other than you, my new friends, and my brother."

"Trust me, there is a reason you survived. You have a real purpose in this world. We all do. Maybe I survived the war so I could be here for you when you need me for whatever reasons there are. Your suffering is there for a reason also; maybe it is so you can now help others who are struggling somewhere. You just have to find out what your life's purpose is and go after it. Your pain is not your curse; it's your blessing!"

"Deda, I don't really know yet what that purpose is, but I do know that I don't want any child of any age in any county to go through the torture that I went through. I wish I knew how to help them and to make them all see that their pain is only temporary."

"You know, even though your mother and I don't talk very much, one thing I am very thankful for is that she let our relationship exist and let me see you as much as I am able to."

I could see the happiness in his eyes, but although he was trying his best to stay at the table and talk to me as much as he could, I could also see he was tired and in pain. It was shameful to see someone like him go through a whole war fighting for our country and its people; to be uninjured on the battlefield only to be nearly killed by a few heartless jerks on his own soil and in his own home.

"Vera, what I want you to take away from this conversation is that I am counting on you to live your life with a purpose. One day, when you are older and wiser, you need to remember to help people, especially children, who spent their precious childhood years neglected by their families. Help those who have lost their last hope and who do not believe in better days any longer. You have to show them that they must stay strong and fight for their freedom and for their pain-free lives. Make them trust that they will find peace if they keep their hopes strong and their faith alive."

Those wise words of his, along with many others, are embedded in my mind. Many times I wrote his comments in my miniature diary and I would read them over and over to myself in the most difficult moments.

About a week later, he decided that when I turned seventeen and moved in with him, he would sell his condo and buy a bigger one that had a larger kitchen and three bedrooms, not just two like he had now. I really wanted to tell him about Aslan and his family, but I wasn't ready to do that just yet. I knew that I would need his support and help to make our relationship work, especially since I knew my parents would never agree or help me with it.

As time went on I visited him as much as I could, at least a few times every week. Some days he was OK and on other days he felt worse. He was staying in bed more and getting up much less. I went back to praying every day and I also started to visit a church on Sundays. I felt more connected and at peace there, and it helped being surrounded by other people who were there for the same reason I was.

I started to talk to my grandma at the cemetery when I went there to clean, usually right after church. Although some people who saw me might have thought I was crazy, I still talked to her picture on the gravestone and asked her to watch over her husband and to help him get better.

Nothing anyone did was really helping him very much, including my prayers or his medications. And it was taking a toll on me as well, really wearing me down. I was constantly sad, crying, or lost in deep thoughts. The only time I smiled was when I could visit with Aslan and Asmat.

Despite not feeling well, my grandpa still tried teaching me life lessons, and he talked to me every time I went over to see him. I loved just sitting next to him on his bed or even on the floor, just listening to his stories and all the things he wanted me to remember or learn.

There was one short, interesting story he told me that I will never forget. He said it took place in the Middle East a long time ago. It was a story about a spy who had been captured and sentenced to death by a general in the Persian Army. The General had been conducting a very powerful mind test with his prisoners. He would give them the opportunity to pick their punishment by giving them two choices. They could either choose to go in front of the firing squad, or they could choose to open and go through a small black door in the corner of a room on the first floor in that same building. He locked the spy in a cell alone and gave him time to think about it. He let him think it over through the night and was told he had to decide by the time the general returned the next morning. The next day, a few minutes before the execution, the general conducted his final interview with that spy.

"So, spy, which shall it be; the firing squad or the black door?" After taking another minute or so to think, the prisoner said, "I choose the firing squad."

A few minutes later, he was taken into the courtyard and a volley of shots was fired and the spy was killed. The General stared at his boots and then turned to his aide and said, "You see how it is with men; they will always prefer the known way, to the unknown, even if the known way means certain death. It is a characteristic of people to be afraid of the undefined and yet I gave him the choice."

"So please tell me, General," the aide asked, "I must know. What lies behind that black door?"

"Freedom and I've known only a few men brave enough to take it."

After a pause, and with my eyes opened wide, I asked, "Deda! This story is just so crazy! Why would that spy choose sure death versus the chance to live?"

"You see, sweetheart, it sounds to you like it is an easy choice, but it's not, especially if you are facing it like that. The reason I wanted to tell you about it is because that's what you are facing right now, in the next couple of years and most likely many times in the future," he said sadly.

"But I don't see any connection between the story and me, Deda!"

"OK, think of it this way. A majority of people will often choose the familiar things instead of the unknown, even if they are making a choice that they know will harm them. People are afraid to take chances, to try or to fight. People pass countless opportunities in their lives just because they are scared to make a move or do something out of character. There were many times when I was faced with hard and risky decisions, but I picked the unknown if the familiar sounded too dangerous. Do you know what? Every time I did that, something great came out of it. Pease use my experience to your advantage and believe what I am saying."

"But what am I supposed to choose between?"

"I think you know the answer. I think it's time for you to be brave and strong, to take chances in life and then see where it will take you. You stayed with your parents for many years despite the abuse. I know you were too young to run away and you didn't want to leave you baby brother behind. You chose the familiar and harmful, versus freedom, every time. Now you are not a little girl anymore and you are almost at the legal age.

Whether I am with you or not, you have to have a mindset of choosing freedom, if the other choice will harm you. Do you understand me?" he asked.

"I understand what you mean. What I don't like is you saying that you might not be with me, because that isn't an option. I'm not sure why you would even say such a thing."

"There is one last important thing today that I need you to remember. No matter what happens, you need to dream big, unrealistically big! Even if its sounds totally crazy to you, I need you to still dream it and visualize it. If you come across challenges on the way to your dreams, do not go around them. Do not try to skip or leave them for later. Face them, fight through them and win. Get to your goal no matter wha, and never lose hope or faith in a positive outcome. When you achieve it, move on to the next one."

"OK! "I've got it and you will be there by my side to see it all."

"Oh. There is one more thing that I completely forgot to mention. When you are dreaming and visualizing what you want, you should do it at a specific time of each day. That way, it will stick with you and you won't forget."

"Hmmm, well, every time I look at the clock, the TV, or the radio, it always seems to read 11:11. I see it a lot. I think I will pick that time in the morning and at night."

"Perfect! That's a great universal number. Start wishing for things as much as possible at 11:11, and don't give up, even if it takes years for the wishes to come true."

After I turned sixteen, many things were already going well and getting better in my life. I had developed great relationships in college and my grades were better than ever. I even substituted for my mother when she was sick, just like any other real teacher would. I was respected by other students and all the faculty members. My brother was now nine years old and he was becoming a very respectful young man, making me proud in many ways. I built a strong bond with Aslan and his family, and I even had my first kiss the day after my sixteenth birthday, and it felt so good and loving. Overall, I was feeling good and hopeful.

The only bad thing was that my grandpa still had cancer. I asked my dad on many occasions if he thought there was a way to get rid of grandpa's cancer, but he would just say that he and his doctors were trying their best. Needless to say, I never got a positive or optimistic answer. To me, my Deda looked worse and worse with every passing month. It seemed like my prayers were working just enough to keep him alive and not enough to get that disease out of his body. He was now seventy-one, which was still young in my mind, and I hoped he had at least another ten years to live.

When my freshman year in college was over, I proudly brought him my grades to show that I had earned all "A's" and "B's". He was very proud of me. He decided to tell me how sick he was feeling and he said that his colon cancer was really taking over. He even said that he had been seeing visions of his late wife. She told him that she loves him and misses him.

I never liked hearing that, and I always told him that he needs to stop thinking about the dead world. But I did see his face light up every time he talked about my grandma. I knew he still loved her but I needed him now much more than she did.

I decided to tell him what had been on my mind and share my life plan that both Aslan and I had developed. He had a right to know who I loved and who I wanted to spend my life with. I made him a hot tea and sat at the foot of his bed.

"Grandpa, you know I love you and will be moving in with you next year, right after I turn seventeen, right?"

"Yes sweetheart, I know and I can't wait. It will be fun."

"Well, there is someone I need to tell you about and that someone is a boy who I met couple of years ago. It was love at first sight. I am sorry I couldn't tell you before but no one, not even my parents, really knows the details."

"I am so happy for you. Feelings of true love are something rare that not everyone gets to experience, especially at such a young age. It's a rare phenomenon and some people go through their entire lives without it. I'm living proof of the existence of it, so I know how you feel. Bring him to meet me in a few weeks."

"Thank you so much! I KNEW you would understand! I just KNEW it!" I said with genuine joy. "But there is one important thing you should know, Deda. He is not Armenian. He is Georgian."

"Well who cares? Georgia is right next to Armenia and we are two very similar nationalities. True love doesn't pick with whom to bless itself. Did you know my brother married a Georgian girl, Auntie Tsiso? You met her many times and you liked her. She is simply an amazing wife and mother. As long as there is love, the rest will follow."

"But you know what my family will say. You know that my dad won't talk to me or come to my wedding."

"I know, but don't you worry about that. If he turns his back on you, I will walk you down the aisle in his place and will give you my blessing."

"I will definitely bring him in three weeks to meet you, just please try to get better. We have lots to do. I was even thinking that after we get married we could live with you while I try to get accepted medical school. As you know, although I love music, my true passion is biology and medicine. I really would love to be able to save peoples' lives just like my dad. My mom said that I am not smart enough for medical school, but I always got "A's" in all my science classes. I truly care about human beings, especially small children who are so helpless."

"Listen, you are stronger and more powerful than you might think. I don't know what exactly happened to you through the years because you hid it from me, but I know you have had a very hard life. Despite all that, you are still happy, laugh quite often, are helpful, kind, and generous. You have a strong will and want to help others. If you want to be a doctor, you will be a doctor! Only you, can stop you. All of your kind deeds affect people. You may not even see it or realize it, but even small acts can change someone's mood, belief or faith. It's a chain reaction. Don't you ever give up on your passionate desires! Never ever give up; that is something you have to stay true to and keep after!"

When he was done, I felt like a different person. He made me see that I am capable of bigger and better things. For the first time in my life, I had no doubts about the possibilities that my life could bring to me. I wanted to do great things and I knew that I was put through all the pain and suffering so I would know firsthand how it feels, how to live with it, and how to survive it.

Knowing that medical school was something that I would try to get into only after I finished at the music college, I decided not to waste time and do something else in the meantime. The very next day I signed up for more classes which I was going to attend in the evenings and on weekends. One of the classes was a law class called "Intellect" where different law professions were taught. I applied and was accepted that same day to start my freshman year in September.

I wanted to get a second degree as a lawyer. I wanted to be able to influence the judicial system, or at least have access to powerful people, and to make new laws that would be there to protect minors from abuse and neglect. I didn't want anyone to feel what I felt, year after year, physically and emotionally. I didn't want people trying to kill themselves, just like I did, because they couldn't deal with the mistreatment or because they lost their hope.

About three weeks later, on the last Wednesday in July, I decided to talk to Aslan and to invite him to meet my grandpa for the first time. After we spent most of the day together we went to the beach to talk and to stare at the beautiful and calming waters of the Black Sea. I told him about my conversation with grandpa and that grandpa wanted to meet him. He was super excited and we decided to meet the next morning to go there.

I was beyond happy and smiled all the way home. Other than my grandpa getting healthy and beating the cancer, this was my next best wish: Aslan in the same room with me and my Deda.

When I got home that night, no one was there. I didn't see any notes left on the door or under the doormat. I walked to the nearest payphone, only about five minutes from the building, and called my grandpa's house. My dad answered.

"Hello?"

"Hi Dad, do you know where Mom and Tigran are? No one is home and I can't get in"

"Vera, they are all here. Come here, Grandpa is not well"

"Oh. No! Please tell him I will be right there and see if he wants me to pick up some of his favorite fruit on my way."

"Don't pick up anything. Just get here right away."

After I hung up the phone, I knew that something was very wrong. I never ran so fast in my life.

When I got to his house, the front door was open and a bunch of people were standing in the hallway. I didn't even know most of them and was confused as to why they were all there.

My dad met me as soon as I arrived and grabbed my hand. He walked me into the living room and then towards my grandpa's bedroom. I didn't see my great grandma or my mom, but I think they were in a smaller bedroom next door because that door was closed.

"Vera, Grandpa got worse two days ago after you saw him last. He lost the first fight of his life, but he is now free of pain and cancer," he told me as we came up to the door of grandpa's bedroom.

I didn't say anything because it seemed like a bad dream or a cruel joke. I slowly walked into the bedroom and looked at the bed where my grandpa was lying. He was fully dressed in his favorite black suit and had black patent leather shoes on his feet. His hands were placed on his stomach and his eyes were fully closed. He had a smile and a very peaceful look on his face.

"Deda! Deda! Why are you lying in bed fully dressed?" I walked up to him and grasped his hand.

"Deda, Is this some kind of joke? Answer me! Please!"

I turned towards my dad and said, "What is this all about? Is this some kind of sick joke because it's not funny at all!"

My father didn't answer and instead just turned his head away as he stood in the bedroom doorway. I turned back to my grandpa and grabbed both of his hands.

"Deda! Wake up! Stop playing around like this! Get up now! You are scaring me! Open your eyes," I said as I became angry. Without getting any reaction from him, I moved very close to his face and started to shake his whole body to wake him up.

"You feel so cold, Deda! Stop pretending to sleep and get off your bed! I have something very important to tell you!" I put my left ear onto his chest.

"Deda, why is your heart not beating? I can't hear it at all! Why? Can you please get up? Dad, make him get up right now!" I screamed out loud as tears flowed uncontrollably from my eyes. I was too shocked to face the fact of what had happened, but I knew. I started to scream in hysterical ways and I shook him back and forth as hard as I could.

My dad pulled me away from the body. "Vera, stop it. He is OK now. He can't feel the pain anymore. Look at his face. He is smiling just like when I first found him. The pain is gone and he is now happy and in heaven, reunited with his loving wife. I know you want him to be happy, don't you?"

"He lied! He lied to me, Dad!" I screamed and dropped to the floor right by my father's feet. "He lied about everything! He told me that he would always be there for me. He said he would be there to witness all the important things in my life and he would help me every time I needed it. He said he would be by my side no matter what!"

My father pulled me up off of the floor and escorted me out of the bedroom. I was fighting him, trying to get out of his hands. Strangely, just now I noticed all the other people – about two dozen of them spread all over the place — crying, mourning, and talking.

My dad took me to the bathroom and splashed cold water on my face. "You have to be strong. It's hard on everyone here, so try to control yourself when you around our other relatives, please. He died yesterday morning but we didn't want to tell you until he was prepared and dressed. I knew you would take it hard, and we wanted him to look as good as he could for you."

"Dad, I am OK. I am calm now and I just want to go back there to sit near him again. I promise I will not scream," I said as I wiped my face with a towel.

"OK then. Go in, but close the door. I don't want people to get any more emotional than they already are. It's hard on me as well. People die all the time, but I took care of him for the past two years, almost every day," my dad said. I could see that his eyes were teary.

I went back to the bedroom, passing by dozens of people, but I did not look at any of them. I closed the door behind me and came up to his bed. He looked so peaceful and relieved. I knew that he was now gone forever and free. I fixed the laces on his shoes and sat on the floor right next to his bed, putting my face next to his body. My right hand was on top of his hands and I just started talking to him as if he were still alive and listening.

I sat there for at least an hour until my dad walked in and told me that I had to go home with my mom and my brother. I didn't want to leave, but my dad insisted and said that I would be able to say goodbye to him again the next day at the cemetery, before they closed the coffin.

The funeral was scheduled for the next day, not that it mattered much because I was not able to close my eyes that night even for a minute. To me it was like one long, horrific day that must have been the work of the devil. All I kept thinking about was that my grandpa knew he was going to die any day. He must have known it and that's why he said all those things to me.

When we got to the cemetery, the grave was already prepared right next to his late wife's. I was in a daze and walked around like a numb zombie. My brother was also sad and I saw him cry from time to time, but he was not as close to Grandpa as I was. He really had no clue as to what I felt inside.

My mother cried nonstop -- not loudly -- just to herself. I didn't even feel bad for her, and I actually thought of asking why she didn't keep a relationship with her own father for almost fifteen years, and then cry now that he had passed on.

When they pulled the coffin out of the car and placed it on chairs just a few feet away from the grave, my heart sank to the floor. I saw different people coming up and saying their goodbyes as well as kissing him on his forehead. There were hundreds of people there from all over the city and the region.

After about an hour, only our immediate family members were left to say their final goodbyes. I was the last one. I knew that as soon as I did it, they would close the coffin and I would never see his loving face again.

My dad took my hand and said, "You can now go to kiss him goodbye and say your last words."

When he said that, it set me off, and I ran up to the coffin as fast as I could like I was a wild animal.

"Deda! Get up! Please get up! It's not real! Please don't leave me," I screamed as I tried to climb inside the open coffin. "Please don't do this to me! I don't have anyone left! Please don't go! Don't leave me!"

It took four men to hold me down and push me away. As soon as I was a few feet away from the coffin, the cover closed shut and nails were hammered in quickly. Each sound of the hammer was going right through me and each stroke created more and more pain for me. The image of my angel, Deda, peacefully lying there with a smile, is my last visual memory of him.

The men held me down for several minutes, until the coffin was in the ground with lots of soil covering it. As soon as I was free, I started to run away from the funeral, and from everyone else. I didn't want to live anymore. I was done. It was over.

I ran like someone was trying to kill me. All of my dreams were shattered and all of my hopes were gone. I had a long way to go but I knew where I was going: the Black Sea.

Drowning was the only thing on my mind and I did not care about anyone or anything at that moment. I ran, then walked, and then I ran some more. It took me over two hours to get there, but I finally made it to the shore.

I went to that peaceful spot where Aslan and I had sat the day before. There were a dozen or so people scattered around the beach. No one would think much if they saw me swim out into the water.

I took off my shoes, looked up into the sky, and walked into the sea. It felt peaceful and I started to slowly swim away.

A few moments later, when I was about twenty feet away from the shore, I heard a very familiar voice. "Where are you going my Armenian princess? Swimming without me? That's not very nice," Aslan shouted sarcastically.

I couldn't believe my ears and I abruptly stopped swimming. I was angry that he had shown up there at that exact moment. I turned around and saw him spreading his hands apart in the air above his head. "What is that all about? Did you get tired of me or something?"

"I am sorry, I, I, I..." I screamed back but I didn't know what to say. I surely couldn't continue swimming away since I knew he was going to jump in at any moment and swim right after me. I waited a few more seconds and headed back toward the shore.

When I came out of the water, Aslan was looking at me in a very puzzled way. "Why did you go into the water fully dressed?"

"Aslan, I don't know what I was thinking or doing. I do know that you and I are doomed and nothing good is ever going to happen again."

"What's gotten into you? What are you talking about and why are you saying these things all of a sudden? Aren't we going to see your grandpa today? I was waiting for you to come and get me this morning but you never showed up!" He grabbed my face with his hands.

"He is dead! Aslan, he is gone! He died a couple of days ago! It's over."

"Oh! My God! I am so sorry sweetie! I am sooooo sorry." He hugged me tightly. "He is never gone though. It's just his body that has left us. He will always be by your side. He will watch over you for the rest of your life, just like he promised. I am sure of that."

That day on the beach, Aslan saved my life without even realizing it. I promised myself that it was the last time I would ever try to end my precious life again. It wasn't a fair thing to do, not when there are so many innocent people that are fighting to take one more breathe or live for just a few more minutes. I had to be strong and responsible not just for myself but for my brother, my love, and my future.

A little over a month later, I attended my first classes at the law school. I tried to balance my time and fit it into the second year of classes at the music college. It was not easy, but nothing was ever easy for me anyway. My grades were still all "A's" and "B's" and I kept myself focused by blocking everything out and concentrating on my future goals. I wanted to get these two professions completed and then get into medical school.

I visited the cemetery at least two or three times per week and talked to grandpa about all the things going on in my life. I also checked in on my great grandma at least once every week. She was still at their house and her daughter, my grandpa's sister, was watching after her. It was heartbreaking to watch her look for him around the house, calling his name. She would open the front door every hour while I was there and would shout, "Sergey, my son, where are you? Come home! Mommy made you dinner sweetheart!"

It was very sad, but I think it might have been the best way for her to cope with the loss. We all let her believe that he was around and let her call his name. We even let her ask us when we thought he would be home.

When I visited his home, everything reminded me of the great and amazing times we had together. I would think about all the irreplaceable knowledge and wise teachings he shared with me. It was a priceless treasure that I will cherish for the rest of my life and I will use it to help others.

Three months after my grandpa died, my dad found my great grandma in her bed. She had passed away in her sleep, which, in my mind, is the best way for someone to go. She didn't have any diseases or sicknesses and was as healthy as a young woman. The report, after her death, simply said that she died from OSA – Obstructive Sleep Apnea — but in parenthesis next to it, the doctor wrote, "died in her sleep from a broken heart."

As my seventeenth birthday approached, I started to spend even less time at home. I tried living my life doing what felt right because I promised my grandpa that I would. I was brave and I worked hard on building a strong future for myself.

Aslan and I decided that when I turned seventeen, I would leave my home and we would rent an apartment together. We were going to get married after we both graduated from college. I told him that I would like to give my parents one last chance to bless us and to help us. He didn't think that I could change their minds, but he told me it was OK and to go for it.

When I sat my parents down, along with my brother, I told them everything. I said that I loved Aslan and wanted to be with him.

I said that I really would love to get their blessing. I even said that grandpa promised to bless me even if they didn't; but Aslan was right and they were not going to change their minds. My dad was livid and told me that I was only allowed to marry an Armenian boy so that my children and his grandchildren had pure blood. He even said that if I disobeyed him, he would never talk to me again.

"Do you remember the wedding of your cousin, Lusine, who is in America right now?" my dad screamed out at me at the end.

"Yes I think so. Is she, the one who got married three years ago?"

"Yes that one! She married a very good Armenian man and do you remember the picture of his brothers that I showed you?"

"No dad, I don't. I was only thirteen and didn't pay any attention to those things. I don't even remember what they looked like."

"Well, you should really pick one of them to marry, not some poor Georgian boy who has no chance to ever give you a good life."

"Dad, I love him and he is who I want to be with. I'm sorry." I left the kitchen in a very sad state of mind. I wasn't surprised at their reaction. I realized that it was pointless to ask for their blessing but at least I gave them their chance to bless me. It was their loss; not mine.

***

About a week later, out of the blue, something very strange happened. My parents sat me down and said that they wanted to talk to me.

"We have discussed our last conversation in depth and have had second thoughts. Although it is not what we believe in, we will support your decision about that boy," my mother began in a calm voice.

I couldn't contain myself and was literally going to explode with excitement from such an unexpected blessing.

"But there is one thing we need you to do for us first" added my father in a serious manner.

"Of course, anything you want, anything at all!" I answered, almost jumping out of my chair.

"I need to go to America to visit my mother and my sister and I want you to come with me," he said with a smile.

"America? Oh My God! Wow! Yes of course! I would love to," I screamed out just like I had won the lottery. "How many days will we be gone, Dad?" I asked. I wanted to be sure I wouldn't be away from Aslan too long.

"Well, we have to first take a train to Moscow and go to the American embassy for our visas, and then as soon as you finish at the colleges in May, we can fly to New York."

"Wow! That sounds great! I can't believe I will be going to America! This is so unreal! I am so happy! Everything is coming to a happy ending for me in all the areas of my life!" I said out loud and ran out of the kitchen, grabbing the house phone to call Victoria, Asmat, and Aslan. I couldn't wait to tell them the great news.

A month later we took a train to Moscow and got our tourist's visas stamped into our international passports. I couldn't have wished for a better birthday present than this, especially since it was the first year that I had to celebrate without my grandfather. Ironically, Asmat's birthday was the same day as my grandpa's and her mom's was the day before. This seemed like a very strange but amazing coincidence.

A few days before I turned seventeen, my dad showed me our round trip tickets to the United States of America. They were real, and I couldn't believe that I was holding them in my hands. I was so fortunate to have an amazing opportunity like this and be able to see that country. I didn't really speak any English, but I studied hard to learn a few important words just before we flew out.

Our departure date was May 15th, 1998, a few days after the end of my sophomore year in both my colleges. I was on schedule to graduate from The Sochi College of Music in the year 2000 and the Law School in the year 2001. It was all going to work out perfectly because I wanted to get married in the new century as well as in the new millennium. I just always thought that it was breathtaking to be so lucky as to live in two different centuries and two different millenniums.

All the things I had been wishing for at 11:11 were starting to become a heavenly reality. It was all almost too good to be true. I was even becoming optimistic!

One day before our departure, my dad told me that our tickets had an issue with them and had to be changed a bit.

"Vera, there are no available flights back one week from now so I had to change our return date to three weeks from the departure," he said.

I became a little upset and I didn't feel like leaving anymore; but Aslan and his sister reminded me that it would be well worth it. Besides, for my dad to keep his word, I had to keep mine.

Though I was only leaving for three weeks, for some reason, it was hard for me to say goodbye not only to Aslan and his family, but also to my friend Victoria and my baby brother. He was ten years old and he had developed into a great young man. He was kind, helpful and always treated everyone with respect. He didn't want me to go either, but he knew that he couldn't do much about it. I think he was upset because he was now old enough to understand what role I had been playing in his life since the day he had been born.

My mother gave me only a small hand carry-on that was packed with one pair of underwear, one top, and one skirt. Even with me leaving for three weeks, I was stunned she couldn't find it in herself to buy me a few nice outfits so I would look presentable to my relatives in the U.S.

"They will buy you new clothes there. It's America! Everyone there is rich!" she insisted.

"OK mother, that's fine I guess. I suppose it doesn't really matter."

When we arrived at the train station, our train was already there but we had another half hour before it was scheduled to depart. Although I had been holding up OK up to that point, when I saw the train and all the other people saying their goodbyes, I became upset. Many sad and anxious thoughts rolled through my mind all at once. I realized no one was going to go to the cemetery and no one was going to watch after my brother or help him if he needed anything. I most likely wasn't going to be able to talk to Aslan over the phone either. Not to mention, I didn't even speak English.

Even though I was excited to go, I was really only going through this for one ultimate outcome: to be with the one I truly loved.

It was now time to board the train. I had to hug my mother who had not hugged me since I was seven. I did it, but I barely touched her body for that split second. I then had to hug my baby brother, who I hugged almost every single day for ten straight years. He was bawling his eyes out and would not let me go. It was a heartbreaking moment for both of us. It looked like one of those scenes from a book about the concentration camps in Germany and the mothers who were being separated from their children by the Nazi soldiers.

My dad told me that the train was leaving and we had to go. I forcefully pushed my brother away from me after giving him a dozen kisses all over his face and his hair.

We quickly went into the train and into our assigned cabin. There were four beds, two on each side, arranged in a bunk bed style. In the middle of the cabin and right in front of the large window there was a table attached to the floor. My dad told me to take the top bunk and I climbed up there and lay on my belly, so I was able see outside.

My brother was still crying and waving to me. My mother, who had showed no emotion just a few minutes before, had started to cry as well. It took me by surprise, since the last time I saw her cry was at grandpa's funeral. She wasn't the type to cry much. I was surprised by her reaction.

"Why are you crying mother?" I felt compelled to shout through the window. "I will be back in just three weeks!" I was quite sure that she could not hear me, and as I expected, she did not answer.

I really wished I knew why she was so upset because it made no sense to me at all. It was like the time she cried after her father died even though she hadn't talked to him for over fifteen years. Maybe it's possible that she felt bad for the way she treated him, and maybe also how she treated me. Maybe she had become accustomed to knowing that we were there in case she needed us, and now we would not be. Still it was suspicious and it bothered me.

The train gave a signal and moved forward. My tears flowed from my eyes uncontrollably. I tried to keep my eyes on my brother but I couldn't. A few seconds later, the station completely disappeared out of my view. All I could now see was full-green trees and the random houses built away from the center of the city.

My dad was silent. He sat and stared out the window from the bottom bunk. I wished I knew what he was thinking.

"Dad, why are you so quiet? Do you know why Mom was crying? It's not like I am leaving forever!"

He didn't answer me and I decided to leave him alone. I figured he was also quite anxious about going away for three weeks. It was a big, stressful trip for him, too.

Only after I asked him about my mother crying did I realize how sad that question really was. Any normal mother would cry if her child was leaving, but to me she was not my mother and was surely not normal. Such a simple explanation didn't even cross my mind.

Our train was skirting the coast of the Black Sea and I was still lying on my belly admiring Mother Nature's beauty. I felt lucky to behold it. Although it was already dark outside, the big moon brightened the night sky and bounced off the seawater like it was a mirror.

I pulled out my miniature diary and started to flip through it. Most of the pages were filled with the things my grandpa wanted me to remember. The entries were positive and full of hope for the future.

On a few of the pages, I noticed pictures of an eagle that I had drawn down in the corners. It was still a mystery to me what exactly my eagle was trying to tell me. Why hadn't he been back to visit these past few years? I never did figure out if he had come to help me die or to help me live. If he wanted me to die and be free, then why didn't he show up when I tried to overdose on the sleeping pills or drown myself in the Black Sea? Maybe he was there and I didn't see him or maybe he only showed up when there was no one else to help me. I hope one day that secret will be revealed, or maybe it doesn't matter. Yet, I still look for him to this day.

After reading through a few more pages, I again glanced through the window and out at the moon. It looked like a human face smiling down; maybe it was my grandpa still watching over me.

All the pain and suffering I endured, all the tears, all the screams, and all the times I wanted to die were behind me now. I was proud to call myself a true survivor who made it out alive and beat an extraordinary and unfair set of destiny's odds. The hands of the heartless and lost souls who tortured me for all those years were not going to touch me again. My little self, once buried deep inside, had survived a brutal siege — just as my grandfather once did with his comrades at Stalingrad — and won an epic battle.

The train started to curve inland, away from the shore. The tranquil sea was becoming smaller and smaller behind us, and the moon was disappearing far into the horizon. Soon, neither would be visible anymore. Exhausted, I rested my head on the pillow. My father was now asleep, and other then the rhythmic sound of the train hitting its rails, all was very quiet.

The train was taking me into the unknown, and I believed I was prepared for whatever adventure was coming my way. In ways that I could not yet hope to understand, this train was taking me through that secret black door my grandpa told me about in the story.

I didn't realize it at the time, and wouldn't for many years to come, but true to my grandfather's prophetic words, I would need to use every one of his lessons in the days, weeks, months and years that lay ahead of me. And I would need them to overcome deceptions, obstacles and heartbreaks so devastating that I couldn't yet begin to comprehend them.

I did not know that night that I had been betrayed yet again, and that I would never return home.

I did know that right now I had so much to live for.

I looked down at the face of the silent clock radio on the table and smiled. It was 11:11.

Me, with my grandpa, when I was 2 years-old.

For more information on the sequel to *Mother at Seven* – visit www.MotheratSeven.com/new-and-event.

Acknowledgements

I am so happy and grateful for so many amazing people in my life. Without them, this book would not have been possible.

First, I want to give the highest honor to two people who are not with us anymore.

With a heavy heart, I give a loving thank you to my grandpa, Sergey Movsesovith Israelyan, who died on July 30, 1997. He was the only person who was there for me from a young age until he took his last breath when I was 16 years old. He kept me going and taught me endless life lessons that I still use and live by. He is my guardian angel and watches over me every day.

I give a unique and never-ending thank you to my college professor of English, Richard J. Walton, who died on December 12, 2012. He was the first person who taught me how to write full English sentences and who made me promise him that one day I would tell my story and write a book. He is gone, but never from my heart and soul.

I would like to express the deepest appreciation to my publishers, Steven and Dawn Porter at Stillwater River Publications, for holding my hand every step of the way and guiding me patiently throughout the whole publishing process.

A special and positively charged thank you to Bob Proctor, from Proctor and Gallagher Institute — an expert in law of attraction, a professional speaker, and coach of human potential — whose teachings inspired me to go after my dreams, believe in myself, and build my success, so in return I am able to help others build theirs.

I wish to thank my close friend Lisa Saglio Casinelli, the owner of Sapphire Star Designs, who encouraged me to keep going when I had my doubts and who was there for me day and night when I needed advice or a friendly ear.

Thank you to Alda Medeiros from Just Breathe Massage for keeping me physically healthy and well, especially after those long ten hour days of writing.

A cozy and warm thank you to my mentor and true friend Diane Lupo, Reiki Master and teacher, for keeping my mind clear and focused from the first chapter to the last.

Blessings, and a full thank you to my two sons, Daniel and Rafael Ayriyan, for believing in me and for being my heart and soul.

A special thank you to Robert Oglakhchyan, the president and CEO of Artn-Shant TV for his tremendous help with the release of the book and for getting the Armenian community familiar with it, as well as for inviting me to the New Day Show.

In addition, a special thank you to Arman Adamyan from Armount TV for producing a video preview for this book. Also a special, warm thank you to a beautiful young actress, Michelle Sahakyan, for playing my role in the movie clip. Thank you to my cousin/God brother Grigor Aghakhanyan, a talented actor, showman, and artist, for his support and guidance with the book release.

Also, a special thank you to English teacher, Elizabeth Pimental, from Smithfield High School, for creating the study guide to be used by schools and colleges.

I would also like to thank Ellen DeGeneres, TV show host, actress, writer, and producer, for being an amazing role model year after year and showing me how selfless acts of kindness can change the lives of good and humble people. *And thank you, Ellen, for inviting me to your show so I could spread the message of positivity. You don't know that you did that yet, but I had a vision about the future and in it we were sitting and chatting about things right on the sofa at your show!*

And, thank you to all the others who contributed to this book in any way. I truly appreciate everyone's help and I am very blessed to have an endless number of supportive friends in my life.

About the Author

Veronika Gasparyan was born in the beautiful city of Sochi, Russia in 1981 and is a proud descendant of many generations of Armenian ancestors on both sides of her family. Today she lives in Rhode Island, United States of America, with her two sons. From a very young age, Veronika enjoyed playing piano which resulted in her attending a music school for ten years, and eventually, the prestigious Sochi College of Arts and Music. Other than the music, Veronika has always displayed a profound love of reading, and at a very young age, read dozens of books from her grandfather's vast, personal library. She considers herself to be a true survivor of what many would call a traumatic and brutal childhood, but has still found a way to not lose her kindness, patience or hope for better days. Veronika is a strong believer in laws of attraction and positive thinking and is working on other books that she hopes will provide emotional support to those who are in need — those who have given-up or have already lost their hope for better days and a joyful life.

Made in United States
Orlando, FL
05 March 2024

44407096R00168